The Forgotten Christians of Hangzhou

THE
FORGOTTEN
CHRISTIANS
OF HANGZHOU

D. E. Mungello

University of Hawaii Press

Honolulu

94 95 96 97 98 99   5 4 3 2 1

Library of Congress Cataloging-in-Publication Data
Mungello, David E., 1943–
The forgotten Christians of Hangzhou / D. E. Mungello.
p.   cm.
Includes bibliographical references and index.
ISBN 0-8248-1540-8
1.   Christianity—China—Hang-chou shih—History.   2.   Christianity—
China—History.   3.   Jesuits—China—Hang-chou shih—History.
4.   Hang-chou shih (China)—Church history.   I.   Title.
BR1295.H36M86   1994
275.1'242—dc20   93-36553
CIP

University of Hawaii Press books are printed on acid-free paper and meet the
guidelines for permanence and durability of the Council on Library Resources

Designed by Paula Newcomb

CONTENTS

ILLUSTRATIONS

The drawings found at the beginning of each section portray the West Lake at Hangzhou and are reproduced from the opening chapter of the *Qiantang-xian zhi* (Local history of the Qiantang district), 1718 edition.

ACKNOWLEDGMENTS

With each new book my indebtedness to others grows broader and deeper. This book would not have been possible without the contributions of colleagues in China, Europe, and the United States. The work began in the fall of 1986 with a trip to Shanghai in an attempt to gain access to the former Jesuit library of Zikawei (Xujiahui). Any foreign scholar who has attempted to do research in mainland China knows just how complicated and frustrating this can be. Without friendly Chinese scholars to smooth one's way, it is practically impossible.

One colleague who smoothed my path was Mr. Hao Zhenhua of the Institute of History, Chinese Academy of Social Sciences (Beijing). Mr. Hao traveled from Beijing to Shanghai in order to help me. Although I was not given access to the building where the Xujiahui Library was housed, I was given a seat in the Rare Book Room of the Shanghai Municipal Library several miles away while Mr. Lü Miangang plied his bicycle back and forth between the two libraries, seeking to satisfy my requests for books. In addition, Mr. Fei Youloong of the Shanghai Municipal Library staff shared his knowledge of the Xujiahui Library with me. The history of the Xujiahui collection is still largely to be culled from individual memories of a generation that is rapidly fading from this world. I am grateful for information about the Xujiahui Library from Jesuits such as the late Fr. J. Dehergne, former archivist of the Jesuit materials held at Chantilly, France; Fr. Y. Raguin, head of the Ricci Institute in Taipei; the late Fr. J. S. Sebes, former professor in history at Georgetown University; and Fr. J. W. Witek, professor of history at Georgetown University. These Jesuits, apart from the younger Fr. Witek, resided at the religious and academic Xujiahui complex prior to 1949 when it was connected with the French Concession of Shanghai and administered predominantly by French-speaking Jesuits.

It was in Shanghai in the fall of 1986 that I first came upon manuscripts by Zhang Xingyao (1633–1715+), the Christian literatus from Hangzhou. After returning to the States, I began to focus on Master Zhang and found that several of his works were available in microfilm copy from the Bibliothèque nationale in Paris. A second research trip to China followed in May and June of 1989, this time to Hangzhou in search of information about Zhang Xingyao. In spite of the political chaos that was convulsing China at that time, I was able to absorb the atmosphere of this site of tranquil natural beauty, which has been remarkably preserved since Zhang lived on the shores of the West Lake three centuries ago. On this trip it was Mr. Xu Mingde, professor of history at Hangzhou University, who guided me from library to library, clearing away obstacles in my path. After my departure from Hangzhou, Mr. Xu was instrumental in helping me to obtain the photographs of the Immaculate Conception Church and the Jesuit cemetery that are reproduced in this book.

The staff of the Archivum Romanum Societatis Iesu (Rome) provided me with microfilms of several seventeenth-century Jesuit annual letters. Ms. P. Paderni of the Istituto Universitario Orientale (Naples) aided me in obtaining a microfilm copy of Fr. Intorcetta's manuscript of "Compendiosa narrazione dello Stato della Missione Cinese cominciando dalt' anno 1581 fino al 1669." Ms. Mi Chu Wiens, China area specialist of the Library of Congress, was prompt and helpful in helping me to gain access to certain rare works. Ms. T. K. Kitao, professor of art history at Swarthmore College, was very patient in responding to my questions about the artistic and architectural features of the Immaculate Conception Church and the Jesuit cemetery in Hangzhou. Mr. A. Dudink of the Sinologisch Instituut (Leiden) was very generous in sharing materials held at the Instituut and also in helping with several difficult points of interpretation. Mr. E. Zürcher, professor of Sinology at the Universiteit Leiden, read an early chapter of the manuscript and provided me with a detailed written critique.

Mr. P. C. Kroll, professor of Chinese at the University of Colorado at Boulder, assisted me in identifying the poetic form of Zhang's eulogies. Mr. A. C. Yu, professor in humanities at the University of Chicago, corrected my translation of two of Zhang's poems. Ms. L. Struve, professor of history at Indiana University, explained a reference to peasant army resistance to the Manchu conquerers that took place in the region of Tai Lake in 1645–1646. Mr. W. T. Chan, professor of Chinese culture and philosophy emeritus at Dartmouth College, and Mr. D. Bodde, professor of Chinese studies emeritus at the University of Pennsylvania, both assisted me with the translations of certain Chinese terms. Mr. E. Burke, professor of humanities at Coe College, assisted me in translating a Latin inscription. Fr. E. J. Malatesta, S.J., director of the Ricci Institute at the University of San Francisco, provided me with a copy of Zhang Xingyao's essay on Chinese sacrificial rites (Sidian shuo). The staff of the Stewart Library of Coe College diligently fulfilled my requests for (oftentimes obscure) materials through interlibrary loan.

I am particularly indebted to three colleagues who were kind enough to read an early version of the manuscript and provide helpful comments and suggestions. Mr. K. Lundbæk, professor emeritus at the Universitet Aarhus (Denmark), assisted me not only in this way but also through his pathbreaking research into several subjects dealt with in this book. Ms. C. von Collani, Dr. Theol. of the Universität Würzburg, followed up her reading of the manuscript with numerous helpful exchanges by correspondence. Mr. N. Standaert, Dr. Phil., a Jesuit scholastic who is now engaged in theological studies at Fu Jen University in Taipei, read the manuscript. Mr. Standaert was able to assist me through the knowledge he had gained in his study of Yang Tingyun, a Christian literatus of Hangzhou who had preceded Zhang by two generations.

I am indebted to Coe College for providing me with half-year sabbatical leaves during the fall semesters of 1986 and 1991. I am also indebted to the History of Christianity in China Project (funded by the Henry Luce Foundation) for providing the financial means for me to make the two research visits to China. In particular, I feel a debt of gratitude to Mr. D. H. Bays, professor of history at the University of Kansas, who as director of this project recognized the potential in my research proposal. In addition, I thank the Committee on Scholarly Communication with the People's Republic of China (CSCPRC) for assisting in the preliminary arrangements with the Chinese Academy of Social Sciences (Beijing and Shanghai) for the 1986 trip to Shanghai. For the third time, I am indebted to the University of Hawaii Press for its vote of confidence in publishing my books. I would like to express a particular note of gratitude to the religion editor, Ms. S. F. Yamamoto, for the meticulous care with which she handled the manuscript.

Finally, I am indebted to my family and particularly my wife, Christine Mungello née McKegg, who provided indispensable editorial and technical advice on matters large and small. As a historian, I am also deeply conscious of the debt to my family in the remote sense of those ancestors who were blood of my blood. Without them, this book would not have been written. And so it is to them—the Mungiellos of Roccarainola, Italy, who lived in view of the magnificent Mt. Vesuvius, and the Dittmars of Harzgerode, Germany, who lived in the purified air of the East Harz Mountains—that I dedicate this book.

Fig. 1.—A map of China showing the east-central location of Hangzhou in relationship to other important seventeenth- and eighteenth-century missionary centers mentioned in this work. The route by which the Jesuit Father M. Martini traveled from Macao to Hangzhou in 1644 is indicated by a *dotted line.*

Introduction

Three hundred years before multiculturalism became a concern of our world, a small group of Chinese literati struggled with blending loyalties to two different cultures. The seventeenth-century city of Hangzhou was renowned for the tranquil beauty of its West Lake, and it was here that a small community of Christians flourished. They had been introduced to this "Lord of Heaven Teaching from the Far West" by some of the most able and colorful European Jesuits of that age. The literati who led this community were in almost all respects highly orthodox Confucians. They embraced Christianity because they saw its teachings (interpreted through distinctly Chinese eyes) as fulfilling the perennial goal of Confucians to recapture in their own day the True Way of the ancients.

These literati faced obstacles not entirely unlike those faced by Christians in China today. There were strong, ingrained feelings of cultural chauvinism to overcome in both European and Chinese cultures. They faced the intellectual and social animosity of fellow literati, who saw in the Christian literati a betrayal of their own culture. There was the hostility of the political authorities, who saw in these Christians a subversive threat that sprang from a long history of quasi-religious rebel groups in China. What was the outcome of the struggle by these Chinese literati? One cannot say that they succeeded, and yet the continuation of Christianity in China from their time down to today prevents them from being condemned as failures.

The importance of Christianity to early modern Chinese history has been much debated. Among historians who study seventeenth- and eighteenth-century Sino-European contacts from a European perspective, there has been a tendency to bestow upon the Chinese side of the encounter an importance more or less equal to the European side. The Jesuit-stimulated European fascination with

China and the widespread debate involved in the Chinese Rites Controversy have been presumed to have had some form of contrapuntal significance in China.

Recent studies that have examined this Sino-European encounter from a Chinese perspective have come to a different conclusion. They believe that Christianity played an ephemeral and peripheral role in Chinese history during this time. In a widely read book, the Sinologist J. Gernet has argued that Christianity was limited in its impact and assimilation in China because of unbridgeable differences in modes of language and thought between Christianity and Chinese culture.[1] Another eminent Sinologist, E. Zürcher, agrees with Mr. Gernet that Christianity failed to be assimilated into seventeenth- and eighteenth-century China, but for reasons other than unreconcilable thought patterns. Mr. Zürcher draws from his own work on the earlier assimilation of Buddhism into China to conclude that Christianity was rejected by the Chinese because of the overly centralized manner in which the Jesuits were directed by a Counter-Reformation church and because of the incompatibility of the Jesuit roles of scholar and priest in China.[2]

The experience of the Christians in Hangzhou offers evidence that, though it does not challenge the judgment that the influence of Christianity in seventeenth- and eighteenth-century Chinese culture was limited, nevertheless contradicts the belief that Christianity was not and could not be assimilated or inculturated into Chinese culture. It also contradicts the widely held image of the Sinocentric Confucian literatus whose mind was closed to foreign influences.

The recent study of Sino-Western contacts has given rise to words that express new ways of viewing these contacts. One such word is "inculturation." The word originated in the early 1970s at the stimulus of Christian thinkers in Asia and Africa. Inculturation refers to the absorption of Christianity into a culture to the degree that it not only finds expression in the elements of that culture but also becomes an animating force that transforms the culture.[3] The facts are that the Christian teaching was to a significant degree inculturated into seventeenth-century China by a small group of Hangzhou literati. Furthermore, when viewed from the perspective of history, this inculturation process could be seen as the early phase of an ebb and flow process of assimilation of Christianity by Chinese culture that is still under way today. Consequently, any final judgment that Christianity has not been assimilated into Chinese culture must await the outcome of long-term developments that are still unfolding.

The historical setting of this book is the city of Hangzhou during roughly one century extending from the early seventeenth to the early eighteenth centuries. The book begins with the arrival of the first Jesuits in Hangzhou in 1611 and ends with the conversion of the Hangzhou Church of the Savior to a temple for the Goddess of Sailors in 1731. This period of Chinese history is often referred to with the hyphenated title of Ming-Qing because it is a transition period. The transition from the Ming dynasty (1368–1644) to the Qing dynasty (1644–1911) involved prolonged and profound effects on political culture and society caused by the invasion and conquest of the Manchus.

The decline of the Ming was hastened by a series of ineffective rulers, including the reclusive and eccentric Wanli emperor (reigned 1572–1619), who was on the throne when the first Jesuits began penetrating China from the Portuguese colony of Macao on the southeastern tip of the mainland. Throughout their history, the Chinese were threatened by nomadic tribes on their northern borders. In occasional periods of internal weakness these tribes succeeded in conquering parts or all of China and in establishing foreign dynasties. The Manchus, a virile and intelligent group of hunters and horsemen, had been pushing beyond the limits of their homeland in present-day Manchuria and threatening the northeast border of Ming China since early in the seventeenth century.

Meanwhile, in northwestern China repeated famines had given rise to a breakdown in governmental authority and to the development of peasant rebellions. As peasant armies grew, their leaders began to contemplate displacing the Ming and establishing a new dynasty. In 1644 a peasant leader named Li Zicheng suddenly marched his bandit army into Beijing and took control, causing the Ming emperor to commit suicide. The Ming armies on the northeastern front were forced to conclude a hasty alliance with the Manchus, who, together with the Ming armies, marched southward to Beijing to free the capital of its rebel occupants. The Manchus cleverly exploited the chaotic situation to depose the Ming rulers and establish their own dynasty. In many ways, the Manchus tried to minimize the effects of the transition, and their attempt to promote continuity is shown by the euphemistic affinities in the names of the two dynasties: the dynasty of "brightness" (Ming) gave way to the

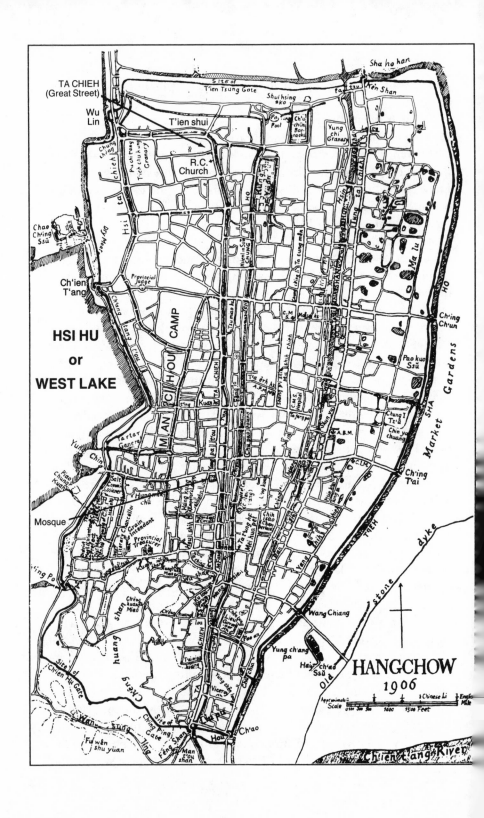

dynasty of "purity" (Qing). The Ming imperial family continued to resist the Manchus by elevating a series of male claimants to the throne. However, the Manchus were firmly in control of the seat of the imperial government in Beijing, and the Ming heirs were nothing more than pretenders, whose courts were perpetually in the process of fleeing for their lives from the advancing Manchu troops. A series of Ming courts were forced to move farther and farther south until the last Ming pretender to the throne was assassinated in pathetic circumstances near the border of Burma in 1662.

The political changes in dynasties had a profound impact on the cultural atmosphere of China, though the shift was one of degree rather than kind. The followers of Confucius, more properly called literati than Confucians, continued to be the dominant cultural force in China. However, in the late Ming the literati experimented with innovative syncretism in which Confucianism was blended with Buddhism and Daoism under the popular slogan "the three Teachings [of Confucianism, Buddhism, and Daoism] are really one." There was even an attempt by the Jesuits and their literati converts to partially follow this pattern in blending Confucianism with Christianity, but this was a minor movement of the time.

The Manchu conquest produced a backlash against this sort of innovative blending. There was a widespread return to the most orthodox of Confucian teachings by Chinese literati, who blamed the experimental cultural atmosphere of the sixteenth and early seventeenth centuries for the fall of the Ming. This return to orthodoxy was reinforced by the Manchus, who suffered from a sense of sharp

---

Fig. 2.—A map of Hangzhou in 1906 showing the city wall and other seventeenth-century landmarks that have since disappeared. Note in the upper left corner the Wu Lin [gate] and, proceeding from it, Ta Chieh (Great Street), which, after running briefly in an eastward direction, turns to the south. It follows the traditional Chinese pattern of main streets in running through the center of the city on a north-south axis. Just before turning to the south, Great Street is intersected by the T'ien shui (Heavenly Water, Tianshui) bridge. After it turns to the south, one finds the Roman Catholic Church (Immaculate Conception Church, formerly Church of the Savior) on its west side. The Islamic mosque is located on the western side of Great Street, near the center of Hangzhou. The Manchou Camp (Manchu Garrison) occupies the west-central portion of the city with Ch'ien T'ang gate lying to its west. The district of Ch'ien T'ang (Qiantang) lies just beyond the Hangzhou city wall and stretches westward around the shore of the West Lake. Reproduced from G. E. Moule, *Notes on Hangzhou Past and Present,* 2d edition (Hangzhou, 1907).

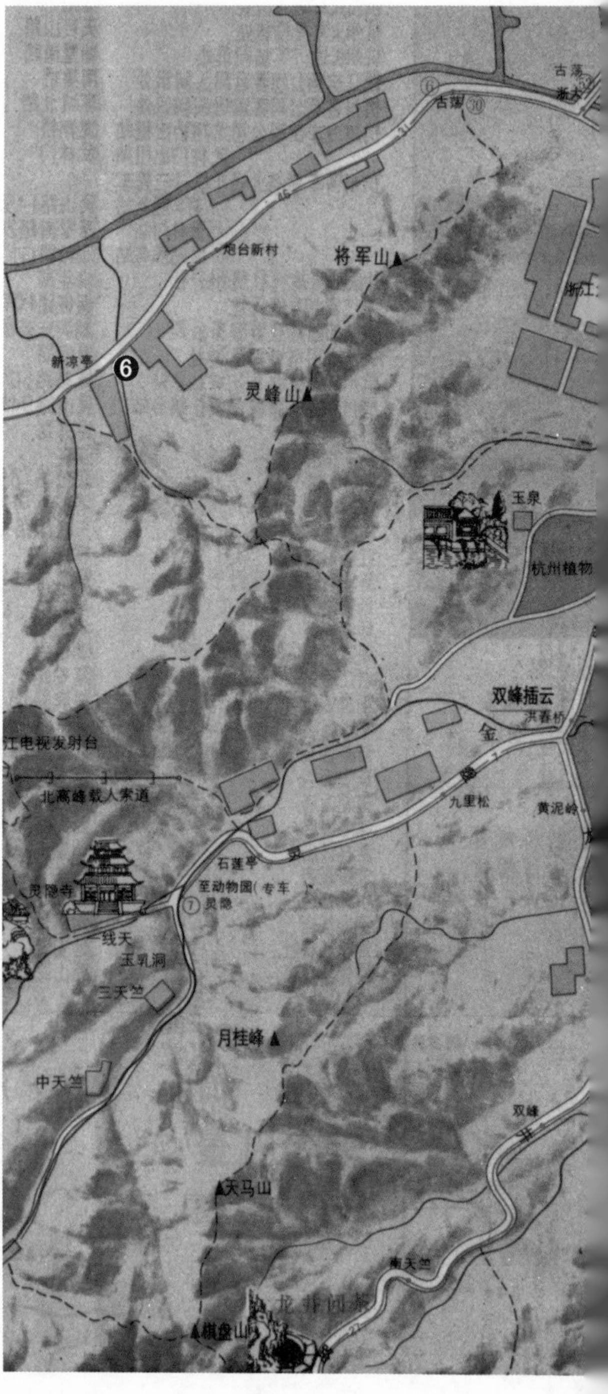

Fig. 3.—A map of contemporary Hangzhou (north is at the top) with the major sites in this work marked as follows:
(1) West Lake,
(2) Guan Gate (site of the first Christian church, built 1627–1633),
(3) Heavenly Water (Tianshui) Bridge,
(4) Immaculate Conception Church, formerly Church of the Savior (built 1659–1663),
(5) Wulin Gate,
(6) Dafangjing Jesuit Cemetery,
(7) Qiantang Gate,
(8) Fengshan Gate, and
(9) Thunder Peak Pagoda.

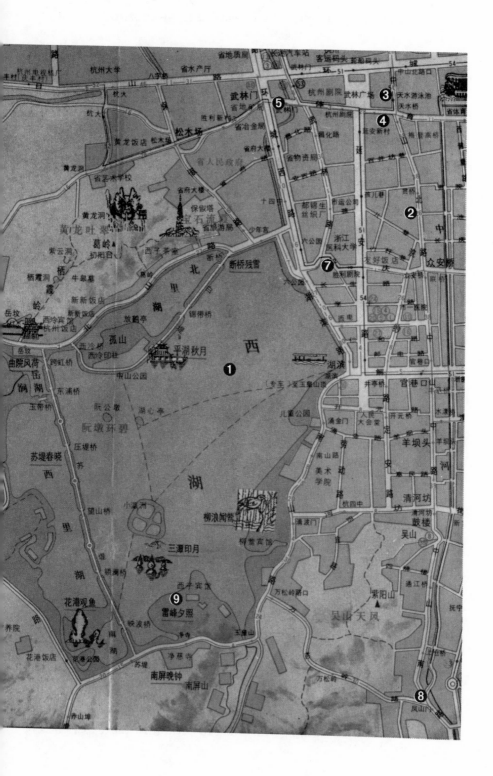

insecurity as uncultivated foreign rulers over a sophisticated culture and a population in which they were vastly outnumbered, by approximately 150 million to one million. In their cultural insecurity, the Manchus embraced the most orthodox Confucian philosophy available.

The Manchu conquest also produced a great social upheaval that disrupted the careers of several generations of literati. In the immediate aftermath of the conquest, many mature literati called "Ming loyalists" withdrew from governmental service and refused to serve the Manchus out of loyalty to the Ming. Younger generations of literati, who came to maturity in the immediate aftermath of the conquest, encountered difficulty in obtaining official degrees and posts because the Manchus had severely cut back on their opportunities. Nevertheless, China as a whole experienced a period of great stability during the first half of the Qing period because the Manchu emperors of this period were diligent, talented, and conscientious.

The first Manchu ascended the throne as a boy and ruled as the Shunzhi emperor from 1644 to 1661. Because of his deep sensitivity to religion and to the powerful character of the Jesuit Father A. Schall von Bell (Tang Ruowang), this emperor came closer to conversion than any other ruler in Chinese history. The greatest Manchu ruler was the Kangxi emperor (reigned 1661–1722), and he was deeply tolerant of Christianity, though less susceptible to its influence than his father. However, by the end of the Kangxi emperor's long sixty-one-year reign, the Christian religion and its missionary representatives had fallen from favor, in part because of persistent literati hostility toward Christianity and in part because of a political struggle between the popes in Rome and the Kangxi emperor over who had ultimate authority over the Christian church in China. The Yongzheng emperor (reigned 1723–1735), whose reign concludes the period covered in this book, was a far less magnanimous and successful ruler than his father. He was hostile toward both the missionaries and their foreign teaching because of the political threat that they posed. As a result, the Christian church and its followers suffered increasing persecution.

The subject of this book is the people who formed the Christian community in Hangzhou from the early seventeenth to the early eighteenth centuries. It includes both the Jesuit missionaries who brought Christianity to Hangzhou and the Chinese literati who embraced that teaching. In order to recapture the experience of these largely forgotten Christians of Hangzhou, I have used two different forms of writing. The core of each chapter is composed of standard historical writing in which statements are traced to footnoted sources or the tentative nature of the material is indicated by cautionary phrasing. The second form of writing involves imaginative reconstructions of the thoughts of three central figures in this work: the Jesuit Fathers M. Martini and P. Intorcetta and, above all, the Confucian literatus Zhang Xingyao (1633–1715+). Each of these reflective elaborations is based on some historical kernel of fact. Although each of the elaborations is, at the very least, highly plausible, I cannot present them as always having the same degree of historical certainty as the cores of the chapters. Consequently, I have distinguished the two forms of writing by the use of different type, and I have excluded the imaginative reconstructions from the numbered sections of each chapter, treating them as chapter preludes and postludes. While some of the reconstructions follow the historical documentation quite closely, others diverge in varying degrees.

The preludes and postludes also include poems by Zhang. In order to allow Zhang to speak for himself, I have translated his poems on "The Four Last Things" (Death, Judgment, Hell, and Heaven). These poems formed part of a collection of thirty-eight eulogies entitled "Inscriptions in Eulogy of the Sage Teaching" (i.e., Christianity) *(Shengjiao zanming)*.[4] In or shortly after 1678 Father Intorcetta apparently asked Master Zhang to compose the inscriptions to accompany and elucidate the paintings on Christian themes that were eventually hung in the Church of the Savior. The paintings were probably destroyed by the fire of 1692.

Not all of the figures treated in this book have been forgotten, but most of their activities in the Christian community of Hangzhou have been lost to our historical memory. Martini is actually famous for his travels and writings on China, but he is rarely associated with Hangzhou even though Hangzhou was his major missionary base in China. Intorcetta remains a largely unrecognized and unstudied missionary whose activities in China are recounted only for the period before he went to Hangzhou. However, it was in Hangzhou over a period of twenty-one years that he made his major contributions as a missionary. Zhang and the Christian literati of his time in Hangzhou have been almost entirely forgotten. I have tried to retrieve these forgotten Christians of Hangzhou from their obscurity, and this is the result of my efforts.

CHAPTER I
In the Beginning

The Manchus are coming! Father Martini, the burly Jesuit, heard the shouted warning while sitting at the dinner table. The streets outside were filled with the cries and screams of the people of Wenzhou fleeing in panic. Inside his large house the rooms were filled with townspeople seeking the refuge that they believed the foreign scholar-priest could provide.

So they are coming, thought Martini. Still, there is no reason not to finish a good meal that Wang went to a lot of effort to prepare. The chicken is superb, almost like in Trento. Too bad there is so little wine left, but if I drank it, there would be nothing for the Eucharist, and who knows how long it will be before I get back to Hangzhou.

It is time, I believe, to cut ties with Prince Tang. The Ming star is descending. I think it would be best to quietly forget about this vague assignment from the court of the supposed Longwu emperor. A fine leader, but my call is to God, not to the Ming pretender. It is time to bury part of the past. The Manchu star is rising.

I have heard stories about the Manchus—that they are rustic but not barbarian in character. The rumor is that they are impressed by learning and are awed by the long-nailed literatus types, even if they despise their weakness. I am not weak and I have a beard that I doubt that any of them has seen. I am ready to shave my head in their manner and wear their "coin-sized rat's tail," though I have heard many Chinese are rioting over the head shaving because to cut away any part of the body is considered an unfilial desecration of what our parents have begotten.

I know what we will do! Li, come! Bring out a table to the front of the gate and also the large leather-bound books. I will set up the telescope, prism, and mathematical instruments. Wang, bring the altar with the image of the Lord! I will announce myself in the manner of newly arrived officials. Where is the large roll of red paper that I have been saving for the New Year's celebration? Li, get the inkstone and brush. What shall we write? Yes, yes, I know, write this: "Here lives a doctor of the Divine Law of the Far West *(Daxi Tianxue xiushi yu ci).*" It would be offensive to the literati, but you don't impress hicks with modesty. Now, Li, help me to attach the sign to the gate. . . . All right, let's wait inside.

Oh, I forgot! Wang, bring me my scholar's robe. Hurry, I hear horse hooves! Yes, that is the right robe. Here they are. They are stopping! They are looking at the table and altar. They are entering the gate and coming to the door. They are knocking. Yes, I am ready. No, wait! (Holy Mary, Mother of God, pray for us sinners now and in the hour of our death). All right, open the door.[1]

I

The rise of Hangzhou belongs to the middle ages of China's long history. The cradle of Chinese civilization lies in the north near the Yellow River, and only gradually was the frontier pushed south to the Yangzi River. The village of Qiantang, which later became absorbed into Hangzhou, had been founded by the third century B.C.[2] Later, around A.D. 600, the autocratic emperor of the Sui dynasty undertook a vast public works project to build a canal linking the north of China with the central regions. This Grand Canal became one of the world's earliest and longest canals and enabled countless barges loaded with surplus rice and tax grains to flow northward to support the army and imperial officials. At the southern terminus of the Grand Canal arose the city of Hangzhou. Favored by human ingenuity as a commercial center and by nature as a setting of great physical beauty, Hangzhou became a place where fantasies were realized—among its exquisite scenery, its Buddhist pagodas, its fabled cuisine, and its orchidaceous singsong girls. Throughout China, it was said that "Heaven has paradise, but the earth has Suzhou and Hangzhou."[3] So fantastic did Marco Polo's fourteenth-century eyewitness accounts of Hangzhou seem to European readers that they were widely regarded as pure fantasy.[4] They were not.

Geography more than any other force has shaped Hangzhou. It belongs to the east-central part of China and lies over a hundred miles (one hundred and sixty kilometers) south of the great Yangzi River. It is a hundred miles southwest of modern Shanghai, though Shanghai remained a fishing village long after Hangzhou had become a world-famous metropolis. Hangzhou emerged on the northern banks of the Qiantang River, just before the river enters into the Hangzhou Bay, whose waters mix with the East China Sea one hundred miles to the east. Eventually, the Hangzhou outlet to the Qiantang River silted up and a seawall was built. This separated the city from the Qiantang River, with its regular tides, including the spectacular Hangzhou Bore, and irregular flooding. A large lake formed that eventually became completely desalinized fresh water. Over the years the city became more and more oriented toward the large lake that lay directly to its west, which became known as the West Lake (Xihu) (see figs. 2, 3 and 4).

The Song dynasty (960–1279) is famous for its aesthetes and philosophers rather than for its soldiers. When the northern capital of Kaifeng was overrun by the Nuzhen tribe the Jürched in 1126, the Song court was forced to flee southward to Hangzhou. The founding of the Southern Song capital at Hangzhou—officially called Lin'an—inaugurated a period in which the city became synonymous with thriving art, literature, scholarship, and commerce.

In the two centuries between 1100 and 1300, the population of Hangzhou expanded from 200,000 to over one million. The multistoried houses, which were unusual in China, enabled this large population to be crammed into the limits of a city wall that had been built to encircle a small town.[5] The problems of supplying such a large, dense population with food and other necessities were solved by the system of roads and canals that crisscrossed Hangzhou. However, rents were high and fires were frequent. Homeless families were squeezed by the high rents or forced by destructive fires into the streets, which overflowed with people. Parts of the population found relief in the canals, where whole families lived on boats.[6]

Hangzhou was a sensual city. People tended to bathe there more frequently than in the northern and western parts of China.[7] The large number of refugees produced a cuisine that was remarkably varied and included seasonings such as pepper, ginger, pimento, and soy sauce. Even human flesh was available in restaurants opened by northern Chinese and was commonly referred to as "two-legged mutton" after the similarity in preparation to the flesh of sheep. For more discriminating palates, there were different names

Fig. 4.—A view of the West Lake, looking toward the south with Hangzhou at the left. Qiantang Gate is visible at the far left, opposite the two docked boats. From the *Hangzhou-fu zhi* (Local History of Hangzhou), compiled by Shao Jinhan (1743–1796), 178 *juan* (1898 edition), 1, pp. 59b–60a.

for dishes made from the flesh of children, young girls, women, and old men.[8] Prostitution was widespread in Hangzhou and infiltrated all classes of society, ranging from lower-class streetwalkers to pampered women whose beauty was celebrated in society and reserved for wealthy Chinese males. Variety in Hangzhou extended to prostitution. Some male prostitutes impersonated females. Laws were passed against such female impersonators, threatening caning as a punishment and offering monetary rewards for their discovery, but detection was no easy matter.[9]

By 1275 Hangzhou had become the largest and richest city in the world, and it remained so under the Mongols when Marco Polo visited it. The people of Hangzhou delighted in the joys of religion as well as the joys of sensuality, and the city's exotic tastes extended to include a large Islamic mosque (see fig. 2) and a Nestorian Christian church, both built in 1281.[10] The West Lake terrain was especially conducive to the building of Daoist temples and Buddhist monasteries and pagodas, all of which dotted the hillsides surrounding the lake. In later years the Confucian literati were especially prominent in Hangzhou and throughout the surrounding province of Zhejiang. Scholars from Zhejiang along with those from neighboring Jiangsu province dominated the lists of successful candidates in the official examinations for many years. The literati of this region became so famous that they were memorialized in the famous eighteenth-century satirical novel *The Scholars (Rulin waishi)* by Wu Jingzi.

II

In the spring of 1611 three Jesuits arrived in Hangzhou to found the first Roman Catholic mission there.[11] They came at the invitation of the recently converted literatus Li Zhizao (d. 1630) and with the blessing of the new Jesuit superior, Fr. Niccolò Longobardo (Long Huamin, 1565–1655), who had succeeded the famous Fr. Matteo Ricci (Li Madou, 1552–1610) at his death in Beijing the preceding year.[12] Li Zhizao had resigned from his post in Nanjing in order to return home to Hangzhou and observe a period of mourning for his father.[13] The trio who accompanied him consisted of a fifty-one-year-old priest from Tuscany (in present-day Italy) named Lazzaro Cattaneo (Guo Zhujing, 1560–1640), who had been in China for eighteen years, mainly in the central and southern provinces. Fr. Cattaneo had a very musical ear finely tuned to languages and he had, together with Ricci and Zhong Mingren, produced a romanization of the Mandarin dialect and its five tones.[14]

The second of the trio was a forty-nine-year-old Jesuit brother named Zhong Mingren, also known by his European name of Sébastien Fernandez (1562–1622). Zhong was born at Xinhui, just south of Canton, and on New Year's Day of 1591 he had become the first Chinese admitted into the Jesuit order.[15] Brother Sébastien had a close relationship with Ricci and was with the latter for several periods in Beijing. He had experienced severe persecution, including several imprisonments and floggings, for his faith. It was a sad fact that such harsh punishments were more likely to be administered to Chinese converts than to foreign priests. The third member of this trio was the Belgian Nicolas Trigault (Jin Nige, 1577–1628), who had been in China for less than one year. Although Fr. Trigault was destined for a prominent role in the China Mission, at thirty-four years of age and still new to China, he was the very junior member of this trio when it traveled from Nanjing to Hangzhou in 1611.

By some irony, Hangzhou was to remain a magnet for all three of these men, although Trigault returned only sporadically from his extensive travels while Zhong and Cattaneo remained in residence there. By December, Trigault had been sent on to Beijing and then back to Europe as procurator. At that time a representative, called a procurator, from each province and vice-province of the Society of Jesus was sent back to Rome every three years to discuss the state of the Society at the Procurators' Congregation.[16] Trigault returned to Hangzhou in 1622 and, after mission work elsewhere in China, returned once again by 1628. All the members of this founding trio died in Hangzhou—Zhong in 1621, Trigault in 1628, and Cattaneo in 1640—and all three are interred in the Jesuit cemetery there.[17]

The Hangzhou mission depended heavily on the patronage of literati. The firm foundations that the Church put down in this region are closely related to the fact that two of the "Three Pillars of the Early Christian Church" (Kaijiao san dazhushi) were Hangzhou residents. The origin of this term "Three Pillars" is unclear, though Ricci referred to Xu Guangqi in his journals as "a great pillar" (magior colonna).[18] Xu Guangqi of Shanghai was the first of the Three Pillars to be baptized. Xu had been influenced by Ricci and was baptized by Fr. João de Rocha (Luo Ruwang, 1565–1623) at Nanjing in 1601.[19] In comparison with Xu, Li Zhizao's path to baptism was slower, but his journey was more linked to Ricci personally. Li met Ricci while serving as an official in Beijing. Over a period of nine years they grew closer together, though as late as the beginning of 1610 Li still resisted baptism.[20] Then Li fell mortally ill and Ricci nursed him for weeks. At a critical point in his illness, Li accepted the faith and was baptized. Ricci died two months later, in May of 1610.

Yang Tingyun was the last of the Three Pillars to be converted. He had briefly met Ricci in Beijing around 1602 when Yang was called to the capital to assume the post of censor.[21] Yang heard Ricci teach about the Lord of Heaven but initially was unmoved. Later in 1611, when he went to the home of Li Zhizao in Hangzhou to convey his condolences on the death of Li's father, Yang met the three Jesuits who had just arrived and began serious discussions with them about the Lord of Heaven Teaching. In response to Yang's invitation, the Jesuits joined Yang in his home, which was more conveniently located on the outskirts of the city. After lengthy intellectual struggles in detaching himself from Buddhist beliefs and after personal struggles in which he (like Li Zhizao before him) had to send away his concubine, Yang was baptized in 1611.[22]

The Three Pillars had all attained the highest literati degree (*jinshi*) and had received prominent official appointments. Xu Guangqi had attained the highest office in the land by becoming one of the grand secretaries (*da xueshi*). Each of the three used his position to support and defend the Western priests. Yang sheltered missionaries in his home during the anti-Christian movement of 1616–1617 and funded the building of a Christian church in Hangzhou. As long as the Three Pillars lived, Christianity could rely on the support of these powerful patrons, but when they died (Yang in 1627, Li in 1630, and Xu in 1633), the Church lost its most eminent group of defenders. The Jesuit leadership turned its attention increasingly to the court in Beijing, where, working through its astronomer-mathematicians at the Bureau of Astronomy, such as Frs. A. Schall von Bell and F. Verbiest, it sought to cultivate support at the very top of the Chinese political structure.

The importance of Hangzhou and surrounding Zhejiang province to the China Mission can be seen in the fact that sixty-five Jesuits (both European and East Asian) passed through the region in the century after the first Jesuits came to Hangzhou (1611–1707).[23] These Jesuits included some of the most prominent of the seventeenth-century mission, such as G. Aleni who came as early as 1617, L. Buglio in 1637, G. de Magalhaes in 1640, F. Verbiest in 1657, and C. de Visdelou in 1691. None of these Jesuits was closely identified with the Hangzhou region, yet their brief visits there indicate the importance of the region at that time. In addition to the Jesuits who focused their efforts in northern Zhejiang province, the Dominicans and Franciscans were active in southwest Zhejiang during the early Qing period.[24]

The gradual shift in Jesuit attention from Hangzhou to Beijing is reflected in the number of Chinese works on Christianity printed at the mission centers in China. From 1623 to 1628 at least seven works by the Jesuit Father Giulio Aleni (Ai Rulüe, 1582–1649) and Li Zhizao were published in Hangzhou.[25] Also, the first edition of the Chinese prayerbook *(Tianzhu shengjiao nianjing zongdu)* was printed at Hangzhou in 1628.[26] In the following years the number of these works declined until apparently the last work published in Hangzhou by a missionary in the seventeenth and eighteenth centuries was *On Friendship (Qiuyou pian)* by M. Martini in 1661. By contrast, from 1662 until 1758 Beijing had a virtual monopoly on the publication of works in Chinese written by missionaries. This monopoly is clearly revealed in lists compiled around 1715 of Chinese works on Christianity that were engraved and printed at churches in China. These lists show that the three major printing centers were Beijing (listing 124 works), Fuzhou (listing 51 works), and Hangzhou (listing 40 works).[27]

However, works on Christianity by literati working independently of missionaries continued to be produced outside of Beijing and at Hangzhou in particular because the seeds of a Chinese Christian Church had been well planted. If later baptized literati at Hangzhou were not as prominent as the Three Pillars, these neglected figures were no less assiduous in carrying forward the inculturation of Christianity into Chinese culture.

In the years following the deaths of the Three Pillars, a number of Jesuits were active at Hangzhou in addition to Fr. Cattaneo. Most of them are among the twenty-one Jesuits buried at the Dafangjing cemetery. The Sicilian Fr. Longobardo, who was superior of the China Mission from 1610 to 1612, briefly visited Hangzhou in 1621.[28] He was succeeded as superior by the Portuguese Father da Rocha, who had first visited Hangzhou in 1616.[29] Da Rocha later returned to Hangzhou and served as superior for less than one year, from June 1622 until his death in March of 1623. He is buried at Dafangjing cemetery. The Portuguese Father João Fróis (Froes) (Fu Ruowang, 1591–1638) was rector of the seminary at Hangzhou in 1624.[30] Although Fr. Fróis died in 1638, Rome was still not aware of his death in 1640, when it named him vice-provincial of northern China. He, too, is buried at Dafangjing. In 1631 the twenty-two-year-old literatus named Zhu Zongyuan was baptized at Hangzhou with the baptismal name of Cosimo (Gesimo).[31] Zhu was born around 1609 in Ningbo and attained the *gongsheng* (senior licentiate) degree in 1646 and the *juren* (provincial examination) degree two years later. He became a distinguished literatus of the second generation of Christians in China, although his life and works have been little studied.

The Italian Father Ludovico Buglio (Li Leisi, 1606–1682) was sent from Nanjing to assume Fróis' duties, but he did not remain at Hangzhou for long. Shortly afterwards, the Portuguese Father Manuel Dias the younger (Yang Manuo, 1574–1659), who had previously visited Hangzhou in 1634, arrived from Fuzhou to head the Hangzhou mission.[32] In 1639 he was invited by Zhu Zongyuan to come to Ningbo, in eastern Zhejiang province, where he consequently founded a Christian church. Dias served as visitor of the mission from 1614 to 1615 and later as vice-provincial of China from 1623 to 1635 and again from 1650 to 1654.[33] Fr. Dias' most enduring contribution to the China Mission was his revision of the Chinese account of Jesus' crucifixion first written by Fr. D. Pantoja. The Passion account appeared in the Chinese prayerbook of 1628 and in the edition of 1665.[34] He visited Hangzhou in 1634 and helped in the establishment of a seminary there.[35] He apparently spent his last years at Hangzhou, where he died in 1659. He, too, is buried at Dafangjing. The Swiss Father Nikolaus Fiva (Xu Risheng, 1609–1640) was in Hangzhou for less than two years before succumbing to an early death in 1640.[36] The Portuguese Father Pedro Ribeiro (Li Ningshi, 1570–1640) died at Hangzhou in 1640 and is also buried at Dafangjing.[37]

III

One of the most famous Jesuits to be active in the development of the Hangzhou mission was the Italian-German (actually from the independent border region of Trent) Father Martino Martini (Wei Kuangguo, 1614–1661). Martini had an intense energy and a charismatic personality. Given his love of excitement, it was his good fortune to have arrived in China at the height of one of the greatest upheavals in its history. With such a mixture of bright talent, powerful personality, and chaotic times, it is not surprising that Martini became the subject of numerous legends. During his training at the Collegium Romanum, he had been tutored by the prolific polyhistor Fr. Athanasius Kircher. Later, during a return trip from China to Rome between 1654 and 1656, Martini provided enough information on China to become the primary source of information for Fr. Kircher's widely read *China illustrata* (1667).[38] Martini arrived in China in time to witness the collapse of the Ming dynasty, the treachery of the bandit leader Li Zicheng, and the conquest of China by the Manchus. Although Martini's primary residence in China was at Hangzhou, this fact has been obscured by his numerous travels throughout China and his production of books, such as a popularized history of the Manchu conquest and an atlas of China, that gave the misleading impression that he traveled throughout more provinces of China than he actually did.[39]

It took Martini three years to travel from Europe to Macao (1640–1643).[40] After one year of preparation in Macao, he was sent to Hangzhou in 1644. This was a very dangerous time for a foreigner, particularly an inexperienced missionary with undeveloped language skills, to be traveling in China.[41] The large, rag-tag army of the bandit-rebel Li Zicheng had taken over the capital, Beijing, on April 25. In order to secure revenge for the murder of his father by Li, the Ming commander Wu Sangui made an alliance with the Manchu forces. In return for Manchu assistance in driving Li out of Beijing, Wu agreed to the Manchus' wish to establish a new dynasty.[42] The Ming court was fleeing southward to Nanjing and attempting to regroup. These chaotic conditions forced Martini to travel from Macao to Hangzhou by the fastest and safest route. This was the so-called ambassador's route, which had long been used for travel between the major Chinese entry point of Canton in the far south and the capital cities in the north. (Martini's route is marked in fig. 1.)

In the spring of 1644 Martini boarded a boat at Macao and passed through a port so crowded with boats that he appeared to be "in a forest of timber."[43] He traveled northward on the Pearl River to Canton, which he probably avoided for reasons of speed and safety. By means of the canals north of Canton, Martini's boat entered the North River and, two weeks later, transferred to the Zhen (Shui) River. At the important transition point of Nanxiong, Martini was impressed by the restrained behavior of the customs officials, who did not hinder ordinary travelers from passing. Martini noted that "Europeans would have a lot to learn from these people, who were once thought of as barbarians."[44]

The open seas were avoided in travel between the north and south of China because of the danger of pirates. Consequently, the transportation system of China had been constructed on inland waterways, such as rivers and man-made canals. Nanxiong had long been an important point of passage in this north-south transit. It sits at the most northerly point of one of the prime navigable waterways in Guangdong province and near the Meiling (Plum Tree) Pass. Located at an elevation of 1,000 feet (305 meters), this was the main pass through the mountains from Guangdong to Jiangxi province. Martini probably crossed the Meiling Pass in a sedan chair carried by Chinese coolies. Here he observed a "nine story tower" and temple dedicated to the imperial minister of the Tang dynasty who had commanded that the road through the Meiling Pass be leveled and paved with cobblestones.[45] At Nan'an (modern Dahu), Martini boarded a boat on the Zhang River, and, after three days, he reached the city of Ganzhou. Here he saw a pontoon bridge made from 130 boats linked together with iron chains, one boat being detachable in order to allow other boats to pass through the bridge. On the Gan River northward, Martini described the danger of "underwater sand banks and sharp rocks . . . accompanied by the speed of the current; I have crossed them not without fear, coming out of them safe and sound thanks to God's will, but I saw many boats which were wrecked after being beaten against the rocks."[46] Martini observed paddle wheels used to transfer water from the Gan River into the surrounding irrigation ditches that flooded the rice fields.[47]

Soon after reaching the Jiangxi provincial capital of Nanchang, Martini's boat entered the vast Lake Poyang. At the point where the north-south waterway of Lake Poyang intersects the east-west flow of the Yangzi River, there is a city called Jiujiang.[48] Martini was struck by the number of boats that docked in this town and by the abundant fish available in the market, including salmon, trout, and sturgeon, some of which had swum up the Yangzi River one hundred leagues from the sea. Martini continued in a northeasterly direction on the Yangzi River and was amazed by the vast number of boats on the river: "It seemed as if all the boats in the world had gathered together in this province."[49] After passing through Anhui province, he entered Jiangsu province and arrived at the Southern Ming capital of Nanjing, probably in April or May (see fig. 5). Through the assistance of a local Christian official, who was a eunuch, Martini was able to visit the tombs of the first Ming emperors.[50] However, the disturbing news from the north that the Man-

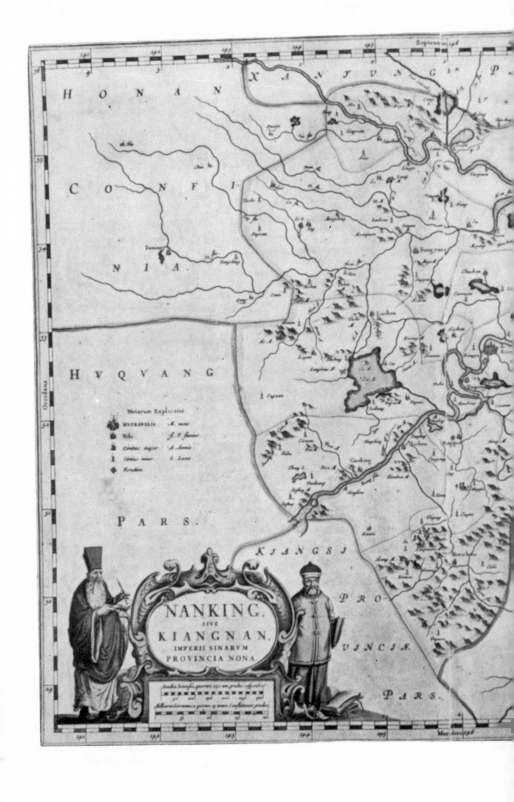

HONAN

CONFI

NIA.

HVQVANG

PARS.

XANTVNG

Occidens

Notarum Explicatio.
METROPOLIS
Vrbs
Civitas major
Civitas minor
Fortalitia

KIANGSI

PRO-

VINCIÆ

PARS.

NANKING,
SIVE
KIANGNAN,
IMPERII SINARVM
PROVINCIA NONA

Fig. 5.—A map of the Ming dynasty province Nanjing (Nanking) or Jiangnan (Kiangnan) which includes contemporary Anhui and Jiangsu provinces. It contains the Ming southern capital of Nanjing. Nanjing is found in the central part of the province on the Yangzi River and is designated "Kiangning" (Jiangning). From M. Martini's *Novus atlas Sinensis,* inserted between pages 94 and 95.

chus had captured Beijing in May filled the city with fear and consternation, and Martini was probably forced to cut short his stay in Nanjing.

After departing from Nanjing, Martini sailed eastward on the Yangzi River to where it intersected with the north-south running Grand Canal.[51] Turning from the northern branch of the canal to Beijing, he took the southern branch and three days later reached Suzhou.[52] Martini described Suzhou as having numerous bridges, though "not as many as in Hangzhou," and as being "superior to Venice" since it was built over fresh water that was pure enough for human consumption.[53] He ate in one of the gaily painted floating restaurants and noted that this was the only place in China where he saw butter consumed.[54] Martini continued southward, entering Zhejiang province and, shortly thereafter, Hangzhou.

Although Hangzhou was Martini's main residence in China, he has been little associated with the city because of the attention focused upon his travels and adventures throughout China as well as Europe. In his widely read books, Martini fostered this image of a daring, peripatetic man of God. Consequently, Martini has been seen as a priest in perpetual motion, a "gunpowder mandarin" who forged cannon for the desperate Ming cause while serving the court of the Ming pretender to the throne, as an "admiral" who marshaled his shipmates against pirates, as an adventurer who could travel throughout north China in the midst of the Manchu conquest, and as a foreign sage who could cow invading Manchu troops into docility.[55] But even if some of these events did not actually happen in the way they are described, Martini was far from being an imposter. There is little doubt that he was an extremely talented and dynamic figure. The image that he cultivated served the cause of the mission —*ad majorem Dei gloriam* (to the greater glory of God)—at least as much as it served himself. His identification with the cause of the mission was so complete that he fused his personal glory with that of the mission. If Martini had had a colossal ego, he would have been inclined to excuse it on the grounds that God's work required it.

Nevertheless, when Martini arrived in Hangzhou in 1644, his image as a great figure had not yet been established. He was barely thirty years old, still struggling with learning the Chinese language, and subject to the strict discipline for which the Society of Jesus is famous. It is likely that he stayed rather close to Hangzhou during most of this time, and he wrote that he spent a total of four years at

Hangzhou between 1644 and 1650.[56] Certainly the Baitou peasant uprising then raging to the north of Hangzhou would have made travel very dangerous. There in the swampy countryside of lakes, rivers, and canals that bordered on the south and east of Tai Lake, a group of fishermen, boat handlers, and lake pirates took their stand against the southward advance of the Manchu army. This peasant army, led by the Ming loyalist Wu Yi (styled Risheng), who had just recently attained the highest literati degree of *jinshi,* put up a stiff resistance to the Manchus around the city of Suzhou and on the border of Jiangsu and Zhejiang provinces.[57]

When the Manchus captured Hangzhou in their southward sweep in August of 1645, Martini was forced to flee the city and hide in the mountainous terrain of southern Zhejiang and northern Fujian provinces. During this time he possibly entered into the service of the court of one of the Ming pretenders, the Longwu emperor (Zhu Yujian), and forged the cannon for the Ming general Liu Zhongcao that earned him the name "gunpowder mandarin" *(huo-yao dachen).*[58] It was also perhaps on this trip while passing through Wenzhou in southern Zhejiang province that Martini encountered the Manchu soldiers and pacified them with his display of learned and sacred objects, an encounter he vividly described in some (not all) editions of his history of the Manchu conquest of China.[59] (See fig. 6.)

Martini returned to Hangzhou in 1646 and remained there until early 1650, when he made a brief trip to Beijing and visited the Great Wall, though not the imperial palace because the trip was abruptly terminated. Martini, who had some ability in mathematics, had come to Beijing hoping to obtain an official appointment assisting Fr. Adam Schall von Bell (Tang Ruowang, 1592–1666) at the Bureau of Astronomy. But Schall was annoyed with Martini's audaciousness and distanced himself from him out of fear that the Manchus would learn of Martini's association with the Ming pretender and that this revelation would damage the Jesuits' tenuous standing with the new rulers of China.[60] Without Schall's backing, the Chinese Ministry of Rites denied Martini's petition to remain in Beijing and ordered him back to Hangzhou. Soon after returning to Hangzhou in the summer of 1650, he was selected as procurator and sent back to Rome.

Martini embarked for Europe in January of 1651 by way of Fujian province, leaving from the port of Anhai (north of the island

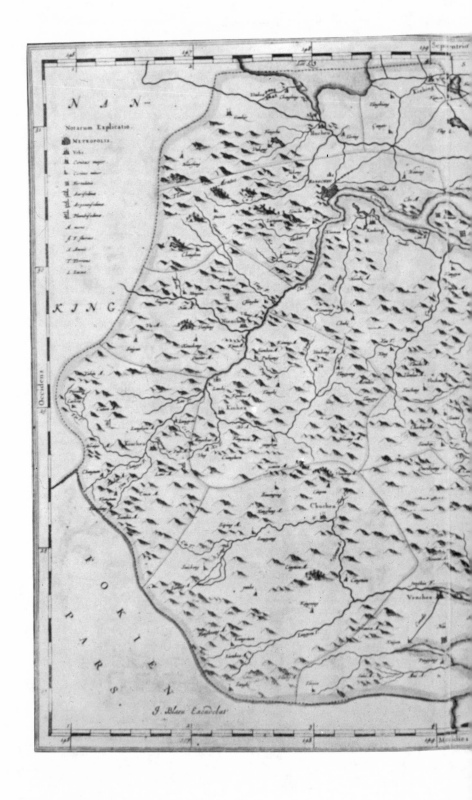

Fig. 6.—A map of Zhejiang (Chekiang) province including the cities of Hangzhou (Hangcheu) in the north-central part of the province and Wenzhou (Vencheu) in the southeast, where Martini is said to have had his dramatic first encounter with Manchu troops. From M. Martini's *Novus atlas Sinensis,* inserted between pages 108 and 109.

Quemoy) on a boat bound for the Philippines.[61] After a whirlwind itinerary that carried him from the north to the south of Europe and after a dramatic return voyage to China in which he was captured by pirates near Valencia (in Spain), Martini arrived back at Hangzhou in June of 1659.[62] He remained there until his sudden death in June of 1661. Added together, Martini spent a total of six years in residence at Hangzhou. If this is a relatively short period, given the long residencies of other Jesuits in China, it is on the other hand a long stay for a man with the restless energy of Martini. Certainly, these six years enabled him to leave his vigorous imprint on Hangzhou more than on any other mission in China. That imprint took the form of a remarkable church and a nearly incorruptible body.

IV

Martini's legacy is visible in Hangzhou today in the form of a European-style church. The first Christian church in Hangzhou had been built in 1627–1633 by Fr. Manuel Dias the younger (Yang Manuo) through the generosity of Yang Tingyun. This church was located just west of Guan Bridge (Guan qiao) on Guan Alley (Guan hang) (see fig. 3).[63] When most of Hangzhou's canals were filled in during the late nineteenth and early twentieth centuries, the canal bridges lost their function. Consequently, "Guan Bridge" today is simply the name of a site on North Zhongshan Road (Zhongshan bei lu) that is designated with the character *guan* (a different character from that of Guan Alley). The church on Guan Alley was apparently just inside Qiantang Gate and within the walled city of Hangzhou.[64] The Jesuits located their residence just southwest of this church and near the West Lake. However, after the Manchu conquest of Hangzhou in 1645, this area around the church became the Manchu garrison city (see fig. 2).[65]

After returning to Hangzhou from Europe in 1659, Martini was filled with great plans for mission work and was supported in his plans during the years 1658–1660 by such influential people as the governor of Zhejiang province, Tong Guoqi. Tong was a member of the famous Tong clan of Fushun in the region of the Liaodong peninsula. Although descended from Jurcheds, the clan had adopted a style of life indistinguishable from that of the Chinese.[66] In the early Ming period the Tong clan was awarded hereditary rank.[67] The clan was notable for producing soldiers and officials, but its ascent to national prominence came with the Manchu conquest of China. After the capture of Fushun by the Manchus in 1619, the Tong family collaborated with the Manchus, initially in administering the Chinese population of Liaodong peninsula and later in the conquest of the Ming.[68] The Tongs served initially in the Chinese Bordered White Banner and later in the Chinese Plain Blue Banner. The family was rewarded for its support by having one of its daughters chosen as an imperial secondary consort of the Shunzhi emperor (reigned 1644–1661). In 1654 she gave birth to a son who would eventually become one of the most capable rulers in Chinese history —the Kangxi emperor (reigned 1661–1722). During the Kangxi reign, the Tong family became so influential and filled so many offices in the palace that it enviously became known as the family that "fills half the court" *(Tong ban chao)*.[69] Tong Guoqi was a paternal first cousin of the Shunzhi empress, Xiaokang (1640–1663), and so was a distant uncle of the Kangxi emperor on the maternal (and less significant) side.[70]

Tong Guoqi was introduced to Christianity when the Manchus conquered Beijing. Although he hesitated to make a final commitment to the new faith, his wife was baptized with the Christian name of Agathe (Yajiada). As part of the Manchu conquest, Tong was sent to the south as an army regional commander and passed through the provinces of Jiangsu, Zhejiang, Fujian, and Jiangxi, where he encountered Christian churches.[71] After the cessation of hostilities, Tong was appointed governor of Zhejiang province. Though he was eventually impeached and removed from office, Tong continued to have an interest in Christianity and was baptized late in life. As was typical of both Chinese and Manchus, several members of Tong's family accompanied him in embracing the new faith. Consequently, when his younger brother (by the same mother) Tong Guoyin became governor of Henan province, the latter was able to assist the mission work of the Jesuit Father C. Herdtricht (En Lige, 1625–1684) in the years leading up to the anti-Christian persecution of 1664.

Tong Guoqi disliked the cramped Hangzhou church in Guan Alley, and he urged Martini to build a new church.[72] Moreover, the stationing of Manchu troops in the area of the church after the fall of the Ming dynasty had frightened the parishioners.[73] In preparation for building a new church in Hangzhou, Martini acquired a plot of land in the northern part of the city near Heavenly Water Bridge

(Tianshui qiao) and just inside North Wall Gate (Beiguan men) (see figs. 2 and 3).[74] This site was quite close to the Grand Canal and only a short walk north from the site of the earlier church in Guan Alley. With the financial support of the governor's wife, Madame Agathe, and also of Madame Judith (Youdida; Su Qinwang), who was a concubine of a Mr. Zhao, Martini began construction of the new church in 1659.[75] One can imagine the stir created by the visit of Governor Tong to the construction site to consult with Martini on the progress of this foreign-style church.[76]

During the course of the construction, Martini's obesity and constipation led him to consult a Chinese physician about his severe indigestion. Impatient and fearful of complications should the problem not be promptly cured, Martini rejected the mild remedy prescribed by the Chinese physician. Instead, he decided to use the more potent cathartic drug rhubarb (a species of Rheum as opposed to garden rhubarb) that he had in his possession. However, he overdosed in the amount of one drachm (drachma)—an ambiguous measurement that as an apothecary unit amounts to one-eighth of an ounce—and his illness worsened. When the Chinese physician was recalled and learned of the large dosage of rhubarb that Martini had taken, he regarded the situation as hopeless.[77] Martini died soon thereafter, on 6 June 1661, three months shy of his forty-seventh birthday.

Martini's premature death disrupted construction of the church, but the work was eventually taken over by Fr. Humbert Augery (Hong Duzhen, 1618–1673) and completed by 1663.[78] Although the original church structure was damaged by fire, it has been rebuilt and is found today on North Zhongshan Road. The church is approached through a noisy, tree-shaded street, brimming with people and shops that spill out into the road. The walled site is marked with the number 415. Upon entering the gate, one finds a typical Chinese courtyard with the church standing at the end of the courtyard facing east (see fig. 7). Initially, the structure was dedicated to Jesus and was referred to by Europeans as the "Church of the Savior" (Templum Salvatoris) and the "Church of the Holy Name of Jesus."[79] The original Chinese name of the church was Chaoxing tang (Church of the Supernatural).[80] It was apparently not until the mid-nineteenth century that the church was given its present name of Immaculate Conception Church (Shengmu wuyuanzui tang).

This church has long been regarded as one of the most beautiful

Christian edifices in China. Its beauty lies not in an imposing size, which is dwarfed, in any case, by the newer cathedrals of Beitang in Beijing, Xujiahui in Shanghai, and others. Even in the late seventeenth century, it was smaller and less imposing than the main Islamic mosque in Hangzhou.[81] The beauty of the Church of the Savior is rather one of form and style in the Baroque sense. The facade, today painted in pale blue with white columns and pilasters (flat columns), presents the image of a European Baroque church with a slightly Chinese cast.

The facade was based on a Baroque design that was reduplicated in Jesuit churches throughout seventeenth-century Europe.[82] Martini had certainly seen churches of this design in Rome, probably in the form of the famous Chiesa del Gesù, which was the prototype of many Jesuit churches. The Gesù facade was built by Giacomo della Porta in 1575–1584 as a transition form from the Renaissance to the Baroque styles (see fig. 8).[83] The Gesù has possibly had the greatest architectural influence of any church since its construction four centuries ago, and there are numerous other examples of this type of facade in Baroque churches throughout Italy.[84] The facade was developed to accommodate a tall and wide nave flanked by aisles outside the rows of columns. The interior of the church in Hangzhou has a typically Jesuit barrel-vaulted nave with lower side aisles (see fig. 9). Although this cross-section would have called for a three-part facade, the Renaissance impetus for classical order dictated that the columns near the center of the facade and the pilasters at the sides be of equal height. The discrepancy in height between the two-story nave section and the one-story side aisles was harmonized in the facade by the use of parapets (walls), which often took the form of scrolls, though these were less accentuated in the Hangzhou church. In some features, such as the use of Chinese circular windows *(oculi)*, the Hangzhou church differs from its European counterparts.

The structure of the Church of the Savior in the late seventeenth century was very similar to what one finds there today, although the interior coloring and decoration were quite different.[85] Previously, the interior walls and ceiling were plastered and painted in very vivid shades of gold and blue using the Chinese technique of high glosses. This bright coloring has been entirely lost in today's church, which is painted in muted pastel blue and white shades. The walls were made of brick, which would have resisted destruction by

Fig. 7.—The facade of the former Church of the Savior, today called the Immaculate Conception Church (Shengmu wuyuanzui tang), Hangzhou, 1990. It was initiated by Fr. M. Martini in 1659 and completed in 1663. The exterior cross seen at the peak was omitted from the original church because of geomantic (*fengshui*) fears expressed by nearby residents. The church was damaged by fire in 1692 and its rebuilding was completed in 1699.

Fig. 8.—The facade of the Church of Jesus (Chiesa del Gesù), Rome, built ca. 1575–1584 by Giacomo della Porta. The design of the Gesù had a tremendous influence on Baroque architecture and was reduplicated throughout Italy and elsewhere. The Gesù was the model for the Church of the Savior in Hangzhou through the inspiration of Fr. Martini, who quite probably had seen numerous examples of this style in Italy. Alinari/Art Resource, New York.

Fig. 9.—Interior of the Immaculate Conception Church (formerly Church of the Savior), Hangzhou, 1990, looking toward the altar.

fire and eased the task of restoring the church after the severe fire in 1692. There were then, as today, four rows of wooden columns that framed three aisles to match the three doors in the facade. The outside rows of columns were anchored to the walls, in accordance with the Chinese style.[86] Each of the columns in the two center rows supported the jams of the high barrel-vault that covered the nave and the two smaller barrel-vaults that covered the side aisles.

The Church of the Savior was part of a Christian college or complex of buildings that included a seminary, a dormitory, a library, and a separate chapel for women called the Church of the Blessed Virgin.[87] In 1624 Hangzhou was chosen for establishing a seminary because of its central location in China.[88] The seminary continued to function for approximately seventy years, from the time of Fr. Aleni to the death of Fr. Intorcetta in 1696. After the

Church of the Savior was constructed, the seminary was moved to this site.[89] The social customs of seventeenth-century China called for a fairly strict separation of the sexes in most activities. Seventeenth-century Confucian attitudes emphasized this separation, and so these customs were rigorously observed in literati families. It was difficult for the Jesuits to observe this custom fully, because only male priests could perform rites such as baptism, distribution of the Eucharist, and administration of the last rites, which required physical contact. However, the Jesuits did establish a second church in Hangzhou exclusively for women, who would gather there each month to hear the mass and receive the sacraments.[90] It is difficult to pinpoint the exact location of this women's church, but it is likely that it was only a short distance from the Church of the Savior.

V

Two portraits of Martini are preserved in Trent.[91] Both are oil paintings by unknown painters, perhaps European painters in China. The larger painting (fig. 10) dates from the seventeenth century, whereas the smaller painting, which is unfortunately too dark to be reproduced, originated in the eighteenth century. Both present a standard portrait form showing the upper part of the body positioned at a slight angle to the viewer with the head and especially the eyes turned and focused straight ahead. The inscriptions on both paintings indicate that they are portraying Martini at the age of forty-seven, when he died.

The seventeenth-century portrait presents Martini as a commanding figure with full beard and learned stature, dressed in the exotic scholar's robe of China. This portrait is intent on commemorating Martini's achievements. It was probably intended to reflect the missionary spirit of *ad majorem Dei gloriam* and to publicize the Society of Jesus, whose insignia is prominently displayed in the upper-left corner. Below the Jesuit insignia is an astronomical instrument similar to an armillary sphere with three symbols from the zodiac [the crab (Cancer), the lion (Leo), and the virgin (Virgo)] below it, which would symbolize Martini's achievement in astronomy. Martini is holding a map of China, which would indicate his work as a geographer. In comparison with Jesuit astronomers like Terrentius (Schreck), Schall, and Verbiest, Martini is not well

R.P.MARTINUS MARTINI⁹ TRID. GEOGRAPHIÆ & ASTRONOMI
PERITISSIM⁹ Aᵒ. MDCXLI. IN SINAS PENETRAVIT, A REGNI PRIM
RIIS OB EXIMIAM PRUDENTIAM ET VIRTUTEM HONORAT⁹ A
MDCLI. ROMAM PROCURATOR MISSUS, A PIRATIS ET TEMPE
STATE VEXAT⁹ OB. IN URBE HANGCHEU, VI. JUN. MDCLXI. ÆT XLV

Fig. 10.—Portrait of Fr. M. Martini, an oil painting by an unknown artist dating from the seventeenth century. 91.5 cm. × 66 cm. The Latin inscription states: "The Reverend Father Martino Martini of Trent, a man of extraordinary skill in geography and astronomy, who entered China in the year 1641. Having been honored by the leading men of the realm because of his exceptional knowledge and virtue, he was sent to Rome as a [Jesuit] procurator in the year 1651. [During the journey] he was subjected to hardship by pirates and storms. He died in the city of Hangzhou on 6 June 1661 at the age of forty-seven." Museo Provinciale d'Arte in the Buonconsiglio Castle of Trento, from the archive of documents administered by the Servizio Beni Culturali della Provincia Autonoma di Trento.

known as an astronomer, but his achievements as a geographer and cartographer had no counterpart in the seventeenth-century China mission. Martini is dressed in an embroidered scholar-official's robe of blue with gold or orange braid. He also wears the hat of a Chinese scholar-official. His stance, long beard, and clothing make him barely distinguishable from other prominent China Jesuits presented in similarly stylized portraits. In some ways the portrait conflicts with what is known of Martini. The long, thin face and nose and the slender tapered fingers are at odds with the picture of a man who was quite corpulent at the time of his death and who apparently died from a malady associated with overeating.

If the seventeenth-century portrait is overly idealized, then the eighteenth-century portrait may be excessively realistic in its treatment. Unlike the earlier portrait, which is filled with symbols, the later portrait focuses entirely on the physical appearance of Martini. The scholar-official's robe in the smaller portrait is also in blue hues with gold decoration and bears the insignia of a crane, indicating some official service. Martini wears a scholar's hat, but most noticeable is the round, fleshy nature of the face, revealing a corpulent body beneath the robe. This portrait is not only less stylized than the first but almost brutally realistic. It is not an idealized handsome face, but one that expresses great personality and charm. The nose is too fleshy and the eyes are too large to be handsome, but the large, dark eyes are penetrating. One is drawn to them as windows into a powerful mind and personality, and feels, for a moment, the force of this Jesuit.

The young scholar Zhang felt it was true what they said about this church—it was a very foreign-looking structure, especially in the height of its facade. Yet Zhang felt there was something graceful and soothing about this temple with its three symmetrical entryways. Zhang had just celebrated his twenty-seventh birthday, and he decided to visit this church, which had become the talk of Hangzhou. Even more intriguing than the church was the scholar from the Far West who was directing its construction. This Master Martini had become a famous man during the last two years because of his incredible activity. It is said that just before coming to Hangzhou, he had returned from a long journey to the Far West.

Zhang caught a glimpse of the Western scholar. It was the scholar's movements that most impressed him. He was a dynamic figure with a wonderfully long beard and a corpulent but quick-moving body that bustled from workman to workman, overseeing the building of the new church. He seemed to be everywhere, and as he came to each worker, he talked with his strange-sounding accent, gesticulating forcefully and smiling. Martini was one of the scholars who had come ninety thousand *li* from the Far West to China. These scholars had first appeared in Hangzhou fifty years ago and had been sponsored by important scholar-officials like Yang Tingyun and Li Zhizao, who became their disciples.

These foreign scholars were very different from Hangzhou people. They were larger, their beards were fuller, and they emitted a strange scent. Some had blue eyes, which Zhang had never seen before. Zhang's tutor told him that the Western scholars had come this great distance to teach the Chinese people about the Lord of Heaven. Their teachings were similar to those in the ancient classics, but also different. Zhang wanted very much to talk with this robust and friendly Western scholar, but he did not know how to approach him. It was not so simple to arrange, because he was afraid that if his family or friends were to hear of his speaking with a foreign scholar, they would disapprove.

There was a lot of controversy surrounding the foreign scholars at this time, because some Hangzhou people were upset over the construction of this church, especially the height of the facade. Such vertical height projecting in straight lines was inauspicious in terms of geomantic forces, because it unbalanced the harmony of nature by plunging into the earth's flesh and violating it, producing malign influences. Master Martini had heard of these concerns and had tried to pacify the Hangzhou people. He assured them that the height of the church would not exceed twenty meters and that there would be no high towers in the facade. High towers created especially inauspicious situations. Moreover, he showed the people that the church would have an auspicious rectangular ground plan plus a courtyard in front to allow the *qi* (vital force) to penetrate the building.

Some of the families who lived in adjoining houses had grown nearly hysterical with anticipation that a cross would be erected on the outside of the church, but the Western scholar assured them that there would be no visible cross on the exterior. This cross was a very curious symbol to Zhang. In spite of the Western scholars' efforts to explain that the cross was a symbol of love, nearly everyone in Hangzhou felt that it symbolized death. So great was the fear of the cross' mortal influence that many of the neighbors had spoken of boarding up their windows to thwart the draining of valuable *qi* from their buildings.

It was time for Zhang to go. He thought that maybe he should bring his own father to see this unusual church that the Western scholar was building, and perhaps then they could together arrange to have a chat with this foreign gentleman. He would see.[92]

CHAPTER 2

The Elixir of Immortality from the Far West: Cinnabar from Rome

It was a bright April day filled with the blossoms of the peach trees. Zhang breathed in the fragrant air and felt it was a fine day to be traveling in a sedan chair to visit the new cemetery of Dafangjing, where the reinterment ceremony of Master Martini would occur. Both ahead of and behind him were sedan chairs of several notables of Hangzhou. Master Martini's colorful reputation had grown even larger in recent times because of the rumors that had circulated since his body had been disinterred last August. Perhaps too many had been attracted by the tales of the Western scholar's uncorrupted body; immortality in one form or another had a powerful attraction. Several Daoists were convinced that Martini had secretly practiced the art of immortality, though whether of the inner or outer elixir they were unsure. The procession was passing Wulin Gate, and the cemetery lay ten *li* to the west. There were a few hills to climb, but nothing very steep for these experienced sedan chair carriers and certainly nothing like the steep hills they had to climb in order to reach some of the Buddhist monasteries and pagodas around the West Lake.

It was fitting that Yang Tingyun's son had respected his father's wishes in donating the plot of land to the Western scholars. Zhang recalled visiting the cemetery site nearly three years ago, in 1676, and being struck at the time by the favorable geomantic features of its subtle dragon formation in the hills to the southwest and the many signs of dragon's breath (*qi*) revealed in the auspicious green foliage on the ridges of the hills. To the southeast, the steep wooded hills behind the site formed a harmonious unity that curved around and down to the cemetery site. Beginning with the high ridge in the distance, the hills descended gracefully on the right and left sides to form a valley, at whose base lay the cemetery. The yang force of the hills was balanced by the yin force of a stream that wound its way through the contours of the hills down the middle of the valley and passed to the eastern side of the site. This water combined with the trees to the rear of the site to improve its geomantic features. Some improvement was needed, because the otherwise auspicious dragon formation in the hills unfortunately faced north instead of toward the desired south and even blocked off some of the life-giving rays of the sun, especially in winter.

Zhang, of course, could not discuss these matters with the Western scholars, because they were extremely critical of geomancy. Although they were careful not to violate geomantic principles flagrantly in their buildings, they wished to show by slight deviations from these principles that they did not accept them. Certainly the low flat fields to the north and west of the cemetery site were not auspicious, and the close proximity of the road was regarded by most Chinese as disturbing to the qi of the grave site. However, the Western scholars welcomed this proximity, because they said they wished to have the cemetery site accessible to the disciples who would travel from the surrounding area to visit the grave site and attend mass in the small stone chapel that Master Intorcetta had built over the stone crypt. In the end, the Western scholars succeeded in attaining what they sought while not offending the local people. The locals thought the site odd, but not so odd as to be inauspicious and to bring misfortune to the area.

Zhang looked forward to catching a glimpse of the uncorrupted body of Master Martini. Sometimes he felt that he was too curious about this body that refused to corrupt, but he could not remove from his mind the question that if Martini had not practiced the Daoist art of immortality, what then kept his body from decaying?[1]

I

The dominating figure in the Hangzhou Jesuit community in the late seventeenth century was Prospero Intorcetta (Yin Duoze; styled [the Sage] Juesi, 1625–1696). He was born the third son of an old and honorable family in the small town of Piazza in Sicily.[2] His two older brothers, Agostino and Francesco, entered the service of the church, and it was assumed that young Prospero would remain at home to care for his parents.[3] However, when he contracted a seri-

ous illness and hovered on the point of death, a vision of Saint Francis Xavier (1506–1552), the pioneering Jesuit apostle to Asia, appeared as a healing image.[4] After recovering, he felt called to the
priesthood as a personal obligation to Saint Francis, who had died
attempting to enter China. While his older brothers served God in
the nearby vicinity of their hometown, Intorcetta's service took him
all the way to China.[5]

It is intriguing that while the Chinese biography of Intorcetta
emphasizes his parents' support of his desire to enter holy orders,
the Western-language biographies emphasize the familial conflict
that led to his vocation.[6] The Western sources portray Intorcetta as a
headstrong youth who ran away from school at sixteen years of age
in protest against his parents' wishes that he study law. He came on
the run to the Jesuits in Messina, burning with youthful zeal to serve
in the foreign missions. But the Fathers were familiar with youthful
rebellion, and they would not take him without his parents' consent.
After receiving it, Intorcetta was admitted into the Jesuit order in
1642, at the age of seventeen. He completed the novitiate, studied
theology, and was teaching grammar and humanities when the call
to China came.

The call came through the vigorous form of Father Martini,
who had just returned from China and was passing through Europe
like a clarion, stirring up the dreams of young Jesuits and inspiring
them to carry the Lord's word to remote and exotic places. War in
Europe had diverted Martini from landing in Holland, and so he
had disembarked at Bergen, Norway, and traveled with his usual
energy southward through Hamburg, Amsterdam, Leiden, and
Brussels to Rome. One can imagine the impact that the dynamic
Martini, around whom audacious stories swirled, would have had
on Intorcetta, who at the age of thirty had yet to leave his homeland.
For Intorcetta, Martini was an inspiring figure who fired the young
priest's imagination. Martini became the means of fulfilling his missionary dreams and his vow to Saint Francis. One is hardly surprised to learn that Martini recruited him, along with sixteen other
Jesuits, for the China Mission.[7]

Martini and his contingent of recruits departed from Genoa in
January of 1656, but they were attacked by French pirates and
forced to turn back to Genoa.[8] Later, they reached Lisbon. Because
of the overseas privileges (*padroado*) granted by the popes to the Portuguese, the latter monopolized sea routes to the east, and Lisbon

was the official departure point for all missionaries going to China.[9] Martini and his recruits boarded the *Bom Jesus da Vidigueira* in April of 1657 and underwent a tumultuous journey in which they were buffeted by frightening storms. One by one, the Jesuits died until twelve out of eighteen in their group were carried away by illness.[10] The exhausted remaining Jesuits arrived at the gateway to China in 1659. It was here in this Portuguese enclave of Macao that Intorcetta took his final vows as a Jesuit.

Intorcetta entered China and traveled to Hangzhou in 1659, possibly in the company of Martini.[11] Here he studied the Chinese spoken and written languages until his Jesuit superior sent him to the prefecture of Jianchang in Jiangxi province, located in the south of China (see fig. 1). In Jiangxi province Intorcetta first demonstrated those qualities of leadership that characterized his thirty-seven-year apostolate in China. At Jianchang and Nanfeng as well as in neighboring villages, he oversaw the establishment of churches and in only two years baptized over two thousand Chinese neophytes.[12]

At Jianchang in 1661 Intorcetta took an important role in overseeing the printing of one of the first translations of a Confucian Classic into a European language. He was a pioneer in developing a technique for producing Sino-European xylographic works in which both Chinese and Latin characters were engraved on woodblocks and printed on the same page.[13] The Latin translation of *Sapientia Sinica* (the Wisdom of China) includes the shortest Classic, the *Great Learning (Daxue),* as well as the first five parts of the *Analects (Lunyu).* This work is attributed to Fr. Inácio da Costa (Guo Najue, 1603–1666), but the translation effort was a collaborative project involving all of the Confucian Four Books and had begun with the arrival of the earliest Jesuits, such as M. Ruggieri, in China in the late sixteenth century. Intorcetta, as a newly arrived Jesuit with insufficient knowledge of Chinese to translate, was apparently assigned the task of supervising the printing because of his organizational abilities and because he was located at a mission site where printing in Chinese woodblocks was feasible.[14]

Intorcetta's initial success in Jianchang was aided by a good relationship with the magistrate there. However, when local geomancers criticized the tower in the new church on the grounds that its height upset the natural harmony of the geomantic *(fengshui)* forces, the magistrate took their side against the foreign priest.[15] Moreover, relations between the missionaries and the local magistrates were vulnerable to any suspicious rumor and to the slightest ruffling of the political winds blowing from the court in Beijing. Consequently, it was not surprising when the Jianchang magistrate later turned hostile to the point of seeking to exterminate the Christians and to convince the governor-general of Jiangxi province that Intorcetta was the leader of a seditious band. His actions produced one of the numerous local anti-Christian movements, which shortly afterwards was followed by a nationwide anti-Christian movement (1664–1666) led from Beijing by the scholar-official Yang Guangxian. Intorcetta was arrested and taken as a criminal to Beijing, from which he was exiled along with other Jesuits to Canton in 1665.

At Canton, twenty-five missionaries were confined to the cramped quarters of a small church.[16] Intorcetta took charge of organizing their supplies of food, medicine, and clothing. After he had been in Canton between one and two years, he was recalled to Rome as procurator to report on their difficult circumstances.

Before departing from Canton, he continued his editorial work of producing a translation of the Four Books, this time by producing a bilingual (Chinese-Latin) edition of the *Doctrine of the Mean (Zhongyong)* entitled *Sinarum scientia politico-moralis*.[17] Intorcetta made use of his return voyage to Europe to have this translation printed partially at Canton in 1667 and partially at Goa, India, in 1669. The printer was probably the Chinese convert Paul, who Intorcetta took with him to Goa, but who then returned to China while Intorcetta proceeded on to Europe.[18]

Intorcetta had been delayed for a year in departing from Canton because of the need for the Jesuits to send a substitute Jesuit hostage from Macao to take Intorcetta's place in jail. In December 1667 and January 1668 he had taken part in a forty-day conference at Canton in which the missionaries of different orders debated mission policy.[19] The enforced confinement of the expelled missionaries at Canton did not make them amenable to agreement. Consequently, the Dominican Friar D. Navarrete departed Canton and returned to Europe, where he attacked the Jesuit position in his famous *Tratados*.[20] The financial straits of the Mission were so desperate that the vice-provincial was able to scrape together only twenty gold crowns to give to Intorcetta for the costs of his long and difficult journey.[21] Finally, in September of 1668, he was able to leave Canton and travel the less than one hundred miles down river to Macao. In January of 1669 he boarded a ship en route to Europe.

After Intorcetta left for China, his mother had fallen ill and was cared for by her two older sons, who lived nearby. Madame Intorcetta, who was advanced in years, longed to see her absent youngest son. As she lay on her deathbed with her two older sons beside her, she said that if only all three of her sons would appear before her, she could die content. According to Intorcetta's Chinese biography, his mother's desire for this visitation was so impelling, that the Lord of Heaven commanded an angel to make a revelation of her youngest son to her, although he was far away in China at the time.[22] Madame Intorcetta said that she saw her youngest son, although the vision was not apparent to the other two sons. After experiencing the vision, she died content, and the remarkable story was communicated to Intorcetta in a letter.

After arriving in Rome in 1671, he addressed both the Father General of the Society of Jesus and the Cardinals of the Propaganda and appealed to both for aid for the China mission. The plight of his confreres in China produced a sense of urgency, and he did not remain long in Rome but promptly departed for China with recruits to reinforce the mission ranks. So urgent was his desire to return to China to help his fellow believers that he refused to take time out to visit his brothers, who were forced to come and seek him out in the midst of his preparations for departure.[23]

On the long journey to China, illness struck down his traveling companions one by one, and it is astounding that, once again, Intorcetta was one of the few to survive this ordeal. Out of a total of five hundred people on board the ship, only twenty-seven disembarked, and, out of these, only fifteen survived.[24] He arrived back in China in August of 1674. Only one of his twelve companions had survived, but the news in China was uplifting: the confinement of the missionaries in Canton had ended in 1671. God was indeed good!

II

On his return to China, Intorcetta was sent to the Hangzhou mission, where he lived in the Church of the Savior and assumed his duties at the beginning of 1676.[25] Given the uncertainties of life as a missionary in China, there was no way that Intorcetta could have known that this would be his final and most important mission assignment. The Jesuits were so impoverished that they had been unable to replace Fr. H. Augery when he died in July of 1673. Consequently, the mission post had remained empty for two and one-half years. One can imagine the long list of postponed questions and unresolved matters as well as anticipation among parishioners that would have greeted Fr. Intorcetta on his arrival in Hangzhou. He would remain stationed there until his death nearly twenty-one years later in 1696.

The situation of Christianity in the provinces of China was growing more and more difficult. Although Yang Guangxian had been disgraced and removed from office in 1669, the literati hostility that had fostered Yang's anti-Christian attitudes was merely in a latent phase before surfacing once again in open animosity. Only at the imperial court in Beijing had the position of the missionaries been strengthened, but cultivation of the Manchu court came at the expense of neglecting the ties with Chinese literati, particularly in the provinces. It was with the literati of Hangzhou that Intorcetta worked, and apparently with some success.

Intorcetta's talents were those of an organizer and a judicious, diplomatic leader rather than a stimulating thinker or a creative scholar. One of the first tasks that he undertook at Hangzhou was to revive and realize Fr. Dias' plans for a seminary for educating native Chinese priests on the model of the Society of Jesus.[26] He sought out and produced books for the seminary. He also traveled throughout Zhejiang province and established churches at such places as Jiaxing, Haimen, Ningbo, Pingyang, and Huzhou. Each year he visited these churches.[27] The published works and manuscripts credited to his name, such as his account of the mission in China from 1581 to 1669, tend to deal with the administration of the mission.[28] Intorcetta's role in the Jesuit translation project of the Confucian Four Books may have involved more than producing *Sapientia Sinica* and *Sinarum scientia politico-moralis*. It is quite possible that on his return voyage to Europe in 1668, he carried a manuscript of the translations that were eventually published as *Confucius Sinarum philosophus* (Paris, 1687). Intorcetta appears to have written part of the long introduction *("Proëmialis Declaratio")* to this work.[29] However, his role in the translation project was more that of an editorial organizer than of a scholarly translator. In any case, Fr. Couplet completed the introduction and editorial work on *Confucius Sinarum philosophus* and saw it through to publication in 1687.

The two Chinese works associated with Intorcetta's name involved translation projects dealing with the rules of the Society of Jesus and the *Exercises of Saint Ignatius.*[30] Chinese versions of these works were important to Intorcetta's attempt to develop an indigenous Chinese clergy for the Jesuit Order. In addition, he wrote a long treatise in response to Fr. Navarrete, defending the Jesuit position on the Chinese rites to ancestors and Confucius.[31] Intorcetta served as a novice master for seven years.[32] His administrative and leadership abilities were recognized by his appointment as Jesuit visitor of China and Japan from 1676 to 1684 and later as vice-provincial of China from 1686 to 1689. Rome again named him visitor in January of 1698, unaware that he had died in October of 1696.[33]

In 1678, two years after his arrival in Hangzhou, Intorcetta undertook an extensive interior decoration of the Church of the Savior. His aim was to use paintings with inscriptions to teach the essentials of this teaching from the Far West. During the early Qing period, the ability to read and write extended far beyond the small class of literati.[34] However, many illiterate Chinese were limited to receiving the teaching in oral or visual form. Not only was street preaching ill-suited to the highly educated Jesuits, but it would have been extremely unwise to have foreign priests preaching on the streets in the sensitive political and social atmosphere of late-seventeenth-century China. (Street preaching had been tried unsuccessfully in China by the Franciscans and the Dominicans.) A far less antagonistic way of presenting the teachings of Christ to the Chinese people was through the use of pictures. To this end, Intorcetta organized an ambitious project that involved the production of seventy-two religious images. Not only were painters involved, but Intorcetta arranged with certain sympathetic literati to compose inscriptions that would explain the paintings and simultaneously make them appealing to the literati class. It appears that Zhang Xingyao composed inscriptions for nearly half of these images.[35] (A complete list of the seventy-two images and Zhang's thirty-eight inscriptions is found in the appendix.) By 1683 the project was completed and Intorcetta was able to list each of the paintings with proud satisfaction in a letter to his brother, Father Francesco.[36]

In the late seventeenth century there were three altars in the Church of the Savior. The main altar was dedicated to Jesus as Savior, portrayed in a large painting measuring 3.5 meters × 3.5 meters (11½ feet × 11½ feet).[37] By contrast, today's main altar is towered over by a large painting of the Virgin Mary in what appears to be a

nineteenth-century style (see fig. 11). The seventeenth-century tab-
ernacle that housed the host (i.e., the sacramental body of Christ) at
the main altar was a mixture of European wooden carvings and Chinese ornamentation. There were two side altars (no longer present
in 1989), each dedicated to one of the prime apostles Saint Peter and
Saint Paul. Painted images of these apostles (each measuring 3
meters × 3 meters) were placed over these altars. Saint Peter was
portrayed with one hand holding two keys and the other hand pointing to heaven, symbolizing the authority of the "keys to the kingdom of heaven" (i.e., papal authority) that Jesus had bestowed upon
him in Matthew 16:19. Saint Paul was portrayed on the other altar
in the act of preaching, with his left hand holding a crucifix and his
right hand pointing to a sign that stated: "But we preach Jesus crucified" (I Corinthians 1:23).[38]

The walls of the church were filled with a total of seventy-two
paintings (including the above three paintings of Christ, Saint Peter,
and Saint Paul) in gilded frames plus images of twelve seraphim
(angels of the highest order). The largest painting in the church
(6 meters × 5 meters) portrayed Christ's genealogy beginning with
Abraham. Most of the other paintings measured between 2 meters
× 2 meters and 2.5 meters × 2.5 meters.[39] These images were
painted by a Chinese painter, working from European models.
Although the paintings were somewhat crude, the subject matter
made them fascinating, and they attracted many curious Chinese to
the church.[40] The paintings depicted scenes from the life of Jesus
from his birth to his ascension into Heaven; the life of the Blessed
Virgin; the Four Last Things (Death, Judgment, Hell, and Heav-
en); the apostles (including ten of the original Twelve Apostles plus
Saint Paul and Saint Barnabas); the Four Evangelists; the martyrs
Saint Stephen and Saint Lawrence; the founders of various religious
orders (including the Jesuit founder Saint Ignatius of Loyola), each
depicted in the habit of his order; memorable scenes from the Bible
as well as from church history, such as the conversion of the Roman
emperor Constantine the Great.

Figures of more recent times among the paintings included the
three Japanese Jesuits who were martyred in Japan in 1597. (These
Japanese Jesuits had been beatified in 1627 as a prelude to their can-
onization in 1862.) Several eminent female saints were portrayed,
including Saint Catherine of Siena (1347–1380) and Saint Theresa
of Avila (1505–1582). The inclusion of the pioneering Jesuit in Asia,

Fig. 11.—The altar of the Immaculate Conception Church (formerly Church of the Savior) in Hangzhou, 1990.

Saint Francis Xavier, is no surprise, given the important role he played in Intorcetta's sickbed apparition and consequent vow to become a Jesuit. In addition, there were several less famous saintly figures, such as Saint Stanislaus Kostka (1550–1568), an extremely devout youth who became the patron saint of Poland. Kostka had been beatified in 1605 (and was later canonized in 1726) and was the patron of Jesuit novices. Intorcetta's Sicilian origins are betrayed in his inclusion of an image of Saint Rosalia (died 1160), an object of. legend and cultic worship among Sicilians who became the patroness of Palermo.

Below each of the seventy-two images was a written explanation of the mystery that each image represented, conveyed in an elevated literary style on a glossy white background.[41] These images filled the Church of the Savior and, along with the bright blue and gold paint and the candles used to illuminate them, created a beautiful, glittering effect, which conveyed miniature lessons in the basic elements of the Lord of Heaven Teaching. To the uneducated, these elements were conveyed visually, while to the literate, who included town merchants as well as literati, they were conveyed through the inscriptions. Many Chinese were led by their curiosity to visit the church and see the paintings, even if they did not become Christians.

III

One of Intorcetta's most enduring achievements as an administrative leader in Hangzhou was the establishment of a Jesuit cemetery. The site that he chose just northwest of the city was called Dafangjing, which might loosely be translated as "bountiful well."[42] Sometimes it was called Fangjingnan (South of the Well).[43] This site had first become famous in the Han dynasty when the recluse Wang Fangping extolled the drinking of its spring water.[44] The famous Song calligrapher and painter Mi Fu (Nangong) wrote an inscription for the site. Later, in the early Ming dynasty, a calligrapher from Qiantang named Hong Zhong wrote a five-character inscription, naming the site "The Great Peach Blossom Well at the Mountain" (Fangjing taoyuan ling), which signified a fantasy land of peace and quiet away from the chaos of the world. In the Later Jin dynasty (936–944), the Monastery of the Gracious Buddha (Fo hui si) was built near the spring. Although the buildings on the site had by the seventeenth century become ruins, it remained a scenic spot of historical interest and people often visited it. The spring water was so clear that the fish and even the pebbles in the water could be counted.[45]

One of the Three Pillars, Yang Tingyun, bequeathed the Dafangjing to his eldest son, who later gave the land to the Hangzhou church. In 1676 Fr. Intorcetta bought an adjoining piece of land in order to increase the size of the plot and began building a crypt and chapel in order to reinter the Jesuits buried in Hangzhou.[46] The damp and low-lying terrain in the city, with its numerous canals, had produced deteriorating conditions in the Jesuit grave sites. He undertook to transfer all of the bodies of Jesuits buried in Hangzhou to this new site on higher and drier ground. The transfer was completed in 1678, and the site was dedicated with a reinterment ceremony.

Today, if one bicycles less than one hour into the western suburbs of Hangzhou on Hanghui Road, one will encounter the Dafangjing site on the south side of the road surrounded by a high iron rail fence.[47] The cemetery is hidden from view from the road by thick shrubbery and trees, and, in any case, one requires a note of introduction to the groundskeeper before the gate will be unlocked for entry. To the northeast lie flat planted fields, while to the southwest, rising behind the cemetery, are steep hills with dense green vegetation. One wonders what kind of geomantic (*fengshui*) qualities were attributed to this land by seventeenth-century Chinese. Certainly the Chinese Christians would have been cautious in raising the issue with Intorcetta, because the Jesuits had voiced strong opposition to geomancy as a diabolical superstition.[48]

In the seventeenth century Dafangjing was apparently part of a large field, but the visitor today sees a small cemetery reduced in size to a flat rectangular area whose lateral sides are each less than 200 feet (61 meters) long. The cemetery is now bordered by two very mundane enterprises—on the west by the Number Two Chinese Pharmaceutical Factory (Di'er Zhongyao chang) and on the east by the Hangzhou Beer Factory (Hangzhou pijiu chang). The cemetery is boxed in between them as a verdant peaceful isle. The vegetation in the cemetery is dense but controlled.[49] There are two stone structures on the site, both of which date from Intorcetta's time. The Dafangjing is still beautiful today, although the setting would have been more pristine and picturesque in 1678. The remarkable fact is that the cemetery has survived the severe devastation of the Hangzhou area by the Taiping rebels in the 1860s and the desecrations of the Red Guards a century later. One suspects that the fairly new iron rail fence that encloses the cemetery was built to protect the site from any future anti-Christian desecration.[50]

Intorcetta had two stone structures built on the cemetery site— one in a blended Sino-European style and the other in a distinctly Chinese form (see fig. 12). The first was a small church, referred to in the Jesuit annual letters of 1678–1680 as a "chapel" *(Sacellum)* called "the new Temple of the Savior" *(novus Salvatoris Templum).*[51] The prefix "new" implied a comparison to the older Church of the Savior within Hangzhou. The small structure at Dafangjing served not only as a chapel but also as a sepulcher.[52] In Europe it was common to find a crypt built under an altar. However, unlike in Saint

Fig. 12.—The memorial gateway *(paifang)* and the Temple of Our Savior (built 1676–1678), in which twenty-one Jesuits are interred, at Dafangjing Cemetery outside of Hangzhou.

Peter's in the Vatican, where a vast crypt is found under the altar, it was typical in small chapels for the crypt to occupy a mere half-story below the church floor in which the bodies of the deceased were sometimes stacked in bunkbed fashion.[53]

Though the form and interior of the Dafangjing chapel is European in design, its external appearance, with its rounded roof and windows *(oculi),* is more Chinese in style. The flat, rectangular facade is slightly more than twenty feet (six meters) in length and ten feet (three meters) in height. The chapel is capped by a rounded cement roof, commonly found in Chinese tomb architecture. A vertical tablet projects from the roof above the door and is topped by a cross. Here in the remote area of Dafangjing, unlike at the Church of the Savior in the city, an exterior cross was permitted. The inscription below the cross, arranged vertically on the tablet, claims that this building houses the "Public Graves of the Lord of Heaven Teaching." Under each of the windows is a small inscribed stone tablet *(mubiao),* which was typically placed above the ground in front of the grave or on the path leading to the grave.[54] The two tablets list the names and give brief biographical information for nine of the Jesuits buried within the chapel.[55]

One enters the chapel by descending six steps into a room that rises into a vaulted ceiling.[56] This room is the largest of the three inner rooms and measures twenty square meters in surface area. Because of the few windows in the chapel, very little light enters the interior, which is so dark that even during the daylight hours a lamp is necessary to see. A low shelf runs around three sides of this middle room, and on this shelf are found coarse, glazed earthenware ossuaries of various sizes, which were typical of seventeenth-century Chinese burial practices.[57] Of the twenty-one Jesuits buried in the Chapel of the Savior, seventeen are identified with a name either inscribed or written on the top surface of an ossuary.[58] Four of the ossuaries are unmarked. Two smaller rooms, one on each side, flank this middle room.

The interred remains of Jesuits in Hangzhou began to be transferred to this Chapel of the Savior in 1678. The two tablets in front of the chapel list the names of the nine Jesuits in the following order: Frs. da Rocha, Trigault, Ribeiro, Fiva, Cattaneo, Fróis, Dias (the younger), Martini, and Augery. The Macaoist Jesuit brother Zhong Mingren (S. Fernandez) was also reinterred, though his name was omitted from the tablets. Jesuits continued to be interred in the

Dafangjing chapel in subsequent years, including the Italian Fathers Intorcetta, Antonio Faglia (Fa Anduo, 1663–1706), and Agostino Barelli (Ai Siding, 1656–1711).[59]

Unlike the blended Sino-European style chapel, the second stone structure at Dafangjing is distinctly Chinese. Soon after entering the iron gate from Hanghui Road, one sees to the immediate right a memorial gateway or arch that frames the approach to the chapel (see fig. 12). Referred to in Chinese architecture as either *paifang* or *pailou,* these freestanding gateways are built in order to dignify the approach to a tomb or palace.[60] These structures have been used for commemorative or triumphal purposes since the Tang dynasty (618–906), but they became particularly popular in Ming times and have become a distinctive part of traditional Chinese architecture. The most monumental example is the marble *paifang* (1540) that adorns the entrance to the Ming imperial tombs outside of Beijing.[61] A typical Chinese *paifang* consists of two vertical posts that frame one gateway, but one commonly finds four posts framing three gateways or even six posts framing five gateways. The posts are joined at the top by horizontal lintels. The *paifang* may be constructed from wood or stone or even bricks that are covered with decorative tiles.

The memorial *paifang* at Dafangjing consists of four vertical posts that define three gateways. As one stands before it, the archway perfectly frames the chapel, which is raised on steps beyond the *paifang.* The result is a blending of the two structures, whose elegant simplicity is very unlike the elaborate decorativeness of what often passes today for traditional Chinese architecture. The middle lintel of the *paifang* is inscribed "Cemetery of the Scholar-Priests of the Lord of Heaven Teaching" *(Tianzhujiao xiushi zhi mu).* At the entrance, directly across from the *paifang,* is a memorial stone inscribed with characters indicating Martini's grave. This traditional Chinese variation on the grave markers *(mubiao)* in front of the chapel was called "an inscription on the avenue to the grave" *(shendao bei)* and was reserved for people of high status.[62] This stone bears a later dedication by the historical preservation unit of the Hangzhou city government dated May 1987. The passage of 326 years between Martini's passing and the dedication of this memorial shows the respect that his name continues to command in Hangzhou, even to this day.

The most famous reinterment at Dafangjing, by far, was that of Fr. Martini. The opening of Martini's original tomb in August of

1678 had ignited galloping rumors throughout Hangzhou because his body had suffered very little decomposition during the seventeen years since his death in June of 1661. Even if Martini's corpse had been sealed in an air-tight coffin, which was common practice in China at that time, it is unlikely that this could fully account for the lack of decomposition.[63] To understand the fascination of the Hangzhou people with this phenomenon, one must understand that the Chinese have a venerable tradition dedicated to the search for a means of prolonging life, even to the point of achieving immortality. Since the time of the legendary Laozi, who was said to be a sixth century B.C. contemporary of Confucius, Daoists in China have developed a sophisticated body of knowledge surrounding this search for an elixir of immortality. The search branched into a search for an inner elixir through meditative techniques and an outer elixir through alchemy. Although the search attracted an endless stream of charlatans and scam artists, it also embodied the traditional teaching most closely associated with the development of natural science in China.[64]

One of the oldest and most famous elixirs was cinnabar (mercuric sulfide) from which mercury can be extracted. The red color of cinnabar has been associated with blood or life, and since prehistoric times in China, red pigments have been used to paint the tombs of the deceased.[65] Chinese alchemists had distilled cinnabar by the third century B.C., and its consumption was supposed to produce physical immortality. However, the mysterious positive aspects were counterbalanced by the fact that cinnabar is also a poison dangerous to consume. Although the Jesuits vehemently denied practicing alchemy, many Chinese suspected them of having a secret knowledge of this science.[66] Consequently, one could see how the lack of decomposition of Martini's body might be regarded as a sign of the effects of consuming cinnabar, giving rise to intense speculation among the people of Hangzhou. Although the Jesuits endeavored to preach a teaching that offered a *spiritual* elixir of immortality, many Chinese saw the Western scholars through Daoist eyes as bringing a physical elixir, akin to cinnabar, from Rome.

The Jesuit annual letter of 1678–1679 describes in detail the condition of Martini's body in a way that seems macabre to us today, but such details were perceived in a more positive and even inspirational tone in the seventeenth century.[67] Martini's hair, beard, and fingernails were described as being intact, and the tomb was found to contain no unpleasant odor. There was a black mucous clinging to his body, though it is not clear whether this was caused by decomposition or by the damp conditions of the original grave site. Reinterment involved stripping Martini's body, drying it with clean linen, and washing the old burial vestments. The Jesuit annual letter of 1678–1679 implies that Martini's reinterment was the talk of the town within the Hangzhou Christian community in 1678, the year in which the scholar Zhang Xingyao was baptized. The extremely gradual decomposition of Martini's body continued to cause a stir in the Christian community of Hangzhou in later years and was noted with obsessive interest. Missionaries who moved the body during the Jiaqing reign (1796–1820) recorded that it had not yet suffered from decomposition.[68] As late as 1843 a priest who visited Dafangjing observed the lifelike appearance of Martini's corpse. The fascination of Hangzhou Catholics with Martini was such that it became a custom for many years to make an annual pilgrimage to Dafangjing in order to trim Martini's hair and nails.[69]

We find in the Hangzhou Christian community of the seventeenth century a heightened sensitivity to scents connected with death. Not only is emphasis placed on the absence of the sharply unpleasant odor of the decomposition of human flesh in the case of Martini, but there is also an emphasis on the presence of certain powerful and pleasant scents. An "extraordinary and heavenly fragrance" is described in the Jesuit Annual Letter of 1678–1679 as having been present at the deathbed baptism of a woman of Hangzhou.[70] The fragrance was thought to be linked with the presence of the Virgin Mary at the woman's deathbed. The Virgin Mary had a particularly close relationship with the Christian women of Hangzhou, whose bond to her was strengthened by the shared experiences of their sex and reinforced by the exclusively female—apart from the priest—communicants who participated in the masses held in the Church of the Blessed Virgin.

IV

Father Intorcetta's long period of service in Hangzhou was aided by his judicious temperament. This temperament was revealed in his handling of what could have been a very damaging incident for the mission. The experience of Jesuits in China was marked by numerous outbreaks of hostility against their unfamiliar religious teaching, and mishandling of some of these incidents had cost the mission dearly. With its foreign-looking structure, it is not surprising that the Church of the Savior aroused the hostility of Hangzhou residents. In 1679 three brothers from a wealthy and influential family attacked the church, possibly on the grounds that the edifice disturbed the geomantic harmony of the area.[71] Intorcetta responded to the physical assault on the church with faith and good sense by urging the parishioners to remain calm and not to respond with force. Instead, Intorcetta took his case to the magistrate, who found the three brothers at fault and punished them by having them caned and placed in cangues.

In July of 1687 a contingent of five French Jesuits disembarked at the seaport of Ningbo, nearly two hundred miles (320 kilometers) to the east of Hangzhou. They were led by Fr. J. de Fontaney (Hong Ruo[han], 1643–1710) and included Frs. J. Bouvet, J. -F. Gerbillon, L. le Comte, and C. de Visdelou. The French contingent, under the direct sponsorship of the French king Louis XIV, had traveled by way of Siam in an attempt to skirt the previously obligatory Lisbon-Goa-Macao route monopolized by the Portuguese. At Siam they embarked on the ship of a Guangdong merchant named Wang Huashi and sailed to Ningbo. The governor of Zhejiang province, Jin Hong, was disturbed by the sudden appearance of foreigners, who traditionally had entered China at the port of Canton in the far south. He proposed that they be expelled and memorialized the throne in Beijing for confirmation of his expulsion order.[72] The French Jesuits appealed to Intorcetta, who was placed in the difficult position of defending their unauthorized arrival.

Intorcetta appealed to Fr. Verbiest in Beijing. When Verbiest petitioned the throne, asking permission for these five Jesuits to come to the capital, the Kangxi emperor responded with eagerness to utilize the mathematical skills of these highly educated and well-trained Jesuits. Consequently, Verbiest was able to secure an imperial edict that reversed the hostile ruling of Governor Jin and permitted the French to pass on to the capital. Intorcetta sent a Chinese candidate of the Jesuit Order to Ningbo to welcome the Frenchmen and to escort them to Hangzhou. They remained in Hangzhou for three weeks (from 30 November to 21 December 1687) before boarding a canal barge for the northward journey to Beijing, which they finally reached in February of 1688.[73]

These were not the first French Jesuits to serve in China; in fact, Fr. Augery, who had supervised the completion of the Church of the Savior after Martini's death, was French. However, prior to this time the Portuguese and Italian Jesuits had dominated the China Mission, and never before had such a large group of Frenchmen arrived. Their arrival confirmed a shift in the direction of the mission. If Intorcetta had not realized the full implications of this shift at the time, he would most certainly have been aware that something was new. And yet Intorcetta would probably have welcomed the French as fellow Jesuits and as much-needed reinforcements for the China Mission. Possibly at the time, he saw their arrival as a hopeful sign of strengthening Jesuit influence at the imperial court. Certainly Intorcetta looked to the Beijing mission more and more for support against the church's enemies in Zhejiang province. One of these enemies was a strict Confucian and a rising star on the Chinese political scene named Zhang Pengge (1649–1725), who would eventually become a grand secretary under the Yongzheng emperor.

Although the Hangzhou Christian community was remote from the centers of power in Beijing and subject to the sympathies or antipathies of local and provincial officials, there were several occasions when Intorcetta met with the Kangxi emperor. These were not casual encounters, but rather audiences arranged as a shrewd means for the Kangxi emperor to keep an eye on the foreign missionaries in the central provinces.[74] Without formally recognizing the status of the missionaries, it was necessary to develop some informal method for keeping track of their growing numbers and for detecting any suspect political activity. The Kangxi emperor's six southern tours (*nan xun*) in 1684, 1689, 1699, 1703, 1705, and 1707 provided the means for controlling the missionaries through personal contacts.[75] At missionary sites along the routes of his southern tours, such as Nanjing and Hangzhou, the emperor would invite the (mainly Jesuit) missionaries to personal audiences. In an informal setting, the Jesuits felt highly flattered by the imperial attention and small gifts from the imperial table. While the Jesuits were reinforcing their positive impression of the emperor, the emperor was becoming informed of their activities. When what he learned did not suit him, he was capable of cracking down, as he did on the southern tour of 1703 when he learned of missionaries moving about the countryside without official supervision.[76]

Intorcetta's first meeting with the Kangxi emperor was during the emperor's southern tour in 1689.[77] Hangzhou has been called the "Venice of China," but the name is far less fitting today than when Marco Polo visited it and observed all the canals that crisscrossed the city before they were filled in to become streets. These canals were still present in the seventeenth century. Consequently, when Intorcetta prepared to greet the Kangxi emperor, he rented a boat.

Early on the morning of 28 February 1689 Intorcetta set out in his rented boat to pay his respects to the emperor. When he reached the outskirts of the city, he came to the emperor's attention. From the imperial boat, the Kangxi emperor asked his advisers who this exotic-looking gentleman was, and he was told Yin Duose of the Lord of Heaven Church.[78] After ordering that Intorcetta's boat be allowed to draw near, the emperor invited Intorcetta to board the imperial boat, where he was asked a series of standard polite questions.[79] These included how many years Intorcetta had lived in China, what his homeland had been, how many years he had lived in Zhejiang province, and what his age was. After Intorcetta answered these questions, the emperor asked if he could read Chinese characters. Intorcetta responded that he understood just a few characters and that he was not able to read very many because of his age. One must interpret Intorcetta's response in light of standard Chinese etiquette, which demanded modesty in replying. After living among Chinese for fifteen years, Intorcetta probably had absorbed the local etiquette, as had most Jesuits.

The emperor went on to ask about other Jesuits. In response to whether Intorcetta had received a letter from Fr. T. Pereira (Xu Risheng, 1645–1708) of the Beijing court, Intorcetta said that Fr. Pereira had written in December to convey that the emperor would be making a southern tour in the following year, but it had been uncertain whether he would visit Hangzhou. In response to whether Fr. Fontaney was in Nanjing, Intorcetta confirmed that he was in Nanjing with Fr. G. Gabiani (Bi Jia, 1623–1694). The emperor asked if Intorcetta had been to Beijing. Intorcetta—no doubt choosing his words carefully—said that because of Yang Guangxian (the leader of the anti-Christian persecution of 1664–1666), he had come to Beijing and had participated together with Fr. Schall in an imperial audience. A Manchu official of the Imperial Household named Zhao Chang (Pursai) spoke up at this point, saying that although he had often visited Lord of Heaven churches, he did not understand what he saw.[80] After an exchange of pleasantries, the emperor presented Intorcetta with gifts of exotic fruit, special pastries, and a dairy drink.

After determining that the Church of the Savior was located not far inside the Northern Gate (Beiguan men) of Hangzhou, the emperor suggested that Intorcetta's boat lead them there. One can imagine the excitement with which Intorcetta hurried on ahead so that he was able to be kneeling in front of the church as the emperor's boat passed by. The Kangxi emperor was said to be very pleased. Two days later (2 March), the emperor sent his trusted attendant along with Zhao Chang, leading a contingent of five guards, to the church, where they paid respects *(koubai)* to the image of the Lord of Heaven.[81] They presented an imperial decree that made a gift of twenty pieces of silver to the Lord of Heaven churches in both Hangzhou and Ji'nan (in Shandong province).[82] Another imperial encounter was recorded six days later. On 8 March the imperial barge passed the Church of the Savior, and Intorcetta together with Fr. Emanuele Laurifice (Pan Guoliang, 1646–1703) bowed down in front of the gate of the church in greeting.[83] The Kangxi emperor asked various questions about Fr. Laurifice and, at the end of the audience, gave his blessing to Fr. Intorcetta to reside in Hangzhou and to Fr. Laurifice to go by boat to the mission in Suzhou. God was indeed good!

V

The Kangxi emperor's visit to the Hangzhou church did not prevent an anti-Christian persecution from breaking out in the region two years later in 1691. With the support of the governor-general of Zhejiang province, Zhang Pengge, the opponents of Christianity attacked the Church of the Savior, where they attempted to destroy the woodblocks that were used in printing Christian literature.[84] They also destroyed religious images and abused members of the church.[85] The women's church, which may have been the origin of the persecution, was consequently converted into a Buddhist temple dedicated to the bodhisattva of mercy, Guanyin.[86] Intorcetta sent news of these dangerous events in Hangzhou to Frs. Pereira and A. Thomas (An Duo, 1644–1709) in Beijing, who on 2 February 1692 petitioned the throne.[87]

The Jesuit strategy in focusing on Beijing clearly proved helpful in this situation. In 1669, after the removal of Yang Guangxian from office, the Jesuits had been restored to leadership of the Bureau of Astronomy (Qintianjian) with the Belgian F. Verbiest (Nan Huairen, 1623–1688) at the helm. At Verbiest's death in 1688, the Italian Jesuit C. -F. Grimaldi (Min Mingwo, 1639–1712) was appointed in absentia to head the bureau. However, because of Grimaldi's absence in Europe from 1688 to 1694, Frs. Pereira and Thomas served as acting heads of the bureau.[88] Consequently, when Pereira and Thomas petitioned the throne in 1692 on behalf of the Hangzhou Christians, they were doing so as prominent officials and with Manchu allies at the court. The power of their allies was shown in Songgotu, a meteoric figure who as uncle of the empress had great influence in the Kangxi court.[89] Later, his fall would be as precipitous as his ascent. As great-uncle to the heir apparent (Yinzheng), Songgotu would be blamed by the Kangxi emperor for the heir's misbehavior and be thrown into prison, where he died in 1703.

This memorial became the basis of the Kangxi emperor's famous Toleration Edict of 1692. Fr. Intorcetta's name is prominent in the petition and appears twice in the Pereira-Thomas memorial of 2 February 1692. The memorial describes Intorcetta's recent message to the Jesuits in Beijing, saying that the governor of Zhejiang province, acting in concert with local Hangzhou officials, had organized an attack on the Church of the Savior. In this attack, the woodblocks used in printing Christian literature had been destroyed on the grounds that Christianity was a subversive religion that should be expelled from the region. If the anti-Christian feelings that inspired this attack had been limited to Hangzhou, then the Jesuits in Beijing probably would not have gone to the effort of expending their precious political capital in attempting to secure a favorable ruling from the throne. Petitioning the emperor in such a way always had its dangers, because when the emperor was forced into taking a firm stand, there was no certainty that the ruling of the throne would be favorable to the Jesuits. Nevertheless, advised by Zhao Chang and supported by Songgotu, the Beijing Jesuits submitted a memorial to the throne in an attempt to preempt another anti-Christian movement from breaking out across China.[90]

In their memorial, the Jesuit authors attempted to rebut the charges that Christianity was a subversive foreign religion by making three different points. First, they noted that the emperor was not biased against foreigners (and thereby delicately raised the sensitive issue that the imperial family was itself non-Han and constituted foreigners in China). Secondly, the memorial reminded the emperor of all the services that the Jesuits had performed for the throne, including the astronomical and calendrical work as well as the manufacturing of weapons by Frs. Schall and Verbiest and the diplomatic services with Russia of Grimaldi, Pereira, and Gerbillon. The memorial noted that the emperor's Jesuit servants did not journey thousands of miles for the sake of glory or wealth. (Here the Jesuits were perhaps distinguishing themselves from the Portuguese and Dutch traders, whose aggressive and acquisitive behavior on the southeast China coast had alienated the Chinese.) Thirdly, the memorial appealed to the precedent of previous honors that the emperor paid to the Jesuits for their services. In a land where precedent received the added sanction of filial respect for the actions of one's ancestors, the appeal to precedent was a powerful force. Finally, the memorial concluded, although the Jesuits were not members of the Han race, the emperor had unified the realms of Han and non-Han (e.g., Manchu) peoples by employing men without regard to their place of origin. How could it be that there might be no place in the realm for Fr. Intorcetta to live in peace? As poor and abandoned servants, the Jesuits appealed to the emperor.

The Edict of Toleration of 1692 consisted of five parts, of which the first and longest part was the Jesuits' memorial to the throne dated 2 February 1692. The second part involved the forwarding of this memorial by the emperor to the Ministry of Rites (Li bu) on 4 February. The third part consisted of the initial decision from the Ministry of Rites dated 19 March and written by Yi Sang'a. Yi was a Manchu of the Plain Yellow Banner who began as an official under the Shunzhi emperor and later, under the Kangxi emperor, became a grand secretary and head of the Ministry of Personnel (Li bu). This decision was not very favorable to the Jesuits, nor did it please the emperor. Songgotu urged the emperor to exert his authority and, consequently, the decision was sent back to the Ministry of Rites for revision.[91] The next day, a more favorable response from the Ministry was forthcoming. It was written by Gubadai (died 1709), the head of the Ministry of Rites and a Manchu of the Bordered Yellow Banner.[92] The emperor approved Gubadai's response without further comment on 20 March.

Gubadai noted that the Jesuits had made important contributions in preparing the calendar, in manufacturing cannon used

against the rebel Wu Sangui, and as interpreters in diplomatic nego-
tiations with the Russians leading to the Treaty of Nerchinsk.[93] His
report further noted that the Jesuits lived in every province in China
and did not teach heretical doctrines *(zuo dao)* or false teachings
(yiduan) that instigated sedition but rather were law-abiding and
peaceful. Gubadai compared the missionaries to Tibetan or Mongo-
lian lamas, Buddhist monks, and Daoists, all of whom had temples
and burned incense. For these reasons, Gubadai recommended that
the missionaries be allowed to carry on their activities without further interference from local officials. A brief memorial in support of
Gubadai's report was issued by Grand Secretary Yi Sang'a and
other members of the Grand Secretariat, who frequently served con-
currently as ministers *(shangshu)* in the Ministry of Rites.[94] Gubadai's report was approved by the Kangxi emperor, and it became
known as the Edict of Toleration (22 March 1692).[95]

The Edict of Toleration represents the high point of the early
modern mission in China. It represents tangible proof of the (albeit
ephemeral) success of Jesuit methods in that the edict was clearly a
reward for services rendered by the Jesuits to the Manchu throne.[96]
The edict removed Christianity from the category of false, heterodox, and seditious sects, such as the White Lotus Society, and placed
it on an equal footing with Buddhism and Daoism. The edict pro-
tected existing church buildings throughout the provinces, including
the Church of the Savior in Hangzhou, and permitted freedom of
worship such that Chinese felt freer to openly admit that they were
Christians. The edict had the immediate effect of giving a tremendous boost to conversions, and the Jesuits recorded more than
twenty thousand converts in the following year.[97] Unfortunately, the
positive situation was not long-lasting and the reasons may be found
in the fickleness of political power. The edict appears to have been
primarily the work of the Manchus on or near the throne. However,
the attitudes of Chinese literati, such as Zhang Pengge, were unal-
tered and would have the more long-lasting effect. Since the Manchus as minority rulers were forced to attune themselves to the cultural leaders of the majority, it was only a matter of time before the
negative attitudes of the literati toward Christianity resurfaced in the
monarch's political policies.

Still, for the time being the Jesuits were basking in the glow of
their success, unaware that the glow belonged to the autumn rather
than the spring. Barely three months after the Toleration Edict was

issued, Intorcetta came to Beijing to thank the emperor for the edict. He was solicitously received at the court by the Manchu official Zhao Chang, who said that, in light of Intorcetta's age and the strenuous journey, the good Father from Hangzhou should first rest and then return to the court in a few days for an audience. Intorcetta was eventually received by the Kangxi emperor in the Palace of Heavenly Purity (Qianqing gong), one of the most important palaces within the Forbidden City.[98] The *Zhengjiao fengbao* records that the emperor asked Intorcetta standard questions about how long he had lived in Jiangxi province and in Hangzhou.[99] Intorcetta was served imperial tea, and then the audience was over. However, the intricacies of imperial politics soon brought him back to court.

The interim appointees to lead the Bureau of Astronomy, Frs. Pereira and Thomas, were anxious to have Grimaldi assume his imperial appointment as head of the bureau. Grimaldi's return from Europe was believed to be imminent, and the throne wished to send Fr. Thomas to Macao to greet him. But Thomas had been ill, and it was believed that the long journey from Beijing to Macao would be too arduous for him. Consequently, the idea was conceived that Fr. Intorcetta should accompany Fr. Thomas on a canal barge south to Hangzhou, where Thomas could recuperate and be cared for by Intorcetta prior to proceeding on to Macao.[100] As part of the preparation for implementing this plan, Frs. Intorcetta and Thomas were received by the emperor at the Palace of Eternal Spring (Changchunyuan), an imperial summer palace located in the western suburbs of Beijing.[101] Here they were entertained with a feast and given valuable presents.

Unfortunately, these plans were disrupted when Intorcetta became ill and was unable to depart. Because he was a venerable sixty-seven years of age, he was shown a great deal of solicitude by both the emperor and the Manchu official Zhao, who both in Hangzhou in 1689 and in Beijing in 1692 had referred to him as *laorenjia,* a title of respect used for the elderly.[102] In any case, Grimaldi's return to China was delayed because, rather than taking the Portuguese sea route from Lisbon to Goa, he had traveled overland through Persia to Goa and consequently did not arrive in Beijing until August of 1694. Eventually Intorcetta and Thomas traveled from Beijing to Hangzhou. Fr. Thomas carried an imperial command that forced the Zhejiang governor-general Zhang to repair the damage done at the Church of the Savior.[103]

On 2 August 1692, ten days after Intorcetta had returned to Hangzhou in triumph, a terrible fire swept through the city and severely damaged the Church of the Savior. The fire spread through the main hall of the church and the dormitory, both of which were destroyed.[104] However, so great were the efforts of those protecting the church that the fire was turned back from the annex in the rear and the library on the upper floor, where the woodblocks used in printing Christian books were stored, was completely saved. Intorcetta overcame his initial despair over the loss of the painted images and dutifully undertook the rebuilding of the church, but the project drained him of his last energy. Four years later, in September of 1696, he was struck by a form of dysentery. After several days he seemed to recover, but he fell ill again soon afterward.[105] He consciously and carefully prepared for death and was concerned that he do so before suffering the confusion or delusion that often occurs on one's deathbed. As his end drew near, he was heard to say: "My work is completed."[106] He waited for death with a composed mind and a peaceful heart. He died during the first watch (11:00 P.M. to 1:00 A.M.) on the morning of 2 October 1696, at the age of seventy-one years and one month.

When Father Intorcetta finished saying the morning mass and the parishioners were leaving, Wang entered the Church of the Savior followed by two catechists, each of whom was carrying a small bundle. They came forward to the altar and placed the bundles on the ground near the baptismal fount, when suddenly a loud wail came forth from one of the bundles. Thank God, thought Father Intorcetta, perhaps at least one might live.

It was the practice of the Jesuits in Hangzhou and other mission cities in China to send catechists out each day at dawn to search for abandoned infants. These infants might be found in doorways or on the side of a foodstall. Most of these foundlings were already mortally ill, but the catechists would gather them before they were trampled underfoot by pedestrians or eaten by dogs or rats. They would be brought in bundles to the Church of the Savior, where they were sanctified with the holy water of baptism. Most of these infants would die before sundown, but none would die without being blessed by the first Sacrament and thereby assured of eternal salvation. A few would survive to be raised as servants in Christian families or as wards of the church, like Wang, who had been found swaddled in a blanket and abandoned on the streets of Hangzhou nearly forty years before.

Some of the Chinese criticized this practice, and there were rumors about why the Lord of Heaven adherents collected these abandoned babies. Some said that the priests enjoyed the infants' eyes as fresh delicacies in their midday soup. Father Intorcetta had heard these rumors, but he ignored them. The saving of souls required that the faithful endure persecution for righteousness' sake. These baptized children would be blessed in the Kingdom of Heaven.[107]

CHAPTER 3

Through a Glass Darkly

I have decided today to be baptized. Master Intorcetta was very pleased and said that he had a special baptismal name for me—*Zhang Yi'najue*, Ignatius Zhang, after Ignatius of Loyola, the founder of the Western scholars' society. I am now forty-five years old, and this has not been an easy decision for me. Certainly it is one that I have meditated on for a long time. Perhaps if Master Intorcetta had not come to Hangzhou two years ago, I would have continued to delay, but he is eight years older than I am and has guided me like a true elder brother.

Each year I have hoped that the times would become more receptive to the Heavenly Teaching, but they have not. When I read the books of the scholars Xu Guangqi and Yang Tingyun, I am amazed by the optimism that fills their writings. Unlike two generations ago, the literati are no longer so receptive to the teaching that the Western scholars have carried ninety thousand *li* from the Far West. But after long reflection, I have become convinced that this teaching is necessary to China, because it will enable us to return to the true path of the ancients. I have decided to commit myself to the task of convincing my fellow literati of the importance of this teaching to China, and to do this, baptism is necessary.

There are some things that I do not understand about the Heavenly Teaching, and there are even some things in which I question the Western scholars' interpretations. I believe that there are things that only Chinese can fully appreciate. But this teaching can return China to the path of truth, and for that reason we need it. I am committed to it, and my baptism will be a mark of my commitment. I pray for a long life to fulfill this task.[1]

I

Zhang Xingyao (styled Zichen) was born in 1633 in the Qiantang district of Hangzhou.[2] He is sometimes said to be a native of Renhe, an adjoining district within Hangzhou that at times in history was absorbed into Qiantang. Zhang came from a literary family. His father was Zhang Fuyan, styled Yinfu, with the honorary name *(hao)* Boyu.[3] Zhang Fuyan might have been exposed to the teaching of the Hangzhou Christian literatus Yang Tingyun.[4] Zhang Fuyan studied with the scholar Ge Qizhan for many years and devoted himself to literary texts, but he failed in several attempts to pass the official examinations. In 1645, with the Ming dynasty collapsing, Zhang Fuyan gave up all attempts to pass the examinations. Whether he did so simply because of the unsettled political and social circumstances or as a form of protest as a Ming loyalist is uncertain. He devoted himself to the Thirteen Classics and the Twenty-one Dynastic Histories, but his writings proved too cumbersome to print. Late in life he fathered a son, whom he named Xingyao. Although Xingyao was born too late to meet his grandfather, he did receive extensive instruction from his father.[5]

Zhang Xingyao had a long and productive life. How long we do not know; the last preface to one of his works is dated 1715, which means that he lived to be at least eighty-two. He had at least one son, whose name was Zhang Youling, styled Dujiu, who also lived in Renhe.[6] We know that he had at least two daughters, because the names of two sons-in-law are known. One was Zhao Feipeng, styled Fujiu, who lived in Qiantang, and the other was Liu Wenbin, styled Sudiao, who lived in Renhe.[7] His son, daughters, and sons-in-law all followed Zhang in embracing Christianity. Although he was typical as a literatus in most respects, his attempt to blend Confucianism with Christianity placed him in a current that was flowing against the cultural tide of his day. As the force of the anti-Christian tide increased in the later eighteenth, nineteenth, and early twentieth centuries, Zhang became a forgotten figure, whose works survived in rare manuscript versions, preserved by the Jesuits in Beijing, Shanghai, Paris, or Rome.

Zhang had little or no contact with the founders of the Hangzhou Christian community. This point is important because it clearly places him in the third generation of Chinese Christians in China. Whereas the first generation of Christians, which included the Three Pillars, has received a great deal of attention, the second generation (which included Han Lin and Zhu Zongyuan) and the third generation have remained shadowy, ill-defined groups.

It is not clear when Zhang was first introduced to Christianity. As a youth he followed the traditional literati path by studying the Confucian Classics and preparing for the official examinations, but the rote memorization and tedious nature of the preparation were dissatisfying for one with his deep spiritual thirst. When a monk was engaged by his family to perform the Buddhist ritual for his deceased parent, Zhang questioned the monk about why he was chanting sutras for the deceased.[8] But the monk's answers reinforced the dissatisfaction that Zhang had felt in his study of Buddhist sutras and, he concluded that Buddhism was illogical.[9] Eventually, Zhang was introduced to Christianity by a fellow literatus.

By the age of thirty-nine he had formulated a sympathetic view toward this teaching and recorded it in a 1672 preface to his *Examination of the Similarities and Differences between the Lord of Heaven Teaching and the Literati Teaching (Tianzhujiao Rujiao tongyi kao)*. He was baptized in 1678, at the mature age of forty-five. Zhang's baptism was one of twenty that Fr. Intorcetta recorded as occurring in Hangzhou during the two years 1678 and 1679.[10] He devoted much of the rest of his long life to studying history and writing treatises that attempted to show how Confucianism and Christianity were in harmony.

Zhang belonged to the ranks of degree-holding literati. Whereas Li Zhizao, Yang Tingyun, and Xu Guangqi had all attained the highest degree of *jinshi,* Zhang acquired the lesser *gongsheng* (senior licentiate). This degree could be purchased as well as attained by examination, and it is not clear how Zhang acquired it.[11] He also prepared for the provincial *(juren)* examination and possibly even competed unsuccessfully, but he eventually gave up trying to pass the exam.[12] Like the *juren* (provincial graduate), the *gongsheng* was an intermediate degree that entitled holders to minor official appointments.[13] As a degree holder, Zhang enjoyed the considerable privileges and status that accrued to such literati, and he belonged to the local elite of Hangzhou. There was often an overlap between degree-holding families and land-owning families, though it is not known whether Zhang's family belonged to the local gentry.

The achievements, whether in attaining degrees or offices, of the third generation of Chinese Christian literati cannot be compared to the first generation, because the Manchu conquest had altered literati attitudes and reduced the opportunities for official service. Certainly Zhang's career was affected by these events in such a way that it is misleading to compare the high official ranking of the Three Pillars with Zhang's modest official attainments. The examinations became increasingly difficult in Zhang's time due to the Manchu government's severe cuts in the examination quotas for Han Chinese.[14] Moreover, throughout the Kangxi period, young scholars found it especially difficult to advance via the regular examination route and to obtain bureaucratic posts.

Zhang did not belong to the generation of high Ming loyalists who had reached maturity by the time of the Manchu conquest in 1644 and whose writings during the 1650s and 1660s were filled with partisan recriminations and collective soul searching in distributing blame for the fall of the Ming. Many of the Ming loyalists expiated their sense of guilt by refusing to cooperate with and receive the benefits of serving the new regime. However, the next postconquest generation, to which Zhang belonged, was more ambivalent in its response.[15] The reaction against and dissatisfaction with Ming literati culture that characterized this generation was certainly found in Zhang's thinking. Using the Lord of Heaven Teaching of European missionaries, Zhang attempted to rectify the lapses of the Ming literati and to return the followers of Confucius to the True Way *(Zheng Dao)* of the ancients.[16]

In trying to determine which missionaries might have influenced Zhang, we can piece together a fairly complete list of Jesuits who were in Hangzhou during Zhang's lifetime. The Jesuit residence at Hangzhou has been obscured by its more famous counterpart at Beijing, and so it is not widely recognized that the Hangzhou mission was served by some of the most capable Jesuits of the seventeenth century. However, after the death of Fr. Intorcetta in 1696, there was a noticeable decline in talent. The growing literati hostility toward Christianity in the provinces combined with the gravitation of the French Jesuits toward the intellectual and political center of China. The result was that most of the best Jesuit minds of the eighteenth century—with notable exceptions like J. de Prémare (Ma Ruose, 1666–1736)—were stationed in Beijing. But in the seventeenth century, the intellectually prominent Jesuits who resided at or passed through Hangzhou included Frs. Trigault, Cattaneo, da Rocha, Martini, Augery, Rougemont, Couplet, and Intorcetta.

The first intellectually prominent Jesuit with whom Zhang

could have had direct contact was Fr. Martini (though we lack clear evidence of such contact). Given the fame of Martini's exploits and the special recognition he received at Dafangjing, it is probable that Zhang, who was twenty-nine years old when Martini died in 1661, heard of the remarkable Martini, even if he had no personal contact with him. The towering figure in the late seventeenth-century Hangzhou Jesuit community was Fr. Intorcetta. Given Intorcetta's broad range of intellectual, organizational, and diplomatic talents, his twenty-one-year residence in Hangzhou from 1676 to 1696, and the small number of Jesuits based at the Hangzhou mission, one can infer that he had considerable contact with Chinese who embraced Christianity during this time. These Chinese would have included Zhang, who was baptized two years after Intorcetta's arrival in Hangzhou.

II

The seventeenth-century Jesuit reports and letters from China contain a host of information about the China Mission but very little detail on individual Chinese converts. This is partly because the purpose of such reports was summary in nature rather than focused on individuals. In addition, there were practical difficulties in transliterating Chinese names for European readers. Nevertheless, one of the richest sources of information about the seventeenth-century mission is provided in the Annual Letters (*Litterae Annuae*) composed by each of the mission centers.[17] For example, the Annual Letters for the years 1678 and 1679 from the vice-provincial of China contain reports from Beijing, Nanjing, Hangzhou, Fujian province, Shanxi province, and Huguang province.[18]

During the Qing dynasty, governmental administrative units were arranged in prefectures *(fu)*, such as Hangzhou, which were subdivided into several districts *(xian)*, such as Qiantang and Renhe. Hangzhou was typical of most Chinese cities in being surrounded by a wall, which is illustrated in local histories dating from the seventeenth and eighteenth centuries (see figs. 13 and 14).[19] The wall around Hangzhou was approximately 11.5 miles (18.5 kilometers) in circumference, not quite 30 feet (9 meters) in height, and 35 feet (11 meters) wide at the top.[20] The city was entered by road through ten main gates or by canal through six gates.

The district of Qiantang comprised an area of land that stretched

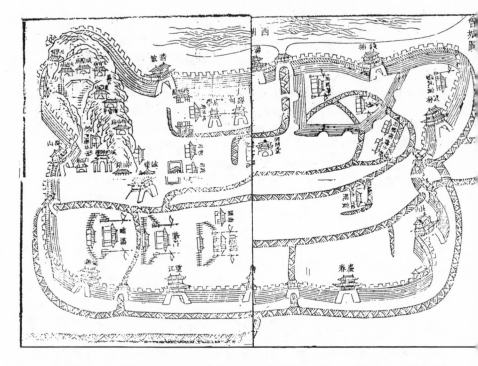

Fig. 13.—An illustrated map of the city wall of Hangzhou. North is at the right of the map. Note Qiantang Gate on the northwestern side of the wall (upper right on the lake), which led into the external district of Qiantang and to the West Lake beyond. Hangzhou's main street, Great Street (not shown), began from Wulin Gate on the northern side of the wall (upper right on the map), running from north to south through the heart of the city, and terminated at Feng-shan Gate on the southern wall (middle left on the map). The names of the ten main gates portrayed in this map have been retained as street markers in contemporary Hangzhou. This map also indicates the canals, rather than streets, with their six entry gates. From *Qiantang-xian zhi* (1718).

from the eastern side of the West Lake to several miles to the west. The district began as a village outside the northwestern side of the Hangzhou wall, but it grew over the years to become an adjoining section of the city. This section stretched along the shore of the West Lake and was linked with the walled portion of Hangzhou through Qiantang Gate (see fig. 15). The district of Renhe was more centered inside the walled city, though it too may have extended beyond the wall (see fig. 16).[21] Today the name of Qiantang Gate is preserved as an intersection of Hangzhou that lies near the previous gate, though the wall has disappeared (see fig. 3).[22] An illustrated local history of

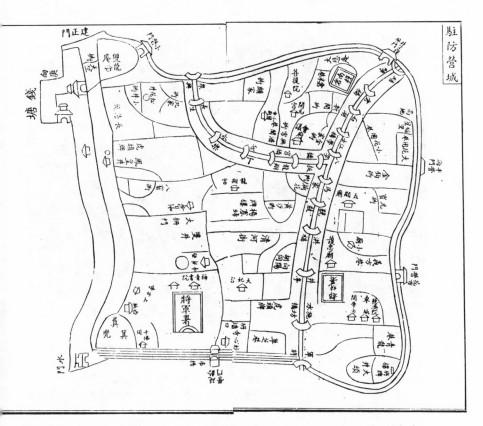

Fig. 14.—A map of Hangzhou in the Qing dynasty as a garrison city *(zhufang ying cheng)* showing the sites of the military barracks. North is at the top of the map and Qiantang Gate is at the upper left. The main entrance (designated *jian zhengmen*) at Wulin Gate is also at the upper left, but on the northern side of the wall. The main street of Hangzhou is designated as running on a north-south axis but on the western side of the city, which is not precise. Some of the main canals with bridges are designated. From *Hangzhou-fu zhi* (1784; 1888–1898), 1, pp. 13b–14a.

1718 shows that Qiantang had become the site of an elaborate literati temple complex during Zhang's time (see fig. 17). The complex reflects the influence of folk religion, for example, the Earth God temple *(Tudi miao)* coexists with the school and the halls for honoring Confucius (Sheng dian and Minglun tang).

The Jesuit Annual Report of 1678–1679 does not mention Zhang Xingyao by name, but there is a reference to a Nicolas Zhang (Cham Nicolaus) as the head of a Christian family that lived outside

Fig. 15.—Qiantang (Ch'ien T'ang) Gate as it appeared around 1906, showing a portion of the city wall that surrounded Hangzhou. This gate linked the inner city of Hangzhou with the village of Qiantang that lay outside of the city wall and along the northeastern shore of West Lake. The gate and wall have since been demolished. Reproduced from Frederick D. Cloud, *Hangchow, the "City of Heaven"* (Shanghai, 1906).

the walls of the city of Hangzhou whose house experienced a miraculous survival from a fire that swept through the area.[23] Since Zhang Xingyao's family home was located in Qiantang, it was beyond the walls of Hangzhou proper and possibly Zhang's father (Zhang Fuyan) was this Nicolas Zhang referred to in the annual letter. If so, not only Zhang but his entire family probably underwent conversion, a phenomenon not uncommon in literati Christian families. However, the character for the surname Zhang was very common in China and one cannot be sure that this reference was to Zhang Xingyao's family. (Similar reasons make it difficult to know if Zhang Anmao, who wrote the preface to Martini's work on friendship, *Qiuyou pian* [Hangzhou, 1661], was related to Zhang Xingyao.) And yet, given the large size of extended families and the fact that the total Christian population in Hangzhou at this time was only five hundred, the likelihood is that this Nicolas Zhang was at least related to Zhang Xingyao.[24]

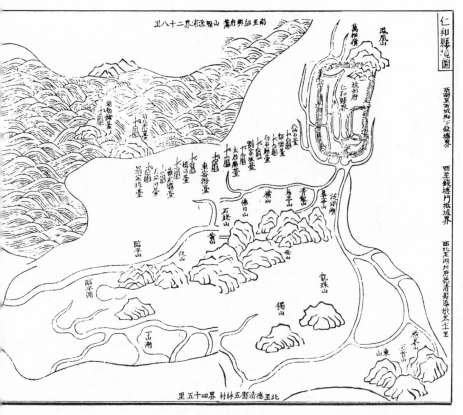

Fig. 16.—A map of the Hangzhou region. Because north is at the bottom of this map, the typical Western perspective would be upside down. The Qiantang River is shown on the upper left side of the map. Hangzhou is illustrated as a walled city at the upper right, and within this enclosure Hangzhou prefecture and Renhe district are labeled. West Lake lay to the right of the walled city, though it is not drawn on this map. From *Hangzhou-fu zhi* (1784, 1888–1898), 1, pp. 30b–31a.

But while the Jesuit Annual Letters fail to mention Zhang by name, so too do Zhang's writings fail to mention specific Jesuits. Zhang's writings do make numerous references to the Jesuits as a group. He commonly refers to them as coming from the "Far West" (Taixi) and traveling ninety thousand *li* (approximately thirty thousand miles or forty-eight thousand kilometers) in order to reach China. The distance of the journey from Europe to China is exaggerated, but the number ninety thousand served as a literary expression to indicate great distance rather than a precise measure. One

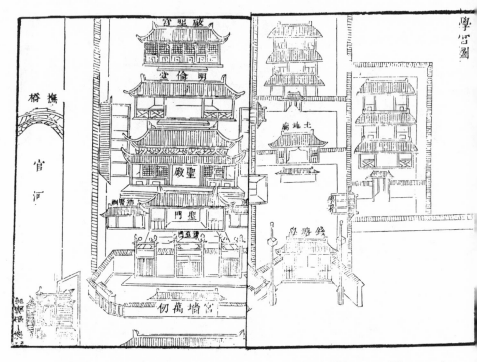

Fig. 17.—An illustration of a literati temple complex in Qiantang. The complex is surrounded by a wall. To the left of the temple complex is the Officeholder's River/Canal (Guanhe) crossed by the Nurturing Bridge (Fuqiao). Directly beyond the main gate, which is labeled "Qiantang School," is an Earth God temple *(Tudi miao)*. A series of halls for honoring Confucius is to the left. From *Qiantang-xian zhi* (1718).

fact that must be understood is that Zhang was not overawed by the Jesuits. He respected them for their knowledge and commitment and he embraced the teaching that they brought, but he regarded them as counterparts to the literati in China. This attitude is shown in the interchangeable terminology that Zhang used to describe them, varying the terms only with prefixes to indicate the different geographical origin, for example, "literati of the Western nations" *(Xiguo Ru)* versus "literati of China" *(Zhongguo Ru)*, or "Western scholars" *(Xi shi)* versus "our literati" *(wo Ru)*.[25]

Zhang's perception of the European Jesuits as counterparts to the elite class of Chinese literati must be seen as a triumph of Jesuit education. Jesuit education melded with the Chinese view that not mere facts but moral and spiritual cultivation were the aim of intellectual study. The Western reference to the school of "Confucianism" is misleading, because the Chinese rarely use such a term. To do so would be to demean the truths that the literati teach by associating these truths with a single individual. Whereas the Chinese tend to accept literally Confucius' statement that he was transmitting rather than creating truth, foreign scholars often misinterpret Confucius' statement to be either a form of Chinese modesty or a delusion.[26] Zhang claimed that the teachings of the Chinese ancients that Confucius transmitted were, in essence, the same teachings that the Jesuits had brought from Europe. Whereas Western references to "Confucianism" obscure this shared heritage of Europe and China, Zhang's references to the "Literati Teaching" emphasized the common heritage. Consequently, the term "literati" *(Ru)* was used for both Confucians and Christians. Zhang also refers to the European Jesuits as "sages and worthies from the Western nations" *(Xiguo shengxian).*[27] "Sages and worthies" is a commonly used Chinese term that refers to the wisest of the literati.

The Italian Jesuit M. Ricci was one of the pioneers in formulating how the Jesuits would present Christianity in China. The advanced state of Chinese culture—in many respects more advanced than European culture in the sixteenth and seventeenth centuries—made this a daunting task. Working together with sympathetic literati, such as Xu Guangqi and Li Zhizao, Ricci came to believe that the ancient Chinese texts revealed the presence of natural religion, that is, moral and spiritual truths discernible through human reason, as opposed to divine Revelation. Jesuits like Ricci argued that whereas the "ancient literati" *(gu Ru)* or "early literati" *(xian Ru)* had adhered to natural religion, the "later literati" *(hou Ru)* departed from it.[28] Ricci claimed that this original Confucianism had been obscured and distorted in consequent years by the entry of Buddhism into China. In this view, Ricci was supported by many literati. On the other hand, Ricci added—with much less support from the literati—that the Neo-Confucians of the Song and Ming dynasties had also obscured and distorted the original teaching.[29] Ricci's point of view dominated Jesuit thinking throughout the early and middle seventeenth century.

Few Chinese Christians supported the Jesuits' negative assessment of Neo-Confucianism. Their distinct terminologies reflected their differences. The term "Neo-Confucianism" evolved from a line of reasoning initiated by the early Jesuits in China, who viewed the thinking of contemporary literati as an intellectually degenerated form of Confucianism.[30] Their view was widely disseminated in Europe in the long preface to *Confucius Sinarum philosophus* (Paris, 1687). In this preface, the Latin epithet *Neoterici Interpretes* (Modern Interpreters)—which is synonymous with "Neo-Confucians"—was applied to the followers of the Song dynasty philosophers Zhu Xi (1130–1200), Cheng Hao (1032–1085), and Cheng Yi (1033–1107). The *Confucius Sinarum philosophus* preface adhered to the viewpoint of Ricci. It found the Song Neo-Confucians, including their all-embracing cosmological concept of the Supreme Ultimate *(Taiji)*, to be superstitious and in irreconcilable conflict with Christianity.

Yet repudiation of the Song Neo-Confucians was something that most Chinese literati could not accept. This limitation was clear in the writings of one of the Three Pillars, Yang Tingyun. Yang's intellectual development was firmly anchored in a late Ming school of Neo-Confucianism, and he saw his conversion to Christianity as complementary to Neo-Confucianism rather than in conflict with it.[31]

The Jesuits in the early and middle seventeenth century were not prepared to listen to the views of Yang Tingyun on this matter. However, when literati receptiveness to Christianity began to decline, certain seminal Jesuit thinkers began to realize in the late seventeenth century that Ricci's strategy needed to be adapted to a new political and cultural environment. One of the elements contributing to their change of attitude might have been the writings of Zhang. Unlike Ricci and most of the seventeenth-century Jesuits, Zhang regarded the literati tradition to have degenerated far more under the literati of the Han dynasty (206 B.C.–A.D. 220) and Six Dynasties (220–589) than under the Song dynasty Neo-Confucians.

It is interesting to speculate on contacts between Zhang and Intorcetta in this regard. Prior to coming to Hangzhou, Intorcetta had been very much involved in the Jesuit effort of producing a Latin translation of the Confucian Four Books that had been initiated by the Jesuit mission founders Frs. M. Ruggieri and Ricci. It has been noted that Intorcetta possibly carried back to Europe the translations of three of the Four Books that were eventually published in *Confucius Sinarum philosophus* and he very likely wrote the first half of the long preface *(Proëmialis Declaratio)*.[32] After Intorcetta returned to China to spend his remaining twenty-one years at Hangzhou and probably had considerable contact with Zhang, it is not clear whether he changed his negative assessment of Neo-Confucianism, because he left few writings on the subject dating from that time. However, it is clear that he did not persuade Zhang to adopt his earlier critical view of Neo-Confucianism. And it is also clear that younger and eventually influential Jesuits, such as Prémare, began to reassess the negative Jesuit views of Neo-Confucianism.[33]

III

One of the most difficult problems that the Jesuits faced in China was in introducing a foreign teaching to a land that believed in its own cultural superiority. For the Chinese to accept Christianity, it was necessary for the literati to concede that China was somehow deficient in its religious teachings. Ricci's attempt to find an indigenous basis for Christianity in China stimulated certain literati, such as Yang Tingyun and Zhang, to formulate ideas that transcended Ricci's views. Seen in this light, the early-seventeenth-century Jesuits in China were ideal teachers whose success should be measured not in terms of transmitting information, but rather in terms of how well they stimulated their students to go beyond the thinking of their teachers. It is in this vein that we are to understand Zhang's statement that the Lord of Heaven Teaching (i.e., Christianity) was not created in the Far West (i.e., in a foreign country) but that Chinese emperors, kings, and sages had honored and served Heaven (i.e., God) from earliest antiquity.[34] This was not the enthusiastic statement of a new convert. It was the carefully considered conclusion of a scholar who felt that he was coming home to the religion of the ancients. The forty-three-year span between his earliest written expression of this view in 1672 and his last (that I have seen) in 1715 shows that Zhang never abandoned this viewpoint, but continued to develop and refine it.

Zhang stated that when Buddhism entered China, truth became confused. Zhang's knowledge of Buddhism was extensive but often distorted by his Confucian prejudices against this teaching. Occasionally his details were inaccurate, as when he stated that the historical Buddha, Sakyamuni, was born during the reign of the Zhou dynasty king Zhao (reigned 1052–1002 B.C.).[35] Today it is believed that Sakyamuni Buddha's life dates were ca. 560–480 B.C., but these dates are only approximate and one cannot assume that they were widely known during Zhang's time. Furthermore, part of

Zhang's misunderstanding may have been due to the intellectual decline that Buddhism in China had suffered since the Tang dynasty (618–907).

Zhang was also critical of Daoism. His approach to criticizing these teachings was characteristically Confucian, and it is instructive that he quoted the most eminent Neo-Confucian, Zhu Xi, to make his criticism. According to Zhang, Master Zhu said that the misfortunes of Buddhism and Daoism were derived from two extremists of the late Zhou dynasty named Yang Zhu and Mo Di.[36] Yang Zhu and Mo Di represent equally undesirable extremes in the spectrum of philosophy. Yang deserted the world to pursue a life of extreme egoism as a hermit, whereas Mo advocated a form of universal love that was undiscriminating in its application. Whereas Yang loved no one but himself, Mo tended to love all people equally and so failed to observe human gradations of devotion appropriate to distinguishing between close relations and strangers. Buddhism and Daoism were said by Zhu Xi to follow Yang and Mo in perverting true principle and damaging spiritual truth. Zhu Xi's point was that Daoism and Buddhism were derived from Yang Zhu and Mo Di not necessarily in the genetic sense of direct historical descent but in the sense that they followed similar patterns of belief.

There is some basis for tracing the reclusive practices of Daoism to Yang Zhu. Moreover, Buddhism was often faulted by Confucians for being, like Mo Di, indiscriminating in its dispensation of compassion and love. The strong monastic tradition in Buddhism was often perceived in family-oriented China as a flagrant self-indulgence. The celibate monk devoted his life to religion while failing to fulfill the responsibility of a filial son to procreate and thereby to provide heirs to care for the family and to continue the ancestral line. In any case, Yang Zhu and Mo Di were code words for heterodox and false teachings; associating Daoism and Buddhism with them painted them both alike with the brush of false heterodoxy. By contrast, Zhang traced the Lord of Heaven Teaching to impeccably orthodox figures in the Confucian tradition, including the three legendary emperors, Yao, Shun, and Yu; the founder of the Shang dynasty, King Tang; the founders of the Zhou dynasty, kings Wen and Wu; the exemplary model of selfless service to the state the Duke of Zhou; and Confucius. Zhang believed that these sages had all transmitted the knowledge of revering Heaven.

But Zhang had a difficult point to reconcile. On the one hand he claimed that the Lord of Heaven Teaching originated simultaneously in China and the Far West. Yet on the other hand he claimed that the Lord of Heaven Teaching contained additional teachings (i.e., the revelations of Christ) that were carried to China by the Jesuit missionaries. It was the need to reconcile these apparently contradictory views on the indigenous origin of the teaching in China with the importation of the teaching from the Far West that led Zhang to divide his *Similarities* into three distinct parts. In these three parts the Lord of Heaven Teaching was said to (a) correspond to, (b) supplement, and (c) transcend the Literati Teaching. Although the *Similarities* is not the most extensive of Zhang's works, it represents his most complete statement on reconciling Confucianism and Christianity because it was written and revised over forty-three years (1672–1715). The last version was written when Zhang was eighty-two years old and clearly looking back on and summing up his intellectual and spiritual development.

In the 1715 preface Zhang reiterated that the Chinese classics contained clear evidence that since the time of the Yellow Emperor (legendary dates 2697–2596 B.C.), the Chinese had understood the meaning of the Lord of Heaven and had performed sacrifices to the Lord-on-High (Shangdi).[37] The first part of the *Similarities* attempts to prove this contention with numerous quotations from the Chinese Classics. Zhang also reiterated that these pure religious beliefs and practices of ancient China began to degenerate when the teachings of Buddhism entered China and were taken up by the followers of the Daoist Laozi. The reference here was apparently to the very early reception of Buddhism in China in which the Buddhists of the third and fourth centuries established a close relationship with Neo-Daoism on the grounds that their teachings held much in common. This close association produced the *geyi* (matching meanings) system of translation in which the Daoist terms were used to render Buddhist concepts into Chinese.[38] As a result, Zhang argued that the early Chinese notions of the Lord of Heaven Teaching became obscured in China, though they did not completely disappear. The Literati school, after a period of decline, underwent a strong revival in the Song dynasty in the form of Song Neo-Confucianism. By this renewal, vestigial notions of the ancient Chinese reverence for the Lord of Heaven were said by Zhang to be perpetuated. For this reason Zhang did not share the Jesuits' criticisms of Song Neo-Confucianism.

Zhang wrote that he had not always been critical of Buddhism. Like Yang Tingyun and other literati who adopted Christianity in the seventeenth century, Zhang had once shown a strong interest in Buddhism and had studied it. During a period of mourning for a parent, he had made a serious study of Buddhist texts, including the *Lankāvatāra Sutra* and the *Vimalakīrta Sutra*.[39] Elsewhere Zhang wrote that he had studied the *Diamond Sutra* and the *Lotus Sutra*.[40] But he found the Buddhist texts deficient in meaning, and he turned back to the teaching of the "two great literati"—the Song Neo-Confucians Cheng Yi and Zhu Xi—and embraced their criticisms of Buddhism.

IV

Zhang wrote that the "Western literati" (i.e., European Jesuits) had traveled thousands of miles in order to "honor the will of the Lord of Heaven and save mankind."[41] However, Zhang's introduction to the teaching of the Lord of Heaven was not from a Jesuit but from a fellow townsman named Zhu Ji'nan, who introduced Zhang to several books about the Lord of Heaven Teaching. Zhang wrote that he had not even finished reading these books when his doubts about the Buddha crystallized in his mind. He seems to be saying that although he was already inclining toward rejecting Buddhism and following Confucianism, his thinking was still in an incomplete form prior to his study of these Lord of Heaven texts.

Like Yang Tingyun, with whom he shared so much, Zhang's final step in converting to Christianity was taken gradually.[42] In 1678, six years after writing the first preface to the *Similarities,* Zhang was baptized with the baptismal name of Ignatius (Yi'najue). His honorary name *(hao),* Master Yi'na (Ignatius), was derived from his baptismal name.[43] Zhang's conversion had a powerful impact on his written works. All of them appear to have been produced after his introduction to Christianity and, as such, his conversion brought his intellectual development to maturity.

There is a memorable passage in I Corinthians where Saint Paul remarks that our present knowledge of truth is obscured by our earthly limitations but eventually we shall understand more fully. He wrote: "For now we see in a mirror darkly, but then face to face. Now I know in part; then I shall understand fully" (Revised Standard Version, 13:12).[44] Saint Paul was the most eminent missionary of the Christian faith, and in this passage he was addressing the fledgling Greek Christian community in Corinth. This passage also reaches across sixteen centuries and the span of Asia to describe Zhang Xingyao, but with this difference: the literati converts, unlike the educated Greek-speaking gentiles of the Mediterranean world after A.D. 100, had access only to bits of the New Testament that had been paraphrased in the Jesuit Chinese prayerbook. Consequently, the Chinese literati were largely dependent on what the Jesuits told them about the content of the Lord of Heaven Teaching.

It is well known that the Jesuits were selective in presenting the gospel in China and that their opponents were quick to accuse them of being crafty and deceptive, i.e., Jesuitical. However, there was a tradition in the early Christian church (ca. A.D. 200–450) that refused openly to discuss certain fundamental rituals, such as baptism and the Eucharist, with unbaptized people.[45] The prohibitions extended in their extreme form to include ritual formulas, the Lord's Prayer, symbols of baptism, eucharistic elements, and writings on essential matters, and even involved excluding unbaptized Christians from the church when these rituals were being celebrated. Although this tradition faded with the demise of Greek and Roman antiquity in the mid-fifth century, elements of it persisted and appear to have been revived in China when the Jesuits encountered a highly developed culture with a prestige akin to the ancient culture of Greece and Rome.

The Jesuits did not emphasize the crucifixion of Christ, because they felt the subject could only be introduced gradually into China without damaging the reception of Christianity among the Chinese. Still, the Jesuits did not totally neglect presenting the Crucifixion in China, and there is a lengthy description of it in the Jesuit Chinese prayer book *Shengjiao rike* (1628; revised 1665).[46] Moreover, in 1640 Fr. Schall presented the last Ming ruler, the Chongzhen emperor, with a sheepskin album in which two of the forty-eight drawings depicted the Crucifixion (see figs. 18 and 19).[47]

In Chinese Christian writings of the seventeenth century, the mention of the Crucifixion is rare, and Zhang's writings are no exception. Even Intorcetta's list of seventy-two images in the Church of the Savior in Hangzhou does not mention a depiction of Christ's crucifixion. By the years 1680 to 1683, when these images were produced, the Crucifixion had become a very dangerous symbol in China. In the pages of an important Chinese Christian work produced nearly

Fig. 18.—An illustration of Jesus having spikes driven into his body as part of the punishment of crucifixion, from Yang Guangxian's *Budeyi* (1665), part 1. This and the drawing in figure 19 were originally numbers 42 and 43 of forty-eight drawings portraying the life of Christ. These drawings were originally presented by Father A. Schall von Bell to the last Ming ruler, the Chongzhen emperor, in 1640. The origins of the drawings are unknown, but the artist was probably Chinese. Yang reproduced these two drawings in his *Budeyi* to support his contention that Jesus had been executed for the crimes of rebellion and subversion. In Yang's view, Jesus was an outlaw who deserved denunciation rather than a divine figure worthy of reverence.

Fig. 19.—An illustration of the Crucifixion of the Lord of Heaven Jesus, from Yang Guangxian's *Budeyi* (1665), part 1.

twenty years earlier, one can find a clear explanation of the crucifixion of Jesus, who as the Lord of Heaven was incarnated in human form in order to save mankind by his act of suffering.[48] This work is the *Tianxue chuan'gai* (Summary of the spread of the Heavenly Teaching), published in Beijing in 1664, which so enraged the Confucian literatus Yang Guangxian that he responded with his famous attack on Christianity entitled *Budeyi* (I cannot do otherwise).[49]

The production of the *Summary of the Spread of the Heavenly Teaching* was a joint effort in which the Jesuit Fathers Buglio and, to a lesser extent, Magalhaes contributed ideas. These ideas were refined and expanded by the Christian literatus Li Zubo, who was a student of Fr. Schall and a prominent official in the Bureau of Astronomy.[50] Yang Guangxian's attack on the *Summary* reproduced the two drawings of the Crucifixion (and only one other drawing) from the collection that Schall had presented to the Chongzhen emperor in 1640.[51] Yang used these Crucifixion scenes to support his contention that Jesus was a seditious rebel who had been executed for his crimes.[52] It seems unlikely to be mere coincidence that, in Hangzhou less than twenty years after Yang's attack, the Crucifixion would be omitted from both the images in the Church of the Savior as well as from the writings of Zhang. Although Yang had been disgraced and removed from power by 1669, the vehemence of his attack lingered, as did the laws decreed in 1665 prohibiting missionary activities. These laws were not revoked until 1692.[53] Although Li Zubo and his four fellow Christians at the Bureau of Astronomy were posthumously rehabilitated, the memory of their execution remained. The idea of the Crucifixion had a particular vulnerability to attack in China, and this vulnerability appears to have made it a symbol too controversial to be treated in a public forum in late-seventeenth-century China, whether in the paintings in the Church of the Savior in Hangzhou or in Zhang's writings.

The Jesuits may have been selective in presenting other aspects of Christianity to the Chinese. For example, Ricci deemphasized original sin in his widely read Chinese work *The True Meaning of the Lord of Heaven (Tianzhu shiyi)* because it conflicted with the Confucian belief in the basic goodness of human nature.[54] Zhang's *Similarities* discussed original sin and regarded it as important, but Zhang did not emphasize original sin because it was not crucial to his blending of Confucianism and Christianity.[55]

Only in his eulogistic poems composed for use within the Church of the Savior did Zhang refer to Jesus (Yesu) by name.[56] In his other writings Zhang avoided the widely used transliterated form Yesu that dated at least to Ricci's *True Meaning of the Lord of Heaven.* Rather, Zhang referred to Jesus using the same term by which he referred to God, namely, "Lord of Heaven" (Tianzhu). In doing so, Zhang's terminology emphasized Jesus as God descended to the earth in human form. This was apparently a point that the Jesuits had stressed in explaining Christianity. Zhang was aware of the distinction between God the Father and God the Son, and he occasionally referred to Jesus as "Son of the Lord of Heaven" (Tianzhuzi).[57] It is also clear that Zhang understood God the Son to be a historical figure, because he referred to Jesus, the Lord of Heaven, as being not yet born at the time of Confucius (551–479 B.C.?) and Mencius (371–289 B.C.?).[58]

Zhang was aware of the difference between the Old Testament *(Gu jing)* and the New Testament *(Xin jing).* He wrote of how the Old Testament speaks of the Lord of Heaven first creating Heaven and Earth out of darkness and making revelations through the prophets and sages.[59] Zhang noted that the New Testament records how the Lord of Heaven descended to be incarnated in the world and how he grew to be a thirty-three-year-old man who taught the faith for three years and had disciples. All of this, he noted, is recorded in the Four Gospels *(Si shengsuo jizhe).* Zhang wrote of how he had heard Western Teachers *(Xi shi)* (i.e., Jesuit missionaries) saying that the Lord of Heaven/Jesus taught for three years and during that time performed numerous healings of invalids, the blind, deaf, dumb, and other afflicted persons.[60]

Elsewhere Zhang spoke of an account recorded in the *Western History (Xi shi)* (i.e., the Bible) in which the Lord of Heaven/Jesus led three thousand followers into a wilderness and, in the absence of food to feed them, transformed five loaves of bread and two fish into thousands of loaves and fish by which the people were fed. This refers, of course, to the miracle of the loaves and fishes in Matthew 14:17–21 and Mark 6:38–44.[61] In telling this story, Zhang was forced to distinguish between God as the Heavenly Father and Jesus, who was praying to God the Father for a miracle. Zhang referred to both as "Lord of Heaven," but added "Holy Father" (Shengfu) as a suffix to distinguish the two. Zhang's account of this miracle made some minor changes in the biblical text: five thousand followers were altered to three thousand and the biblical twelve baskets of leftover fish were altered to "over ten baskets." It is not clear whether these changes were made by the Jesuits in the telling of the story or by Zhang in recounting the miracle. He may have heard the story in an oral form, perhaps in a sermon, rather than read it in translation. Elsewhere, Zhang wrote of the Lord of Heaven/Jesus preaching the Sermon on the Mount.[62]

Although Zhang wrote that all of these events were recorded in the two books of the Old and New Testaments, he did not indicate that he had read the Bible. Indeed, very little of the Bible, apart from the account of Christ's crucifixion, was included in the Jesuit prayerbook. Unlike the nineteenth- and twentieth-century Protestant missionaries, who directed their first efforts toward translating the Bible into Chinese, the Jesuit missionaries directed their initial efforts toward translating the Chinese Classics. The Jesuits did so not because they were less faithful Christians than the Protestants, but because they believed this method to be the most effective way of winning the Chinese to Christ. In fact, in the seventeenth century, the Bible was rarely read by Catholics as a book, but rather was encountered as passages in the missal (a book with prayers used in the mass) or prayerbook. The Protestant emphasis on the Bible as a text was not absorbed into Catholicism until the twentieth century.

The enormous difficulties that the Passion of Christ presented for the Jesuits in China have already been noted.[63] The belief that God took on human form in the person of Jesus was made more difficult for the Chinese to accept by the ungodlike way in which Jesus died. The Jesuits approached the problem by revealing the teaching of Christianity gradually, beginning with what was more similar to Chinese religious teachings and leading slowly up to the more alien and difficult points, such as the Trinity. Zhang did not discuss the crucifixion of Jesus, though he did speak of Jesus teaching for three years and then, after being "unable to overcome his destiny" (bu ke sheng shu), ascending to Heaven. The Jesuits had discovered that the crucifix produced a very negative reaction among many Chinese. Unsympathetic Chinese regarded the crucifix as a form of black magic.[64] Even sympathetic Chinese literati found Jesus' submitting to crucifixion as behavior more appropriate for a slave than for a king or God. Certainly such brutal punishment was viewed with horror by an elite group who regarded their exemption from corporal punishment (secured by their academic degrees) as a precious privilege.

It is clear that Zhang saw Christianity as a dim reflection in a mirror, but if Saint Paul was correct in saying (I Corinthians 13:12) that we all experience God's truth in such an obscure way, we can only distinguish Zhang's perception from that of Christians today as different in degree. In fact, if Zhang was correct in some of his views that the ancient Chinese worshiped the same God as seventeenth-century European Jesuits, then perhaps Zhang saw something of God in his vision in a mirror darkly that is even in some ways superior to the vision of the Jesuits. Whether Zhang read the account of Jesus' crucifixion in the Jesuit prayerbook is unclear, though his poems indicate that his knowledge of Christianity was fairly sophisticated. Even if his knowledge of the Crucifixion and the Resurrection was incomplete, is it not possible that God in his love for Zhang may have revealed to him something unique and special? Some seventeenth- and eighteenth-century Jesuits who lived in China for many years and who acquired a deep appreciation for Chinese culture seem to have perceived the visions of literati such as Zhang in just this way.

Father Intorcetta awoke to the sound of shouting. The shouts were from the elderly gatekeeper Liu, who lived in the small gatehouse beyond the walls of the college and at the courtyard entrance to the Church of the Savior. The night sky was still black, but there appeared to be torches shining in the courtyard. Quickly Father Intorcetta dressed, though arthritis had painfully swollen his fingers at the joints, making them less nimble than they once were. Rushing out the door, he nearly collided with the cook Ma, who was running from his room adjoining the kitchen. Together they hurried out the doorway of the dormitory and into the courtyard.

The southern sky was ablaze with light, and the air was filled with the sound of crisp crackling. The fire was already close by. Intorcetta instinctively took charge and began issuing orders to set up a bucket brigade from the canal in front of the church. The next few hours passed like several moments as the fire moved through the college property, jumping to the neighboring buildings on the north. He could scarcely remember what he had done in this time, except that the heat and the smoke were horrible.

Dawn came with an unusual harshness that day, diffusing a smoky light through the stench of charred remains. When the light was bright enough and the smoke cleared enough, Intorcetta could see the extent of the damage, and his heart fell. The nave of the church, along with most of the paintings, was lost, though the facade was largely intact. The dormitory was destroyed, but the annex and the library in the rear of the church were miraculously spared. He moved up the stairs toward the library.

As he stood in the middle of the library, he felt a sense of exhaustion and despair so overwhelming that he sank to his knees and instinctively made the sign of the cross. For the past sixteen years he had devoted his life to this church and to creating the religious images and inscriptions that had filled the structure. He had fought one battle after another—with hostile neighbors, the lack of funds, stubborn painters, illness, scheming officials, and doubting literati—to build up and protect this church. Finally, after obtaining a great victory in the Edict of Toleration in Beijing, he had returned from the capital in triumph. That was only ten days ago, and now came this devastation. And he could see no meaning in it, because the fire had not been set by an enemy of the Church but was a horrible coincidence and had swept through much of the city.

In a few weeks he would celebrate his sixty-eighth birthday, and he knew that the time remaining in his life was limited. What did God want him to do? When he raised his eyes, he saw on the wall the small wooden cross that he had carried with him on his last long sea voyage from Europe. How many times he had prayed to that cross on that horrible journey, in which nearly all of his young confreres had died of illness while he had been spared. When he looked at that cross, even as he asked his question, he knew the answer. God wanted him to rebuild the church and especially this church dedicated to Christ the Savior.

Intorcetta had always been a doer rather than a thinker, and once he had the answer to his question, he rose from his knees. First he would have to make arrangements for Father Thomas, who needed a quiet place to rest and to prepare for his ongoing journey to Canton to greet the returning Father Grimaldi, whom the emperor was so anxious to have installed in the Bureau of Astronomy. Then he would begin visiting the Chinese Christians to learn of their losses in the fire and, sadly, perhaps to arrange for some funerals. He would discuss with them the rebuilding of the church. He hoped that Master Zhang Xing-yao would be helpful. Below he heard the ever-faithful Ma calling for him. As he descended the steps from the library, he brushed some ashes from his sleeve, and, as he did so, he suddenly had an idea for rebuilding the nave.[65]

CHAPTER 4

The Negligence of Today's Literati

Zhang took another sip of hot tea—it was a good brand of Longjing tea and it helped him to endure the stifling heat. Today seemed to be one of the most humid days of 1705, but the discomfort was increased by the tension between Zhang and his old friend Ji Jiongfan. Zhang had shared so many things with Ji—their childhood tutor, rites of passage in growing up, the marriage of Zhang's grandson to Ji's granddaughter. All these things bound them together, but Ji had never fully understood Zhang's adoption of the Lord of Heaven Teaching. He had been curious about the teaching itself, but he had never fully embraced it. He had accepted Zhang's decision and had even allowed his granddaughter to be baptized before marrying Zhang's grandson, but he had never really understood Zhang's decision to embrace this Lord of Heaven Teaching, and his doubts would surface occasionally in questions such as the one he had just asked Zhang. Their Middle Kingdom, said Ji, unlike the Western nations, possessed Master Kong (Confucius) to teach them the most important essentials of life—to distinguish true teachings from false ones, to honor one's blood more than strangers (or even animals, as the Buddhists did), to guide one's life toward what was right. Why then should there be a need for Chinese to adopt the foreign Heavenly Teaching?

Zhang sat there trying to collect his thoughts and to choose his words carefully. The term "negligent" was, he believed, the right one. It was the negligence of the literati toward the teachings of Master Kong that had caused the literati of today to pervert Confucian teachings by drawing from Buddhist and Daoist teachings, tainting what the Great Sage had taught. Zhang would never slander Master Kong, but Master Kong himself said that he was only transmitting his teaching from the ancients. It was not slander to recognize that the Great Sage was human and so subject to human limitations. However, the Heavenly Teaching reveals to us the source of what the Great Sage received from the ancients. This teaching tells us that Heaven created a sage who was not subject to human limitations and to the misfortunes of life. To recognize that this Lord of Heaven had such power was not to disparage Master Kong, because the Lord of Heaven was not human, even if he had briefly descended to the earth and felt human suffering.

Zhang took another sip of tea and smiled at his old friend. He would try again to answer this most difficult of questions. He prayed that the Lord of Heaven would help him.[1]

I

Zhang Xingyao's life as a scholar was mainly confined to the region around Hangzhou.[2] Most of his scholarly friends and associates, including thirty-seven of his sixty-eight disciples, lived in Zhejiang province.[3] In addition, there were occasional contacts with Christian literati in other regions, such as Ding Yuntai of Ji'nan in Shandong province, who was both a friend and an intellectual influence on Zhang.[4] Zhang devoted a lifetime of effort to researching, defining, and refining his ideas and to expressing them in written form. Apart from his *Refutation* criticizing Buddhism, his works were never printed but were limited to circulating in manuscript form among his associates and disciples as well as Jesuit missionaries. Such circulation of manuscripts was a common practice among literati.

Some of the reasons for not printing his works were practical. Zhang himself spoke of the enormous task of getting the over 1,700 pages of his *History* into print.[5] On the other hand, his major statement on the relationship between Christianity and Confucianism, the *Similarities,* was relatively brief, and yet it too was not printed. There were unstated reasons for having these works remain in manuscript. In the hostile cultural environment the publication of such works might have been viewed as subversive acts. Zhang himself may have felt a certain tentativeness about his ideas. Perhaps he was a perfectionist who felt a compulsive need to revise his works indefinitely in order to meet the ever harsher criticism he knew they would face. Certainly the different manuscript versions of the *Similarities* show that the numerous revisions he made over many years were minor in nature. The changes involved rephrasing passages rather than rearranging the contents of the work or adding substantial new sections.

The Literati Teaching was based on antiquity because the literati believed that the thoughts of the ancients were the clearest expression of truth. Consequently, the most authentic record of truth was believed to be found in the ancient Chinese texts. It is for this reason that Zhang began his major statement on the reconciliation of Confucianism and Christianity with a section devoted to quotations from the Chinese Classics. These quotations were intended to confirm that there were similarities between the two teachings. This was not the first time that such an argument had been made. At the beginning of the seventeenth century, Ricci had been assisted by literati Christians in locating passages from the Classics that supported the argument that there were similarities between Confucianism and Christianity. The results of their efforts were incorporated into the first significant literary attempt to reconcile these two teachings, *The True Meaning of the Lord of Heaven* (1603).

A comparison of the citations from the classical literature made by Ricci and his literati coworkers with those citations by Zhang will show the evolution in thinking about Confucian-Christian reconciliation that occurred in the seventeenth century. In Ricci's *True Meaning of the Lord of Heaven*, the list of Classics cited is similar to that of Zhang's *Similarities*, but the emphasis differs.[6] Whereas Ricci relied mainly on the Four Books, Zhang cited predominantly from the Five Classics. But in another sense, this comparison is misleading because Zhang based his argument far more on the literati tradition than did Ricci, who also drew heavily from European traditions of Aristotelian-Scholastic logic. The 1603 edition of the *True Meaning of the Lord of Heaven* consists of approximately fifty thousand characters, whereas the longest version of the *Similarities* contains only twenty thousand characters. Distributed throughout Ricci's work are eighty-six allusions and citations of classical works, whereas approximately two hundred classical citations are concentrated in the first part of the *Similarities* and about forty-five citations in the last two parts.

Although Ricci was brilliant and had a great deal of help from learned literati, it would have been unreasonable to expect any European who had spent only thirteen years in China to have been able to cite the classical literature in the manner of a native literatus. Ricci's pioneering effort was limited by practical realities. His greater reliance on the Four Books for forty-six out of eighty-six citations (twenty-three citations from *Mencius*, thirteen from the *Analects*, seven from the *Doctrine of the Mean*, and three from the *Great Learning*) was a reflection of the difficulties of the classical Chinese language. The Five Classics are more difficult to read than the Four Books. For this reason the Jesuits had, soon after their arrival in China, decided to focus on the Four Books as classical language primers to provide a practical entry to literati culture. In doing so, they were duplicating the educational approach of the Chinese themselves, who began with the Four Books and worked their way up to the Five Classics.

Consequently, the Four Books were the classical works that Ricci knew best. They also happen to be the classics most identified with the Song Neo-Confucians because of a famous commentary by Zhu Xi on these four works.[7] Ricci was extremely critical of the Neo-Confucian interpretations of the Four Books, because he believed that they contained philosophical materialism and atheism. The Jesuits attempted to provide an alternate interpretation by appealing to the texts themselves on the grounds that they were more primary than the Song Neo-Confucian commentaries.[8] So Ricci's emphasis on the Four Books reflected both his accommodation program for reconciling Confucianism and Christianity and the practical realities of Europeans entering the realm of Chinese culture.

Zhang's *Similarities* shows that although his reconciliation effort continued Ricci's attempt to reconcile classical literature with Christianity, there were also differences between the two efforts that involved more than a shift in emphasis from the Four Books to the Five Classics. Zhang did not echo Ricci's criticisms of the Song Neo-Confucian thinkers. Since antiquity and truth were inseparable for Zhang, he chose most of his quotations from two of the most ancient Chinese texts—the *Book of Documents (Shujing)* and the *Book of Odes (Shijing)*.[9] These works contain numerous references to something very like a monotheistic deity. Of the approximately 245 passages from the Confucian Classics that Zhang cited in the *Similarities*, 181 were drawn from the Five Classics as follows: ninety-two from the *Book of Documents*, fifty-seven from the *Book of Odes*, twenty-two from the *Book of Rites (Li ji)*, eight from the *Book of Changes (Yijing)*, and two from the *Commentary of Zuo (Zuozhuan)*. The remaining sixty-four classical passages were drawn from the Four Books as follows: thirty-nine from the *Analects*, sixteen from the *Mencius*, seven from the *Doctrine of the Mean (Zhongyong)*, and two from the *Great Learning (Daxue)*.

Modern scholars now doubt many of the claims formerly made for the high antiquity of the Confucian Classics. The prevailing view is that none of the Classics represents a genuine text from the Shang dynasty (ca. 1500–1050 B.C.). Although certain passages and general concepts in the *Book of Documents* and the *Book of Odes* may have been derived from the Shang, the present forms of these Classics are believed to date from the Zhou dynasty (1050–221 B.C.) or later.[10] These two works, apart from a small core section of the *Book of Changes,* represent the oldest written works of China.

The *Book of Documents,* although a work of history, lacks a sense of connected narrative. Rather, it consists of a collection of speeches, exhortations, proclamations and edicts, for the most part of a high moral tone. These constitute a category called "recorded words" (*jiyan*), as opposed to another category called "recorded events" (*jishi*) found in the *Commentary of Zuo.*[11] These "recorded words" have been attributed to the period of high antiquity extending from the reign of the legendary emperor Yao down to 626 B.C.[12] The textual analysts of the Qing dynasty (1644–1911) revealed that approximately half of the chapters of the *Documents* (twenty-eight chapters) date from the Zhou dynasty. The remaining twenty-two chapters are forgeries that, rather than dating from the Zhou as claimed, were written in the second or third century A.D. during the Han dynasty. In spite of the spurious chapters, most scholars believe that early Zhou history can be reconstructed from these documents.[13]

Apart from questions of its authenticity, the *Documents* has been a tremendously influential text in Chinese history, particularly in terms of establishing such fundamental concepts as the Mandate of Heaven (*Tianming*) by which Heaven legitimizes a ruler on the basis of his virtuous actions while withdrawing legitimacy from unjust rulers.[14] Zhang, unaware of the spurious nature of half of the chapters of the *Documents,* divided his citations fairly evenly between the forged and the authentic chapters.[15] Zhang's other major source of classical citations was the *Book of Odes,* a poetic collection of 305 folk songs, hymns, and religious odes, some of which date from early Zhou times and all of which probably predate Confucius (551–479? B.C.).[16] According to a disputed tradition, Confucius selected these 305 poems from a larger collection of three thousand poems drawn from the Zhou court.[17]

Zhang's *Similarities* was an attempt to persuade his fellow literati of the truth of his views on the compatibility of Confucianism and

Christianity, and the work was organized with this very clear logical purpose in mind. In the first of the three parts where he sought to show the basic similarities between the two teachings, Zhang arranged the classical passages under fourteen fundamental statements about the Lord of Heaven Teaching. Under the first statement he grouped together passages from the ancient Classics that referred to the idea of a Lord of Heaven.[18] Under the second statement are passages that show that in antiquity the authority of rulers, fathers, and teachers had been commissioned by the Lord of Heaven.[19] Another section contained passages to show that Heaven loved mankind but that Heaven's sympathy for good people was matched by Heaven's dislike and anger for those who were evil.[20] Passages from the Classics were gathered to show that the Lord of Heaven rewarded goodness and punished evil, though the punishment in this world was often dispensed on a public (rather than an individual) basis in the form of natural calamities.[21] Birth and death, poverty and wealth, success and failure all depended on Heaven, although Heaven bestowed fortune and misfortune on the basis of individual human behavior.[22] The inculturation of Christianity into Chinese culture was particularly evident in Zhang's blending of the idea of the Lord of Heaven with the traditional Confucian idea of the Mandate of Heaven *(Tianming).*[23] The Mandate of Heaven was believed to be the blessing of Heaven necessary for establishing the legitimacy of any government in China. The Mandate was bestowed as a reward for unsurpassed ability and morality, and it was revoked for negligence and immorality. Clearly, one who followed Zhang's line of argument in part 1 of the *Similarities* was being led to the conclusion that the Lord of Heaven was not at all alien to the teachings contained in the ancient Classics.

II

Zhang realized that beyond the similarities between Confucianism and Christianity, there were fundamental differences, and he dealt with these in two ways. The most radical differences were treated in the third part of the *Similarities* as ways in which Christianity transcended Confucianism *(Tianjiao chao Ru).* However, the second part of the work is the most subtle of the three, because it deals neither with clear similarities nor with differences, but with ways in which the Heavenly Teaching supplements or completes concepts already contained in the Literati Teaching *(Tianjiao bu Ru)*. It is the bridge linking the similarities between the two teachings in part 1 and the differences described in part 3. However, it is also the intellectual pivot on which the success of the entire work depends.

Most literati would have tended to accept the similarities between Christianity and Confucianism claimed in part 1 because they flatter Chinese culture by claiming that these fundamental truths of the religion from the Far West had been present in China since antiquity. However, most literati would have been resistant to accepting the claims made in part 3 regarding the ways in which Christianity transcended Confucianism, because these claims imply an insufficiency on the part of Chinese culture and require that literati learn from a foreign teaching. Hence part 2 became the main battleground in the battle for literati minds waged by Zhang. If part 2 were convincing, then there was a chance that the literati would be more receptive to the culturally demanding claims made in part 3.

Zhang's three-part teaching was not a missionary strategy for establishing Christianity in China, but rather an attempt by an otherwise orthodox literatus to reconcile the two teachings. From Zhang's point of view, it was not necessary to introduce the Lord of Heaven teaching into Chinese culture, because the basic elements were already present within the literati teaching. Zhang did not see Christianity as a foreign religion that surpassed Chinese teachings. Rather he saw the ways in which Christianity transcended Confucianism as a form of completion or fulfillment of elements already present in China since antiquity. It is on precisely this point that Zhang's ideas have been misinterpreted in one of the most influential contemporary works of Chinese intellectual history. The historian Hou Wailu and his collaborators simplified this three-part teaching by interpreting it as a three-step strategy for establishing Christianity in China.[24] In Hou's interpretation, Zhang's reconciliation of Confucianism and Christianity is limited to the first of three steps and is merely an expedient to the ultimate aim of having Christianity transcend Confucianism. According to this view, the Literati Teaching cultivated a lower stage of truth that was limited to the tangible material world or immanent nature of things, whereas the Lord of Heaven Teaching occupied a higher stage of knowledge that dealt with spiritual and transcendent truths.

In addition to misinterpreting Zhang's three-part teaching as a missionary strategy, Hou and his collaborators misleadingly imply that the strategy originated with Ricci. Although one could argue that Zhang's three parts were implied in Ricci's missionary strategy of accommodation in a general sense, Ricci lacked the knowledge of Chinese history and Confucian philosophy necessary to have formulated Zhang's ideas. Zhang's limited contact and collaboration with missionaries fostered a concern very different from missionary strategy. Zhang was attempting to explain how Christianity's transcendence of Confucianism should be seen in terms of completing certain basic ideas present in China since antiquity. According to Zhang, these ideas had failed to be completed in Chinese culture mainly because of the negligence of literati, who had lost sight of the True Way.

Zhang's awareness of the difficulties he faced explains the many minor revisions he made over the years in an attempt to make his work more convincing. One might argue that his failure to publish the *Similarities* was a sign that he fell short of his aim. Or, it may have been that as the cultural response to Christianity grew more hostile in the late seventeenth and early eighteenth centuries, Zhang felt the need to postpone publication in order to further refine the argumentation in the *Similarities* to counter this rising hostility. Zhang may have felt as if he were swimming against the current and that as he came closer to his goal, the current became stronger.

Zhang spent most of his mature life reflecting on the contents of the *Similarities*. His dated prefaces of 1672, 1702, and 1715 to part 1 mark the evolution of the work.[25] The manuscripts preserved in Shanghai and Paris reveal numerous instances of altered terminology and phrasing that represent refinements rather than substantive changes. The form of the work is not completely consistent, indicating that its three parts were probably written separately.[26] The twenty-one sections of part 2 and the fourteen sections of part 3 are numbered, whereas the fourteen sections of part 1 are not. In addition, there is an appendix on the "Laws of the Western Nations" *(Xiguo xingfa)* and a postscript *(ba)*. Whereas part 1 bases its claim on the Classics, part 2 shifts to a more subtle type of argumentation that draws as much from allusions to Chinese history as from citations from the *Analects* and *Mencius*.

It is Zhang's extensive use of Chinese history to support the inculturation of Christianity in China that makes his work unique. In his attempt to use the Classics to support his argument on the compatibility between Christianity and Confucianism, Zhang was merely extending and refining a practice that dated from Ricci and Xu Guangqi. However, Zhang was essentially a historian. Though the significance of his *Supplements to the History of the Comprehensive Mirror Topically Arranged (Tongjian jishi benmo buhoubian)* has been recognized, the work has not been widely disseminated and manuscript copies of it are extremely rare. His thoughtful application of Chinese history to explaining how the Heavenly Teaching supplements the Literati Teaching in part 2 represents a contribution that has gone unrecognized by both Chinese and foreign scholars.

In his meeting with his friend Ji Jiongfan in the summer of 1705, Zhang expressed his concern with how the modern literati's "neglect" *(shulüe)* of Confucius (Master Kong) might be corrected.[27] This was a perennial concern echoed by literati throughout Chinese history. It was a preoccupation with restoring the original and authentic meaning to the teaching of Confucius and eliminating the distortions to his teaching that had occurred since the sage had died. Though Zhang's concern was a perennial one, his solution was unique. He proposed that this neglect of Confucius be corrected through the adoption of the Heavenly Teaching.

Zhang's friend, Master Ji, posed the fundamental question that many literati might have asked: "Since our China has Master Kong, it has the most important of the essential elements, so why should we serve the Heavenly Teaching?" Zhang replied that Confucius was the highest sort of human sage, but Heaven had created a sage who could transcend human fortune and misfortune. This sage was the Lord of Heaven. Zhang was far more Trinitarian in interpreting the Incarnation of God on earth than we are today. Our cultural perception of Jesus emphasizes his human qualities. Scarcely anyone doubts that Jesus was a historical figure, but only orthodox Christians regard Jesus as a divine manifestation of God, and sometimes even they unwittingly slight Jesus' divine nature in order to make him more humanly approachable in attempting to establish a personal relationship with their Savior. Zhang's emphasis was quite different. When he spoke of the incarnated form that the Lord of Heaven took on earth, he did not use the Chinese name for Jesus— Yesu. Zhang emphasized the *divinity* of the human Incarnation of God, and this is why the sage-incarnation of the Lord of Heaven transcended Confucius as a human sage and yet also supplemented Confucius' teachings.

Zhang's adherence to Confucian teachings was expressed in his quotation from *Mencius* 7a.24: "He who has been a student of the sage [Confucius] finds it hard to think anything of the words of others." However, Zhang explained his position by repeated reference to the term *shulüe,* i.e., a sense of negligence or deficiency or being remiss. It was through their neglect of Confucius that the literati of Zhang's day were said to have perverted *(bei)* the teaching of the great sage.[28] In their neglect, the literati had tainted the teaching of Confucius by borrowing from Buddhism and Daoism.[29] Zhang regarded the Heavenly Teaching as important, because it provided a corrective to this neglect of Confucius' teaching. Adopting the Heavenly Teaching would enable the Chinese to restore the lost and pure sense of Confucius' teaching. It is in this sense that the Heavenly Teaching supplemented the Literati Teaching.

III

In the first section of part 2, Zhang cited two passages from the Confucian Classics to show how the Heavenly Teaching supplemented the Literati Teaching. The *Book of Documents* was cited to refer to the inherent nature (moral sense) *(hengxing)* that the Lord-on-High bestowed on the common people.[30] Zhang believed it was this bestowal of a moral sense as part of our human nature that revealed Heaven to be God rather than just a blue sky. Zhang said that the "Western literati" (i.e., the Jesuits) interpreted the Lord-on-High (Shangdi) found in this *Book of Documents* passage to be equivalent to the Lord of Heaven who was both omnipresent and omniscient. The Lord of Heaven operated in ways that were both unseen and unheard. In order to show how this view supplemented the Literati Teaching, Zhang cited the *Doctrine of the Mean* (1.2) injunction to be watchful while alone and especially sensitive to our actions that are unseen and unheard. It is through our caution and anxious respect that we stand in awe of the Will of Heaven.

One of the most debated questions of nineteenth- and twentieth-century Sinology has involved Confucius' attitude toward spiritual phenomena. Although it is quite clear that Confucius urged that his disciples keep a distance from spirits, it is unclear whether Confucius urged this out of genuine belief or agnostic avoidance. Zhang regarded Confucius as a genuine believer in God, and he cited six passages from the *Analects* to support his claim.[31] For Zhang, the Heavenly Teaching supplemented the Literati Teaching by showing that Confucius did pray to the Lord-on-High and that this realization could help us to see the Lord-on-High as Lord and to reject the falsehoods of Satan (Xiemo).

Some of the points made by Zhang in part 2 of the *Similarities* are surprising. It is to be expected that he should claim that the Heavenly Teaching could supplement the Literati Teaching in the realm of spiritual and moral cultivation. Zhang was well aware that Confucius had urged people to correct their faults, but the need to attain the proper degree of self-examination was a perennial concern in Confucianism.[32] Whereas Buddhism confused people by speaking of repentance in terms of emptiness, nothingness, and quiescence, Zhang felt that the Heavenly Teaching offered a clear method for correcting faults. After daily self-examination and scrutiny, the slightest sin against the Lord should require one to kneel in obeisance before the Lord of Heaven's altar. A feeling of repentance and desire to correct one's fault would produce forgiveness of those sins by the Lord of Heaven.

Zhang believed that in antiquity there had been a balance between honor and affluence in society. However, since then honor had declined while Buddhism and Daoism had fostered the search for wealth and power.[33] Wealth no longer fostered virtue but rather engendered pride, extravagance, licentiousness, and idleness. Criticism of literati corruption in seventeenth- and eighteenth-century China was not unique to Zhang. Echoes of Zhang's criticism can be found in abundance in the satirical treatment of literati by Wu Jingzi (1701–1754) in his famous novel *The Scholars (Rulin waishi)*. Wu's satire portrays how the Daoist alchemical quest for transmuting base metals into the precious metal silver corrupted certain literati, and he also attacks Buddhist morality.[34] Zhang recognized that in a world in which the *Dao* (Way; Truth) was in decline, many people would unjustly suffer from poverty and misfortune. The Heavenly Teaching supplemented the Literati Teaching by giving the proper rewards in Heaven to those good people who had suffered in this life.

One of the ways in which the Chinese inculturated Christianity was by shifting the focus from a European concern for personal salvation to a Chinese social concern for people and culture as a whole. This was a slight shift of emphasis rather than a major distortion of Christian theology. Personal salvation was still crucial, but it was viewed in a wider social and cultural context. Zhang lamented the insufficient welfare and charitable efforts of his own day, and he criticized the inadequacies in transferring funds from the wealthy to the poor.[35] He believed that the charity and welfare system that existed prior to the Han dynasty had declined and had been replaced by a Buddhist system of welfare in which charitable contributions were funneled to the needy by means of monasteries.

Zhang was quite specific in describing this ancient system of charity and welfare that disappeared after the Qin dynasty *(xian zong dang hou lü li)*. He spoke of the government of the earliest kings under which four villages *(lü)* composed a precinct *(zu)*, which took responsibility for funerals. Five precincts composed a ward *(dang)*, which was responsible for welfare-type assistance. Five wards constituted a township *(zhou)* that was responsible for charity. According to Zhang, a precinct had one hundred families, who would help as a group with a funeral; a ward had five hundred families, who would help a single family in difficult circumstances; a township had 2,500 families, who would help a single family in an emergency.

The system that Zhang referred to was associated with the Zhou dynasty and involved the organization of the populace into administrative units for the purpose of self-government. As such, these units were responsible for many things besides welfare. For example, the precincts were responsible to the central government's Ministry of Education *(Diguan)* for local defense, for reporting census data and records on supplies in storage, and for disseminating information about state regulations to the people.[36] Zhang may have idealized the effectiveness of this system in dealing with welfare needs, but his perspective was probably representative of many seventeenth- and eighteenth-century literati. He saw the Heavenly Teaching as helping contemporary Chinese by reviving ancient customs of welfare and charity.[37]

Another aspect of the Chinese inculturation of Christianity is revealed when Zhang speaks of the Heavenly Teaching supplementing the Literati Teaching by teaching the people agricultural rather than military skills.[38] Zhang referred to the legendary figures Hou Yi (the Archer Lord), famous for his skill in archery, and Ao, who had the strength to shake his enemies out of a boat.[39] Both came to a bad end, whereas the legendary emperors Yu and Hou Ji, who labored in agriculture—Yu drained the land and Hou Ji was the patron deity of agriculture—were blessed with the possession of the kingdom.

Zhang noted that sometimes benevolence was not rewarded in this world, and he cited the famous models of propriety, the brothers Bo Yi and Shu Qi. According to legendary history, toward the end of the Zhou dynasty in the twelfth century B.C., in the region of present-day Hebei province, a prince tried to deprive his firstborn son Bo Yi of his rightful heritage by making his younger brother Shu Qi heir to the throne. But Shu Qi's morality was such that he refused to deprive his older brother of his heritage, and so, when his father died, he fled the region. However, his elder brother Bo Yi declared that to accept the throne would be to violate his father's wishes, and so he too fled the land, leaving the throne to a third brother. The two brothers retired to the region of Mount Shouyang in modern Shanxi province, where they starved on a meager diet of wild seeds and later refused to serve the conquerors of the Shang.

The *Analects* and *Mencius* contain numerous praiseworthy references to the purity of commitment of Bo Yi and Shu Qi.[40] Yet their virtue caused them to suffer in this life. By contrast, Zhang noted that the tyrant Dao Zhi killed unfortunate people every day and yet lived a long life, and so his evil deeds appear to have been rewarded in this life. In short, in this life sometimes good people suffer and evil people reap rewards. The Heavenly Teaching supplemented the Literati Teaching by explaining how the virtuous behavior of Bo Ji and Shu Qi would ultimately be rewarded in the afterlife and how the evil of Dao Zhi would be punished in hell. Without the heaven and hell of the Heavenly Teaching, the people would not see that goodness and evil were justly compensated. Zhang believed that the notions of heaven and hell had existed in Chinese antiquity, but the Buddhists had plagiarized *(dao xi)* the ancient Lord of Heaven Teaching and in the process lost the true sense of how heaven and hell were used to recompense good and evil.[41] By introducing transmigration, Buddhism had destroyed the decisiveness of one's acts in life and diminished the finality of judgment at death.

IV

One of the most important filial obligations in Confucian China was to procreate and continue the family line. However, Zhang believed that the procreation of descendants was only part of a deeper truth that was understood solely by genuine, not commonplace, literati.[42] Commonplace literati lived out their lives preoccupied with the mundane concerns of reputation and profit *(ming li)* and with accumulating descendants until one day they died. Although they had anticipated death, they had not prepared for it. They had been preoccupied with the pressing concerns of the here-and-now rather than with ultimate truth. Zhang believed that they had not understood the meaning of Confucius' statement "One who does not consider what is distant will certainly suffer in what is near at hand."[43] By being preoccupied with producing descendants, these literati had misjudged what was important for the future.

The Heavenly Teaching supplemented the Literati Teaching by revealing the deeper meaning of Confucius' statement and the ultimate significance of the future. It taught literati how to attain eternal happiness and joy after death. Zhang believed not only that Confucius taught people to stand in awe of Heaven, but that Mencius had been teaching the particulars of the laws of Heaven when he spoke of the five ways in which a gentleman taught, namely, by exerting an influence like the rain, by helping the student perfect his virtue, by developing the student's talent, by answering questions, and by fostering self-cultivation.[44] Zhang believed that the Lord of Heaven acted out of love in bringing into the world teachers who instructed the people in such things as the Ten Commandments. If these teachings were followed, the most intelligent people could become sages and worthies while the uneducated people could attain a state of moral conduct.

Zhang saw immortality as part of both the Literati and Buddhist teachings.[45] He was aware that both teachings spoke of casting off the present body and seeking some form beyond our body. Zhang quoted *Mencius* 6a.15 in saying that those who followed the greater part of their nature became great, whereas those who followed the lesser part of their nature became mean spirited. For Zhang, the lesser part of one's nature involved the ears, eyes, and flesh, whereas the greater part involved the mind, thoughts, and soul. He believed that the Heavenly Teaching offered a way out of the confusion of Buddhist teachings in regard to the immortality of the soul. The Lord of Heaven was immortal and there was never a time when He did not exist.[46] However, humans have a beginning in time because we are created by the Lord of Heaven. At our creation, He bestows upon us a spiritual as well as a material nature, but it is through our spiritual nature that we attain immortality. Zhang believed that since the soul was indestructible, whoever created us had the power to sentence us to eternal rewards or punishment.[47]

The fundamental distinction between humans and animals is a distinction that both Confucianism and Christianity made, but it is also one in which Zhang believed that the Heavenly Teaching could supplement the Literati Teaching. Both views differ from the Buddhist view, which sees humans and animals as merely different manifestations of sentient beings *(zhongsheng)*, all of whom are related as approximately equal forms of life that are interchangeable at the time of death and transmigration.[48] Zhang claimed that vegetative life had no soul and that animal life had consciousness *(juehun)* but lacked a soul *(linghun)*.[49] Zhang showed that the traditional Confucian view of the relationship between the body and the soul was not so alien to the Western view when he made a clear distinction between the physical body *(rouqu)* and the soul *(linghun)* of each human being.[50]

Western students of Chinese religions are often influenced by Daoist views of the soul expressed by Zhuangzi, but literati like Zhang were less influenced by Zhuangzi. Neither was Zhang's view of the distinction between the body and the soul the elaborate theory developed by European Scholasticism. Zhang was not a wholesale borrower of European culture, and his interpretations nearly always derived from literati traditions. It is unlikely that he borrowed his view of the division of the body and the soul from the Heavenly Teaching; rather, he would have seen the Heavenly Teaching distinction between the body and soul as confirming and supplementing a similar view held by the literati.

Zhang believed that humans were distinguished from animals in their greater degree of choice. A human being who was dominated by the physical body sank into an animal-like state of existence, but one who was led by the soul advanced to a state of sagehood. Zhang made his point here by referring to the famous debate between Mencius and Gaozi over whether morality was internal or external, that is, inherent in human nature or acquired by means such as education.[51] Gaozi argued that the inherent nature of humans was amoral and that morality involved an arbitrary reshaping of that inherent nature. Zhang here followed the Mencian viewpoint that human nature was inherently good, and in doing so he appears to have been oblivious to the Christian viewpoint that all human beings are tainted at conception by original sin, from which they can be saved by God's grace. This shows to what degree Zhang's understanding of Confucianism was orthodox. He viewed Christianity as reconcilable not from the perspective of someone alienated from the literati tradition of Confucius or as one even marginal to the tradition, but rather as someone fully within the mainstream.

For the literati tradition, there was nothing more important than distinguishing truth from falsehood, particularly in a moral sense, and it was in this preeminent quest that Zhang felt the Heavenly Teaching offered the greatest supplement to the Literati Teaching. Repeatedly in the *Similarities,* Zhang spoke of the need to avoid following the false teachings of the "Two Masters" *(Er shi),* Buddha and Laozi.[52] Whereas Buddhism and Daoism conflicted with the teachings of Confucius on the role of morality over self, the Heavenly Teaching supported and supplemented Confucius' teaching. Zhang spoke of the physical body *(rouqu)* as both the helpmate *(zhu)* and the enemy *(jiu)* of the soul.[53] Confucius and Mencius desired people to fully illumine the truth and morality *(liyi)* of their souls and to diminish the lustful desires *(shiyuan)* of their bodies. Zhang quoted from the Song Neo-Confucian Zhu Xi to explain that when Confucius spoke of "overcoming the self," he meant "overcoming the selfish desires of one's own body."[54] Zhang's use of Zhu Xi's interpretation along with his favorable references to Han Yu (768–824), Cheng [Yi], and Zhu Xi show how much he identified with what was regarded as the orthodox Confucian tradition of his day.[55]

In the Confucian tradition, benevolence *(ren)* directed toward others stands in stark opposition to selfish desires. Zhang drew from the *Analects* to explain this opposition: "The determined scholar and benevolent person will not seek to live at the expense of benevolence, but will sacrifice his life to complete his benevolence."[56] Quoting *Mencius,* Zhang made his point: "[If forced to choose] I would give up life and do what is right."[57] Zhang used two examples from antiquity to explain the role of sacrifice in the service of morality. The first was Bigan, who together with Weizi and Jizi represented the three worthies of the Shang dynasty (ca. 1500–1050 B.C.). After repeatedly demonstrating his personal courage in protesting against the evil actions of the tyrannical Shang king Zhou, Bigan was punished by having his heart torn out.[58] Zhang believed that Confucius was emphasizing morality in this example, because although Bigan's physical body died, his soul had eternal life. The Heavenly Teaching supplemented the Literati Teaching in this regard by affirming eternal life.

Zhang used the historical conflict between Xiang Ji (styled Yu) to show how morality *(yi)* overcomes brute force.[59] Xiang Ji (233–203 B.C.) was a giant of a man who possessed great fighting skill, but he is most remembered for his unscrupulous cruelty as exemplified in his mass killing of the Qin armies after their surrender. After murdering the last representative of the Qin dynasty, Xiang agreed to establish King Huai of Chu as the new emperor under the title of Yi di (Righteous Emperor). Xiang later had this emperor assassinated but was eventually himself defeated by Liu Bang. Zhang believed that Xiang Ji's acts of rebellion were immoral and that, although Liu Bang was weak, Liu's greater morality enabled him to triumph over Xiang. Xiang eventually committed suicide and his state of Chu was destroyed, whereas Liu Bang founded the Han dynasty as the emperor Han Gaozi (reigned 206–195 B.C.).

Zhang believed that sages such as Han Yu, Cheng Yi, and Zhu Xi had made great efforts to clearly distinguish between right and wrong, but mankind had not accepted their teachings. Instead, the similarities and differences between the teachings of Master Kong and the Buddha had become confused. The Lord of Heaven created both Confucius and the Buddha, but the Buddha's teachings had been manipulated by Satan (Xiemo) to lead people astray and the true teachings of Confucius had been neglected. Apparently drawing from biblical teaching, Zhang claimed that Satan had existed at the time of the creation of heaven and earth, and had been criticized by the Lord of Heaven for his spiritual arrogance.[60] The Buddha himself is said to have come very close to this kind of arrogance. Confucius was unable to criticize Buddhism, because it had not yet come to China during his time.[61] However, Zhang stated, the Heavenly Teaching could enable people of his day to see that logically the teachings of Confucius and the Buddha should be distinguished as true and false.

V

The arrival of the Jesuit missionaries in China late in the sixteenth century presented a great challenge to Chinese culture. This group that included Europe's brightest, best educated, and most spiritually committed representatives would overwhelm many cultures around the world. China's unassailable cultural heritage and vast resources were such that few Chinese were overwhelmed. Nevertheless, there were a variety of reactions to the missionaries' teachings, ranging from hostility to fascination.

It is difficult to know what Zhang thought about the missionaries' motives in coming to China. First of all, he displayed a remarkable lack of interest in Jesuits as individuals. His extant writings rarely refer to individual missionaries by name, even though it is quite clear that Zhang had contact with the Jesuits in Hangzhou. The sole reference to a China missionary that I have found in Zhang's writings is to Ricci ("Master Li of the Far West"), with whom Zhang had no personal contact.[62] This personal remoteness is one of the things that distinguishes Zhang from the early literati converts, like the Three Pillars who worked closely with the missionaries and were personally influenced in their thinking about Christianity through these close relations. Conversely, Jesuits themselves, such as Ricci, were influenced in turn by their close relations with these literati. By contrast, except for one period in his life, Zhang appears to have had fairly detached relations with the missionaries and to have been less deeply influenced by them. Whether this distance was more the result of Zhang's own personality or of the changing cultural atmosphere and Chinese attitudes toward the foreign teachers is not clear. It is clear that there were far fewer collaborative works produced by Jesuits and literati of Zhang's generation than by their counterparts in the early seventeenth century. The decreasing collaboration of the Chinese Christians with the foreign missionaries was a certain sign of the deepening inculturation of Christianity into Chinese culture.

The one period in which Zhang did collaborate closely with the Jesuits was around and shortly after his baptism in 1678. Two vestiges of this collaboration have survived. The first is a short biography (3,100 characters) of Xu Guangqi.[63] The biography was compiled by Fr. P. Couplet and composed by Zhang in 1678. The second vestige of Zhang's collaboration with the Jesuits was his manuscript "Inscriptions in Praise of the Sage Teaching [i.e., Christianity]" consisting of thirty-eight poems.[64] Each poem consists of sixteen lines with four characters in each line. The poems are written in a very ancient poetic form that can be traced back to the *Book of Poetry*. The form is called a *zan* (eulogy), and it contains patterns using rhymes but not tones.[65] The phrasing of Zhang's eulogies is extremely concise and the vocabulary is far more obscure than in his prose writings, so that only fellow literati would be capable of fully understanding the poems.

Each eulogy is dedicated to one subject drawn from a list of Christian apostles, martyrs, church leaders, angels, Four Last Things (Death, Judgment, Hell, and Heaven), and well-known events drawn mainly from the New Testament dealing with the birth and early life of Jesus and Mary. These eulogies include all the original Twelve Disciples (except for Judas Iscariot and John, son of Zebedee) plus Saint Paul and Saint Barnabas. In addition, Zhang wrote eulogies to the Church Fathers, such as Saint Augustine, Saint Ambrose, and Saint Jerome. Several eulogies are dedicated to founders of religious orders, such as Saint Francis of Assisi, Saint Dominic, and Saint Ignatius of Loyola, as well as to momentous (albeit legendary) events in church history, as when Pope Silvester baptized the Roman emperor Constantine. One is not surprised to find a eulogy dedicated to the pioneering Jesuit apostle to Asia, Saint Francis Xavier, given the important role he played in Intorcetta's religious life. Zhang had dedicated eulogies not only to the first Christian martyr, Stephen, but also to the three Japanese Jesuits who were martyred in Japan in 1597. (A complete list of the subjects of Zhang's eulogies is found in the appendix.)

The eulogies blend historical fact with Christian reverence. Zhang received the facts from the Jesuits, but the use of complex literary language (which was beyond the Jesuits' literary abilities) to express reverence shows that the devotion was his own. The first eulogy, dedicated to Saint Peter, expresses this blending:

> How wonderful was Peter,
> a sage who was a great cornerstone for the Teaching.
> A fisherman who was commanded,
> to leave his family and follow the Lord.
> His love for the Lord was so filled with reverence,
> that he was a great wave hurling onward.
> A massive mountain of shining light,
> he swore an oath to totally commit his time,
> and sincerely believed in complete self-cultivation.
> He underwent all sorts of worldly suffering,
> and the spiritual light illumined his mind.
> He was a sage who spread the teaching throughout a wide area.
> He elevated the Teaching to a supreme position.
> He lived five lives in only one lifetime,
> and sacrificed his life in hurling himself against Satan.
> He had the keys to open Heaven's blessings.[66]

The eulogies were not freestanding poems but apparently were intended to accompany and to explain the paintings of religious images that Intorcetta was preparing for the interior of the Church of the Savior in the years from 1678 to 1683. It is no longer possible to examine the paintings on which the eulogies were inscribed, because they were destroyed by the fire that severely damaged the church in 1692. However, a comparison of a list of the paintings with Zhang's eulogies shows that Zhang's thirty-eight inscriptions almost exactly correspond to the themes of half of the seventy-two paintings (see the appendix). The contents of the eulogies were so detailed and involve historical figures so unknown to Chinese history that Zhang must have received this information from a Jesuit source—either a written source like Fr. Alfonso Vagnone's *Lives of the Saints (Shengjiao xingshi)*[67] or directly from someone like Intorcetta. A project of this nature would have required considerable contact and consultation between Zhang and Intorcetta.

Although there was considerable contact between Intorcetta and Zhang in the years around 1678, Intorcetta lacked the colorful, charismatic personality of Martini. Moreover, he had first encountered Zhang not at a youthful, formative age but rather when Zhang was a mature forty-two or forty-three years old. This timing may have limited Intorcetta's ability to exert great personal influence. In any case, Zhang's writings indicate that he was influenced more by the teaching of Christianity than by the personalities of the Jesuits with whom he came into contact. His treatment of the Jesuits was always general and respectful in terms of their being sagely teachers of the Heavenly Teaching. He used the same honorable terminology to refer to both the Jesuits and the Chinese literati, distinguishing them only by region. He called the Jesuits Western literati *(Xi Ru),* Western scholars *(Xi shi),* Western teachers *(Xi shi),* religious adepts from the Western nations *(Xiguo xiushi),* and sages and worthies from the Western nations *(Xiguo shengxian).*

Zhang believed that the Heavenly Teaching was brought from the Far West to *help* the Chinese in their ongoing attempt to distinguish truth from falsehood.[68] The missionaries did not come to China to teach the Chinese the difference between truth and falsehood or right and wrong, because the basic outlines of what was true and false had been delineated in antiquity and transmitted by Confucius. But Confucius' teaching was incomplete and had been distorted by Satan or by demonic forces, functioning through such figures as the Buddha.[69] The principles of spiritual phenomena were subtle and difficult to comprehend. Confucius had taught the people to revere spirits and to keep them at a respectful distance *(Analects* VI.20), but it was the Heavenly Teaching that completed the Literati Teaching's knowledge of spirits. To do so, it had to struggle against Satanic forces that invaded human minds.

Zhang believed that the Heavenly Teaching came to China not only to clarify what was true, but also to delineate what was false. To this problematic category belonged the astrological selection of auspicious and inauspicious days. Zhang noted that the missionaries had carefully studied the positive customs of China, but they had excluded the astrological selection of auspicious and inauspicious days from their study.[70] The Western literati did so because there was insufficient evidence to support this process of selection. But although Zhang was willing to reject the astrological computation of lucky and unlucky days as false, his attitude toward divination using the *Book of Changes (Yijing)* was more complex.

Zhang noted that the literati did not reject yarrow-stalk divination of auspicious and inauspicious days, but he himself regarded this divination as incomplete.[71] For example, he spoke of the topmost line of the hexagram *Daguo* (Great Passing) from the *Book of Changes,* which "shows its subject with extraordinary [boldness] wading through a stream, till the water hides the crown of his head. There will be evil, but no ground for blame."[72] Zhang explains this hexagram divination by drawing from an historical incident to show that an auspicious divination will sometimes turn out to be inauspicious. In 672 B.C. Duke Xian of Jin led an expedition against a barbarian tribe called the Western Rong. Duke Xian captured and took as his concubine the chief's daughter, whose name was Li Ji, one of the fatal beauties of Chinese history. Through Lady Li's influence, their son Xi Qi was advanced to the throne over several older half-brothers. But when he was placed on the throne in 651 B.C., he was murdered by the minister Li Ke, immediately transforming what was thought to be an auspicious situation into an inauspicious one. Zhang argued that divination was incomplete because it concentrated only on what was auspicious and inauspicious while neglecting what was good and evil. The Heavenly Teaching could supplement the Literati Teaching by teaching the people that good fortune and calamity were not fortuitously ordered by the Lord of Heaven but rather followed from human obedience to or rebellion against the commands of Heaven.

VI

The process of Sinifying Christianity was not always done consciously. The relations between church and state in the history of

Christianity have received a range of interpretations, extending from the extreme separation of church and state by the Anabaptists to the fusing of church and state in Byzantine Caesaropapism. The argument for some degree of separation is usually based on the biblical passage Mark 12:17, where Jesus states: "Render to Caesar the things that are Caesar's and to God the things that are God's" (Revised Standard Version). Zhang viewed the Heavenly Teaching as involving a unity of church and state in regard to China. But there is no evidence that Zhang conceived of church and state issues in universal terms that dealt with resolving conflicts of authority between the pope in Rome and the emperor in China. His view was based on the Confucian perspective in which separation of church and state would have been undesirable, because it would have violated the cosmological unity of the world that existed between Heaven, earth, and man.

In order to show how the Heavenly Teaching could supplement the Literati Teaching in this political dimension, Zhang contrasted how violations of the law were described in great detail in China, whereas in the Heavenly Teaching there were only a few moral laws. Even fewer than the Ten Commandments *(Shi cheng)* were the two fundamental rules *(Er duan)* on which the Heavenly Teaching was based, namely, "to worship the Lord of Heaven and to love other people like oneself."[73] These rules were clearly a paraphrase of Matthew 22:37–40 in which a lawyer among the Pharisees posed a question in an attempt to trick Jesus into incriminating himself by contradicting the Hebrew scriptures. In response to this question asking what was the greatest commandment of the Hebrew law, Jesus answered: "You shall love the Lord your God with all your heart, and with all your soul, and with all your mind. This is the greatest and first commandment. And a second is like it, you shall love your neighbor as yourself. On these two commandments depend all the law and the prophets" (Revised Standard Version). Zhang's shorter translation—which, he notes with characteristic literati pride, was reduced to eight Chinese characters—was most likely made from these words of Jesus.

It was in Zhang's interpretation of this eight-character passage that Sinification took place. Zhang interpreted the passage to mean that Heaven had established and sanctioned the Son of Heaven and rulers generally. Not only had the Lord of Heaven established these bases of political authority, but He had also established the bases of familial authority and hierarchy in giving us father and mother, elder and younger brother, husband and wife, as well as friends. When one adds to these four specified relationships the implied relationship between ruler and subject, it is clear that Zhang was referring to the five fundamental human relationships of the Literati Teaching. Political and familial authority all derived from God and there was no mention of the separation of political from religious authority. Zhang stated that the Heavenly Teaching was "sufficient to supplement the deficiencies" of the Literati Teaching because, whereas the teaching of Confucius was unable to include all people, the teaching of the Lord of Heaven was unable to neglect even a single person.[74]

Most religions have difficulty in balancing love and morality. Zhang stated that the followers of Confucius had been aware of the need for this balance and sought benevolence (i.e., love) by increasing morality (righteousness).[75] Mencius used morality to assist benevolence and to prevent it from degenerating into an indulgent state in which love was dispensed indiscriminately. Conversely, Mencius used benevolence to prevent morality from becoming so strict that it excluded love. Zhang believed that Buddhism failed to maintain this balance and cited as an example monks who excessively followed the bodhisattva ideal in offering themselves as food to a tiger in a compassionate act of self-sacrifice. Drawing again from history, Zhang cited an example of a similar lack of balance in Emperor Wu (reigned 502–549) of the Liang dynasty. Emperor Wu was so absorbed with practicing Buddhist compassion and with not killing sentient beings that he suspended capital punishment and substituted noodles for sacrificial animals in the ancestral ceremonies.

Zhang believed that the Heavenly Teaching balanced benevolence and morality in combining the washing of one's sins clean (i.e., benevolence) with eternal punishment (i.e., moral justice). Zhang spoke of the Lord of Heaven being incarnated and born into the world in order, first, to save people through redemption and to teach them to repent of their sins (i.e., benevolence and morality combined) and, second, to inform people of the death of an emperor (i.e., the Crucifixion of Christ).[76] Zhang then made what would have appeared to the non-Christian reader as a puzzling, if not astounding, statement: he said that we were commanded to eat the Sage's body *(shengti)* and to drink the Sage's blood *(shengxue)* in order to attain immortality.[77] The reference, of course, was to the eucharistic eating of the body and blood of Christ. Zhang cautioned the reader to guard against the deceits of Satan, but he cited the *Book of Odes* to note that the Lord of Heaven was present everywhere.[78]

Zhang continued with a discussion of killing by presenting a fascinating blending of the Literati Teaching and the Heavenly Teaching. He noted that loving one's parents was the beginning of benevolence and that the worst crime in China was killing one's parents, for which the standard punishment was the horribly slow slicing of the limbs prior to beheading.[79] Zhang believed that this extreme punishment was fitting for such a heinous crime, but he noted that the Literati Teaching offered no appropriate punishment for killing one's child or for killing oneself. Under the apparent influence of Christian morality, Zhang called the killing of one's child an inhumane *(buren)* act that deserved punishment.

A traditional Confucian argument against suicide was that one's body was a gift from one's parents and it would be unfilial to harm it. Rather than appealing to this traditional argument, Zhang said that suicide was wrong because we are creations of the Lord of Heaven and suicide violates God's law.[80] The Lord of Heaven created heaven, earth, and the myriad beings all in order to nurture us, and among all the living creatures, we are forbidden to kill only human beings, unlike the Buddhists who are forbidden to kill any sentient being. Zhang believed that the Buddhist teaching on transmigration misled people into the error of striving for a better state of reincarnation. However, the Heavenly Teaching supplemented the Literati Teaching by showing that it was the Lord of Heaven who gives us life, and if we oppose the will of Heaven and commit suicide in this life, then we will indeed suffer the punishment of descent into the pit of eternal suffering that is hell.[81]

Zhang was dripping with sweat from the horrible heat of the fire. Although he was stripped to the waist, the heat was hotter than anything he had ever known. Each time he looked to the right he saw his old friend Ji Jiongfan lying nearly naked, face down in the iron bed of fire. Jiongfan was struggling with the terrible pain, but he could not scream because a demon with an iron pike stood over him to keep his head submerged in the molten liquid. Zhang wanted to run away, but he could not move. His hands were tied behind his back and he was forced to kneel. The small demon across from him smiled, waiting for Zhang to take his turn on the bed.

Jiongfan suddenly raised his head to scream and Zhang opened his eyes. He was in his own bed. It was a dream. He threw off the damp covers and felt the humid night air against his skin. Zhang knew the dream because he had dreamt it before. He was in the Hell of the Iron Bed, where the ruler with three eyes blazing in the darkness had just sentenced him to punishment on the bed of fire for his lust.[82] These were sins that he and Jiongfan had shared in the pleasure houses at the West Lake, pleasures that, to be frank, he had still not entirely given up in his thoughts.

The belief in the Hell of the Iron Bed was shared by many superstitious people and Zhang was not superstitious, so why could he not shake this dream? He knew Jiongfan did not suffer from the same dream, but then Jiongfan enjoyed life more than Zhang did. It was Zhang's dissatisfaction that had led him to the Lord of Heaven Teaching. The Lord of Heaven Teaching did not have a Hell of the Iron Bed, but it did have a hell. He remembered the inscription he had written for the depiction of hell hanging in the Church of the Savior:

The earthly ruler,
has his prison.
How could the Creator of the world
not have His hell?
Pure natures ascend and impure natures fall,
but the natures of things are not "fallen."
And yet humans fall into evil,
because they bring themselves to hell through their own actions.
In hell a fierce fire and all sorts of suffering
are increased by a vicious Satan.
And this suffering is endless and forever,
like a harsh slicing and stripping of the skin that goes on and on.
The Two Masters Laozi and Buddha spoke deceiving words,
because one can indeed die and fall out of the cycle of
      transmigration.
Rely on the Lord instead for protection,
and all these misfortunes can be avoided.[83]

CHAPTER 5

Loving the Lord of Heaven and
Hating the Buddha

Zhang listened as one of his neighbors, standing in front of the smok-
ing embers of his home, sadly explained that the house had burned
because he had failed to pay his annual tribute to the god of fire
(zhurong) last month. Many people believed that the god of fire had a
magical power that prevented these swift and terrible fires from des-
troying homes and even whole neighborhoods. This man believed in the
god of fire, and he also believed in the Buddha.

Zhang remembered how once long ago he and some young friends
had taken a walk on the outskirts of the city. When they came upon the
Sweet Dew of Immortality Monastery (Ganlusi), they had wandered
around the grounds and found some scaffolding left over from a recent
ceremony in honor of the god of fire. His young friend Paoan had play-
fully picked up a piece of wood and struck the monastery bell. Immediately a monk came running over and stopped him, saying that the setting was not fortuitous and sounding the bell would certainly bring harm
to the body of monks. Zhang was puzzled and asked, if the Buddha
were the highest thing in Heaven, why did they need to worry about
the proximity of spirits, such as the god of fire, interfering with the
Buddha's helping them. It was a wasted question. He did not see then
what he saw now. The monks' minds are clouded by a very subtle and
elaborate deception that leads them and many followers of the Buddha
astray. Hong Ji and Zhang had spent a great deal of time unmasking this
deception, and their work was soon to be printed. He wondered if his
neighbor would read it and be convinced. It is sometimes more com-
forting to cling to old beliefs and to remember to placate the god of
fire.[1]

I

In China in the late sixteenth century several Jesuit missionaries, including Frs. Ruggieri, Ricci, and Valignano, made the decision to blend Christianity with Confucianism rather than with Buddhism. This decision followed an unsuccessful experiment in adopting the clothing and spiritual role of the Buddhist monks, and thereafter the Jesuits did not turn back from their decision to identify in dress, thinking, and social status with the Confucian literati. This plan developed slowly and in consultation with the early literati Christians. In 1612 the eminent scholar-official and one of the Three Pillars Xu Guangqi expressed this plan in the form of a short, memorable phrase of the type of which the literati were so fond. In the preface to a work on Western hydraulics, Xu wrote that Christianity should "supplement Confucianism and displace Buddhism" *(bu Ru yi Fo).* [2]

"Supplement Confucianism and displace Buddhism" is a formula for inculturation that may be interpreted on several levels. The technical nature of Xu's work on hydraulics caused it to be placed in the "practical section" *(qibian)* rather than the "theoretical section" *(libian)* of the collection of missionary literature in which it appeared. Consequently, the level in which Xu presented the formula in 1612 was the practical one of blending the scientific learning of Western hydraulics with Chinese culture. In his brief preface Xu did not develop the phrase in any detail or depth, and it has been assumed that the formula "supplement Confucianism and displace Buddhism" expressed an insight so simple and elementary that it belonged to only the earliest stages of the inculturation process. The facts are otherwise.

After the collapse of the Ming dynasty in the mid-seventeenth century, Christianity faced increasing obstacles as the literati sought refuge in more orthodox forms of Confucianism and were less open to accommodating foreign teachings. By focusing their efforts so fully on cultivating the Qing court and Manchu monarchs such as the Shunzhi and Kangxi emperors, the Jesuits had less energy remaining to devote to the literati. So although there was no clear break with the early missionary approach of Ricci and Xu Guangqi, there was, in fact, a shift in emphasis.

Nevertheless, there were regional pockets of Christian activity, such as in Zhejiang, Shandong, and Fujian provinces, where literati carried forward the early orientation of Ricci and the Three Pillars. In the Hangzhou Christian community there were several heirs to Xu's approach. Among them was Zhang Xingyao, who carried Xu's formula of inculturating Christianity by "supplementing the literati and displacing the Buddhists" to a deeper level than had the early seventeenth-century Christian literatus.

Zhang was an accomplished historian, whose knowledge of Chinese history defined his contribution to the inculturation process. In his *Similarities,* the emphasis was on how Christianity completed Confucianism. However, in his *Abridged Refutation of Several Disputable Points [Held by the Buddhists] (Pi lüeshuo tiaobo),* the emphasis was on why Christianity should replace Buddhism. Zhang's heretofore neglected works show that the seventeenth-century phase of the inculturation process continued longer and went deeper than has been realized. One reason for this oversight is that too much scholarly attention has been focused on missionary activity at the Manchu court in Beijing and too little on indigenous Christian activity in these provincial centers.

II

Zhang believed that Christianity reinforced traditional Chinese morality while Buddhism undermined it. In his preface to the *Refutation,* Zhang presented the traditional Confucian viewpoint that morality, more than anything else, distinguished humans from animals.[3] This morality included the Five Human Relationships *(Wu lun)* between ruler and subject, father and son, husband and wife, elder and younger, and friends. This morality also included the Five Perennial Virtues *(Wu chang),* of benevolence *(ren),* righteousness or morality *(yi),* ritual *(li),* wisdom *(zhi),* and belief *(xin).* Zhang believed that the Lord of Heaven bestowed all of these virtues on the human soul and so one could speak of Heaven-bestowed human relationships and Heaven-bestowed human nature. Moreover, many ancient sages and worthies revered and stood in awe of Heaven. However, when the Buddha arose, principles of human relationships were discarded, and when the Chan Buddhist sect flourished, principles of morality were extinguished.

In part, Zhang's criticisms of Buddhism were based on Buddhism's very different ethical principles and the negative effects these principles had on Chinese history. But his criticisms were also based on his conviction, shared by the overwhelming majority of literati, that the Buddhist view of reality was irreconcilable with the Confucian outlook. Whereas Confucianism believes that the world we experience is real, Buddhism believes it to be an illusion. Zhang may not have fully understood the Buddhist teaching of Emptiness *(Kong; Śūnyatā)*, because it is not simply an intellectual concept but an insight so profound that it requires extensive meditation and culminates in a profound experience of enlightenment. However, Zhang had at one point in his life seriously studied Buddhism, and he had a basic understanding of Buddhist Emptiness and of how it differed from the Confucian perspective. Unlike Buddhism, which sees the mountains, rivers, and land masses as the creation of the mind, Zhang believed that Confucianism agreed with Christianity in regarding these things as the creation of the Lord of Heaven.[4]

Zhang believed that Christian creation was in harmony with the Literati Teaching, whereas it is widely believed today that the Christian account of creation is irreconcilable with the Literati Teaching. Even if most Chinese literati held the view that the universe contained its own creative energy and needed no outside creator, Zhang's writings show that this viewpoint was not as unanimous as some have thought.[5]

Zhang believed that whereas Buddhism's arrival in China had led to a degeneration of traditional morality, Christianity's arrival fostered the morality of the ancients. "These gentlemen and masters from the Far West" *(Taixi zhu wei xiansheng)* had traveled ninety thousand *li* in order to implement a teaching that "distinguishes truth from falsehood, teaches people to revere the Lord of Heaven, sincerely believes in the Five Human Relationships, exhaustively practices the Five Perennial Virtues, and transforms evil into good."[6] Zhang noted that all of these teachings were in complete harmony with the words of the ancient sages Yao, Shun, Yu, King Tang, King Wen, King Wu, the Duke of Zhou, and Confucius.

In his *Similarities,* Zhang's criticisms of Buddhism are intellectual and fairly detached from individual personalities, but in his *Refutation,* the hostility has a personal cast. It was produced by a public airing of differences between Xu Guangqi (canonized Wending) and a Buddhist monk. In 1613 Xu resigned from his official posts in Beijing on grounds of illness. He then made a temporary retreat to Tianjin, where he farmed and wrote a number of works until being recalled in 1616.[7] One of these works was titled *A Refutation of All the Falsehoods of the Buddha (Pi shishi zhu wang;* commonly known as the *Pi wang).* After the appearance of Xu's work, a critique was published by a Buddhist monk named Master Jie of the Puren Monastery in Suzhou, who was also known as Jieliu Xingce (1628-1682).[8] This Master Jie had been a student of Ruoan Tongwen (1604-1655) in Hangzhou and was a contemporary of Zhang Xingyao.

Suzhou lies less than sixty miles (ninety-seven kilometers) west of Xu's native Shanghai and approximately ninety miles (145 kilometers) northwest of Hangzhou. In the seventeenth century Suzhou and Hangzhou were major cities, unlike Shanghai, which would not become prominent until the nineteenth century. Suzhou and Hangzhou were linked by the Grand Canal, and the monk Jie probably lived in Hangzhou while studying under Master Ruoan. However, Jie was ten years older than Zhang, and there is no indication that the two ever met. Zhang felt a sense of personal loyalty toward Xu as a fellow baptized literatus, and he took great offense at Jie's attack on Xu's work. Zhang felt called to answer Jie's critique. Consequently, in 1689 Zhang and his fellow villager and Christian literatus Hong Ji, also known as Master Ji, collaborated in writing a rebuttal to Jie that was sometimes harsh and polemical in its criticism of Buddhism.

Unlike Zhang's other works, which remained in manuscript, the *Refutation* was printed. The fact that the printing took place at the Church of the Savior in Hangzhou indicates that Fr. Intorcetta supported it.[9] Zhang accused Jie and his followers not only of ignorance and perpetuating falsehoods, but also of willful deceit. Zhang said that in terms of deceiving mankind and oppressing people, there were none who surpassed them.[10] In saying that he and Hong had undertaken this rebuttal in order to save humanity from drowning, Zhang used a famous phrase that had been used against the Christian missionaries twenty-five years earlier by Yang Guangxian in the title of his anti-Christian work *Budeyi* (I cannot do otherwise) (1664). But here the phrase "I cannot do otherwise" was used in defense of Christianity and against Buddhism.

Hong Ji's preface in the *Refutation* followed lines of argumentation similar to those already presented in Zhang's preface. Hong and Zhang saw themselves as rousing people out of a demonic dream filled with Buddhist illusions. Hong followed Xu in stating that whereas it was important to understand that unrepentant sinning would cause one to fall into hell after death, it was dangerous to believe in the Buddhist illusion that prayers by the living would enable a deceased soul to break out of hell.[11]

The introduction to the *Refutation* was written by Zhang, and it served as a bridge that referred back to Xu Guangqi's refutation of Buddhist falsehood while looking ahead to the refutation by Zhang and Hong. Zhang used the writings of Confucius and Mencius to criticize Buddhism. In one sense his argument was based on a historical anachronism, because Buddhism did not arrive in China until after the deaths of both Confucius and Mencius. However, Zhang was criticizing Buddhism not as a distinct religion, but rather as a type of heterodoxy or fallacious form of reasoning similar to earlier teachings that had existed at the time of Confucius and Mencius.

Zhang was acting here not only as a social critic of the China of his time, but also as a Confucian prophet who spoke for God and called the Chinese people back to morality. This was why he spoke critically of the China of his day for discarding the fundamental (Five) Human Relationships and for lacking truly moral people.[12] The degeneration of Chinese Buddhism in Zhang's time from its earlier vitality gave Zhang's accusations against Buddhism for deceiving the people a plausibility that we tend to dismiss today as the prejudice of a narrow-minded Confucian. But we must remember that, as a Confucian prophet, Zhang was not defending the morality of his day, but was calling people to return to what he believed was an older, lost truth.

For Zhang, civilization was defined in Confucian terms. It did not refer to a high degree of technological achievement, intellectual expertise, or material affluence. Civilization was most essentially defined by morality, and it was morality—in the form of the Five Human Relationships and the Five Perennial Virtues—that most clearly distinguished humans from animals. This is why the literati were so opposed to Buddhism's dissolution of this fundamental distinction between humans and animals. Zhang rejected the Buddhist notion of sentient beings *(zhongsheng)*, divisible into the five incarnations of gods, humans, animals, hungry ghosts, and beings in hell.[13] (Sometimes the category of demons was added as a sixth incarnation.)

Zhang found support for this view of morality in *Mencius* 7a.1: "One who understands his inherent nature will understand Heaven (i.e., God). One who controls his mind and nourishes his inherent nature serves Heaven." In Zhang's perspective, this statement reflected a perfect fusing of the Heaven of Confucianism with the God of Christianity. Zhang believed that the Buddhists were unenlightened about both the creation of living things by the Lord of Heaven and the distinction between the human species and animals.[14]

III

Masters Hong and Zhang divided the *Refutation* into eight sections that were organized around rebutting the monk Jie's criticisms of Xu's *Pi wang*.[15] Their point-by-point rebuttal enhanced the polemical tone of the work. Each section begins with a quotation from Jie's critique. The quotation is followed by a rebuttal by Hong or Zhang or sometimes both.[16]

The first section of the *Refutation* plunges the reader into one of the most abstruse concepts of Buddhist epistemology, namely, the Mind-Only *(Weixin or Weishi)* doctrine. This doctrine is a form of radical philosophical idealism, often (though simplistically) compared to the philosophy of the Irish bishop G. Berkeley (1685–1753) as well as to Christian Science. Although the Mind-Only teaching logically follows from the historical Buddha's original teaching that the world is an illusion, the doctrine was not formally developed in India until the fourth century A.D. by the brothers Asanga and Vasubandha.[17] The school was propagated in China by the famous pilgrim-monk Xuanzang (Hsüan-tsang) (ca. 596–664), who made a long voyage to India in order to study this doctrine. Xuanzang's journey has been immortalized in Chinese culture through the late sixteenth-century satirical novel *The Journey to the West (Xi you ji)*, about a roguish monkey of great spiritual power who accompanied Xuanzang to India.[18] Although the Mind-Only teaching did not prosper in China as a separate school, it was absorbed into other Chinese schools, most notably the Huayan and Chan (Zen) teachings.[19] The Mind-Only doctrine is expounded in important Chinese Buddhist texts, such as the *Laṅkāvatāra Sutra (Lengjia jing)* and the *Huayan Sutra (Huayan jing)*, texts with which Zhang was familiar.

The Mind-Only doctrine teaches that all deeds have effects that are transmitted as a stream of seeds (in Sanskrit *bija*) called the Storehouse Consciousness *(Zangshi;* in Sanskrit Ālaya-vijñāna). This is a universal consciousness from which the other seven forms of consciousness (the mind and the six sense-consciousnesses) are generated. The Storehouse Consciousness is passive but stores all the ideas reflected in the mind.[20]

The Storehouse Consciousness has no self-awareness and functions blindly without self-control. It is a great reservoir that stores all mental impressions of the past and the present. As the inactive seeds of the Storehouse are activated, the seeds are influenced by the fragrance of the Storehouse Consciousness, such that the stored ideas manifest themselves in the everyday world of phenomenal experience and psychic processes. This narcoticlike fragrance stimulates the desire for life and for consequent reincarnations, from which one can be released only through enlightenment. Progress toward enlightenment involves eliminating the defiled seeds and replacing them with pure dharmas. The end result is pure truth, in which there is no discrimination between the subject and the object. In sum, the Mind-Only doctrine teaches that the material world is a projection of one's mind. The physical world that we experience is compared to the images in a mirror, which of themselves have no reality. The phenomenal world that we experience in our daily lives is a result of our desires interacting with the Storehouse Consciousness.

This complex Mind-Only teaching underlies Jie's claim that hell can be viewed as both existing and not existing.[21] Jie stated that one distinguished between principle or noumena *(li)* and facts or phenomena *(shi)*. Principle was linked with the formal cause *(ju gu)*, i.e., the form, pattern, or structure into which something is changed, while phenomena were connected to the efficient or moving cause *(zao gu)*, i.e., the active agent that produces something.[22] In a teaching of radical idealism like the Mind-Only, the mind is the causative force of everything because there is no reality outside of ideation. So Jie argued that if the mind is viewed as a formal cause, then one can regard hell as not existing, but if the mind is viewed from the perspective of an efficient cause, then hell exists. Zhang explained this apparent contradiction by saying that if, on the one hand, the mind is an efficient cause, then things are caused by outside forces and so one can speak of existence because the mind is a real agent that produces hell. Conversely, Zhang stated that if the mind acts as a formal cause, then it is a false creator because hell is changed into something mental that has no existence outside of the mind.

Jie illustrated this distinction with an anecdote in which a scholar asked the monk Huang Nie whether hell really existed.[23] Huang answered that it did not exist, but when the scholar asked the same question of another monk named Da Hui, Da answered that hell did indeed exist and spoke about it in detail. When the scholar confronted Da with Huang's contradictory answer that hell did not exist, Da responded by contrasting a Buddhist layman who had a wife and children with the monk Huang Nie who had none. Whether one had a family or not depended on the status of the individual. By implication, he meant that whether hell existed or not depended on the perceiver, because worldly phenomena (including hell) were produced by the mind.

Confucianism is a tradition that has given great emphasis to morality and spiritual cultivation but (unlike Indian philosophy) has shown little interest in epistemology (the theory of knowledge) and ontology (the nature of reality). The dominant Confucian viewpoint was a form of realism in the sense that the external world was thought to have a reality independent of the observer.[24] This view was clearly the contrary of Mind-Only idealism, which saw the external world as having no independent reality but rather being a product of ideation. The Confucian attitude has been well expressed by the eminent translator of Chinese philosophic texts Wing-tsit Chan, who refers to the Mind-Only philosophy as "completely alien to the Chinese tradition" and "merely an Indian system transplanted on Chinese soil."[25] Consequently, it is not surprising that orthodox exponents of Confucianism like Zhang or Hong would look very critically at Jie's Mind-Only idealist views.

Hong began his critique by stating that various forms of Mind-Only (i.e., idealist) teachings have been confusing the world for two thousand years, that is, since the death of the last great ancient sage, Mencius, and prior to the entry of Buddhism into China.[26] Zhang's response to the Mind-Only school was equally disparaging; he began by emphatically declaring that, with regard to the facts and principles of the world, existence depended on external reality and not on our mental constructions.[27] Showing a typical Confucian disdain for ontological subtleties, Zhang argued that something either existed or did not; it could not simultaneously exist and not exist as the Chan school maintained. Zhang's conviction of the correctness of his viewpoint was based not only on his own mental and logical powers, but also on the test of human experience as recorded in the Chinese Classics. In his mind, the ancient vintage of the views embodied in the literati tradition gave his viewpoint a certainty not found in Buddhism. Consequently, it was perfectly consistent to quote from classical works, such as the *Book of Odes* and *Doctrine of the Mean,* to rebut Jie's Mind-Only argument. Zhang concentrated on the process of creation and stated that things were not created by the mind, but rather had a real and objective existence due to their creation by the Lord of Heaven.[28]

IV

Zhang believed it was possible for one's own mind to create evil and to cause one to fall into hell, but he said it was impossible for one's own mind to be both the formal and efficient causes of hell.[29] It was inconsistent, he said, to believe it was possible to break out of hell with chants and incantations (by the living for the dead) and yet to think that hell did not really exist.[30] Zhang supported his position by again drawing from history. In the Song dynasty, Chen Shidao (1053–1101) had composed a collection of biographical notes called *Hou shan ji* in which he cited the example of the monk Shan Duan, who lived in the Chongdou monastery in the western capital.[31] In spite of his monastic calling, Shan Duan indulged in wine and women to excess. Eventually he became ill, and, as he was approaching death, he worried about how the karmic effects of his misdeeds in this life would cause him great suffering in hell. However, he realized that if hell did not exist, then he would not suffer. Consequently, he prayed that hell was an illusion.

A Buddhist monk tended to view hell in a different way than did a layman. For the latter, the tortures of hell helped him to abjure his sinful ways and embrace the teachings of the Buddha. But a monk tended to see the terrors of hell as the product of his own thoughts and as terrors that could be controlled through meditation.[32] Viewed in this light, the monk Shan is probably less cynical than Zhang implies, though perhaps still as self-deluded as Zhang claims. Zhang believed Shan's attitude was an example of the baseless self-delusion typical among Buddhists.

Not only did Chinese Buddhism contain a clear sense of hell, but it appears that Buddhism introduced the notion of hell into China, where it became fused with indigenous forms of ancestral worship.[33] Long before Zhang's time, Chinese notions of hell were no longer identifiable as belonging to a particular religion but had become thoroughly blended with various forms of popular religion. However, the doctrinal explanation of Buddhist hell remained quite clear: the Buddhist hell was not a permanent abode but a transient state in which one purged oneself of past sins through suffering punishment. Hell was one of the five or six incarnations in which sentient beings were reborn. One passed through one's reincarnation in hell just as one passed through reincarnation as an animal, god, hungry ghost, demon, or human.

The specific conceptions of Chinese hell differed. Buddhism teaches that breaking the chain of life-and-death (samsara) requires a profound individual enlightenment in which the illusory nature of human experience is perceived. Not only is human existence illusory, but so too are the other forms of reincarnation as sentient beings. Enlightenment, however, can come only in the human form. Only with the realization that the chain of life-and-death is built upon an illusion does the release called Nirvana occur. Consequently, Buddhist doctrine saw hell from quite a different perspective than did Christians. However, since the Buddhist hell had become thoroughly fused with non-Buddhist teachings, the Buddhist notions of hell that Zhang encountered were not entirely consistent with Buddhist doctrine.

One of the most fundamental characteristics of Christianity is its two-sided nature with regard to divine forgiveness and punishment. Those who repent of their sins are promised forgiveness and an eternity in heaven, while those who refuse to repent are condemned to an eternity of punishment in hell. Forgiveness is associated with God's love given freely and without being earned (i.e., grace), while judgment is associated with God's justice. The monk Jie criticized the Christian punishments of hell as the work of an oppressive God. In fact, Jie said that the Lord of Heaven's cruelty was "a hundred thousand million times" (bai qian yi bu) greater than the cruelty of the notorious tyrants of Chinese history—King Jie of the Xia dynasty and King Zhou of the Shang dynasty.[34]

Hong responded to Jie's criticism with a very Confucian argument. He compared the Lord of Heaven to parents who give birth to, suckle, and nourish a child. This is a relationship characterized predominantly by love. Hong spoke of the Lord of Heaven as the "common father" (gong fu) of the myriad peoples.[35] The Lord of Heaven created all people and bestowed on each person an eternal and indestructible soul. So if someone was in rebellion against God, he or she belonged to the same category as those who were unfilial toward their parents and so deserved the punishment of descending into hell for eternity.[36] Hong made a very sharp contrast between the single cycle of birth-and-death bestowed upon us by the Creator-Lord of Christianity and the endless cycle of birth-and-death reincarnations found in Buddhism. The Christian conception of a soul who was born, died, and experienced life only once was much more complementary to Confucian ancestral worship, with its strict sense of hierarchy and ordering by age. In contrast, Buddhist transmigration confused the order of generations by introducing rebirth.

Hong continued to blend the Christian and Confucian teachings by claiming that genuine sorrow and repentance of one's sins would enable one to receive—through the infinite compassion of the Lord of Heaven *(Tianzhu wuxian renci)*—an escape from hell and ascent into Heaven.[37] Hong believed that this notion was found not only in the Heavenly Teaching, but also in the Classics of China. The three sage-emperors Yao, Shun, and Yu as well as many of the enlightened kings of the Shang dynasty (ca. 1500–1050 B.C.) and the founder of the Zhou dynasty, King Wen (ca. 1050 B.C.), were said by Hong all to be residing in heaven.

In traditional Chinese culture there were two ultimate sources of living authority—one's parents and the emperor. To his previous claim of a parallel between filial respect for one's parents and respect for God, Hong now added a parallel between obedience to the emperor *(dihuang)* or imperial court *(zhaoting)* and obedience to the Lord of Heaven.[38] Although there were differences in the abilities of the emperor and the Lord of Heaven, Hong argued that rebellion evoked a severe punishment from both, except that with the case of the Lord of Heaven, the punishment was eternal in duration. Zhang's rebuttal to Jie in this section was based on his view that respect for the ruler of a nation was prerequisite to having respect for the Lord of Heaven.[39]

Zhang's criticism of Jie disputed the Buddhist view of hell as the product of our mind and therefore a form of illusion.[40] It is possible to argue that Zhang's rejection of the Mind-Only teaching was based on an incomplete understanding of this complex philosophy. But given his previous study of the *Lankāvatāra* and *Huayan* sutras, it is more likely that his rejection of the Mind-Only teaching was based on a pervasive intellectual disposition shared by many Chinese literati against this teaching. It was this disposition that caused Zhang consistently to reduce Buddhist positions to classical anti-Confucian positions. One example was Zhang's reaction to a particular *gongan*. Chan masters often assigned riddles or *gongan* (Japanese *kōan*) for pupils to meditate on in order to remove all traces of intellectuation in preparation for receiving a profound intuitive insight. One of the most famous of these *gongan* asked what one's original face looked like before one was born. The particular *gongan* Zhang was reacting to involved grasping one's original countenance *(benlai mianmu)* before one distinguished between good and evil. Zhang reduced this Buddhist notion of the amoral original countenance to a variation on the teaching of Mencius' famous adversary Gaozi. Gaozi had opposed the Mencian claim that humans were inherently good by arguing that human nature was inherently neither good nor evil.[41]

In contrast to the subtle epistemology of the Mind-Only philosophy, with its emphasis on perceiving the illusory nature of the world, Zhang compared the clarity and certainty of the Lord of Heaven Teaching to a compass.[42] Instead of pointing toward twenty-four different mountains or 120 different degrees, the Chinese compass pointed south and indicated a fixed direction. The metaphor of a compass would be ill suited for the subtleties of the Mind-Only teaching, but it was well suited to the Confucian desideratum that a teaching serve as a clear, practical guide to morality.

Zhang rebutted Jie's charge that the Heavenly Teaching's hell was created for a cruel purpose by saying that the Lord of Heaven balanced the two primary virtues of benevolence and righteousness.[43] The Lord of Heaven did not allow any imbalance in His distribution of compassion *(renci)* and righteous punishment *(yifa)*.[44] Zhang was particularly concerned about Jie's criticism that the Lord of Heaven was cruel in his creation of hell, and he took pains to argue that Jie's statement was the antithesis of the truth. The Lord of Heaven's compassion was so great that he offered evil people the choice of repenting and avoiding hell.[45] The Lord of Heaven truly had the power to offer people an option of an eternity of punishment in hell or an eternity of joy in Heaven. By contrast, Zhang claimed that the Buddha lacked the spiritual power to send humans to hell or to rescue them from hell's punishments, in spite of the many references in Buddhist literature to Avici Hell *(Abida diyu)*.[46] In regard to cruelty, Zhang believed that the harshness of the Buddha caused numerous repetitions of cruelties of the sort associated with the archtyrants of Chinese history—King Jie of the Xia dynasty and King Zhou of the Shang dynasty.[47]

V

Prior to the entry of Buddhism into China, the predominant Chinese teaching on the soul conceived of a life after death in which the soul split into a heavy yin component called *po* and a light yang component called *hun*. The *po*-soul was an earthly element that descended into the grave of the deceased, where it resided. If the living descendants honored the deceased with an appropriate burial ceremony and sacrifices, the *po* would rest peacefully, but if it were neglected, it would become a demonic ghost *(gui)* that would seek vengeance on the descendants. The *hun*-soul was an ethereal element that ascended into the heavens. If appropriate burial and sacrifices were forthcoming for the deceased, the *hun* would become a benevolent spirit *(shen)* that aided the descendants.[48] Sometimes the soul after death was said to descend into the Land of Darkness or to the Yellow Springs, but there was no notion of judgment or punishment. Vague ideas about reincarnation were contained in early Daoist thought, but they were essentially poetic and part of the cycles of nature, as in Zhuangzi's (Chuang-tzu's) dream of the butterfly, and not tied to working out any karmic retribution.

The idea of a hell in which souls were punished in the afterlife for their evil deeds in life was unknown in ancient Chinese culture. There are references in ancient Chinese literature, such as the *Book of Documents* II.v.6.6, to a god of death. This god, variously known as Youbei and Youhao, was linked with the northern regions because of northern connotations of dark and cold that are associated with the netherworld.[49] Youbei was probably the ruler of the subterranean realm of the dead. In south China a similar ruler was called Tubo.[50] In addition to a spirit of the underworld, there emerged in ancient China a demon of death (or a ruler of one's destiny) known as Siming.[51] It was this Siming with whom the ancient shamanesses achieved mystical union through their ecstatic dancing and singing.[52] However, Siming was a ruler of destiny only in the sense that he implemented the destiny that humans had brought about by their own deeds.[53] He was an underworld deity who eventually was blended with the heavenly deity of Shang times known as Shangdi (Lord-on-High). Continuing during the Zhou dynasty, both Shangdi and Siming were rulers of the dead.[54] In spite of their roles as gods of death, the notion of separating regions in the afterlife into a heaven for rewards and a hell for punishment appears to have been foreign to ancient China.[55]

The idea of a separate heaven and hell did not develop in China until after the introduction of Buddhism.[56] While the most direct source of Chinese ideas on hell was Buddhism, other sources influenced the Chinese indirectly by way of Buddhism, such as the Twenty-one Hells of Vedic literature. Chinese hells also contain features similar to Christian and Islamic hells, though how these features came to China is debatable.[57] Finally, imported notions of hell blended with indigenous Chinese ideas, such as Confucian notions of morality and authority as well as Daoist ideas. The end result was a uniquely Chinese view of hell.

Possibly the first description of the punishments of hell to be translated into Chinese was by the central Asian monk An Shigao, who came to China from Parthia in A.D. 148.[58] Another Chinese translation attributed to An Shigao presents a system of eighteen hells, eight of which are unbearably hot and ten of which are unbearably cold.[59] Another variation on the Chinese hell was the Ten Courts of Hell, which include the eight principal hells of Indian Buddhism plus an entrance hall where there occurs a preliminary classification of souls into good and evil (the ninth hell) and a departure hell from which a soul leaves hell to be reborn (the tenth hell).[60] The presence of the departure hall as the tenth hell makes the point that Chinese hells were not permanent abodes, like the Christian or Islamic hells, but rather one of the five or six transitory incarnations that sentient beings assumed in being reborn. They were akin to the Catholic Purgatory in the limited sense that Purgatory is a transitory abode en route to heaven, where one redeems oneself for unrepented venial sins through suffering punishment. In Zhang's time the two most prevalent conceptions of hell were the Ten Courts of Hell and the Eighteen Hells. Portrayals of the Ten Courts of Hell can be found in Daoist, Buddhist, and popular religious temples.[61] Nevertheless, some maintain that the category of ten hells is predominantly Daoist, whereas the category of eighteen hells is predominantly Buddhist.[62]

Whereas hell held a great deal of interest for the Buddhist laity, monks tended to see hell in a more sophisticated way and specifically in terms of how hell affected their search for enlightenment. The tremendous influence of the indigenous Chinese school of Chan (Zen) Buddhism and its emphasis on meditation also shaped the monk's view of hell. The monk Jie reflected this Chan influence when he interpreted hell as an illusion comparable to a frightening dream in which one is attacked by a tiger or a wolf. He likened this fright to what one experiences in hell until one awakens from the dream.[63] Awakening from the dream is akin to the true enlightenment of Buddhism. Using this Mind-Only perspective, Jie argued that hell was a fabrication of the mind. If hell was a fabrication of the mind or an illusion, it could be destroyed by a truly enlightened mind.

Zhang's realistic perspective was so opposed to Jie's idealistic point of view that it is hardly surprising that he found Jie's reasoning incomprehensible. He was completely unconvinced by Jie's portrayal of the suffering of hell as akin to the frightening experience of a dream.[64] The conflict between the views of Zhang and Jie is not simply a difference between a Confucian-Christian and a Buddhist. Among Buddhists themselves, monks tend to emphasize that the world we experience is controlled by our consciousness, whereas the laity, less attuned to meditative techniques, are more inclined to accept the world around them as real. This difference in perspective explains why the Buddhist laity used the fear instilled by paintings of hell as a means of evoking fear and moving people toward goodness, whereas the monks saw such paintings as reflections of another form of unreality that, like the external world, can be controlled through meditation.[65]

Zhang believed that knowledge could illumine the world but could not destroy a phenomenal reality such as hell. Zhang noted that the *Lankāvatāra Sutra* spoke of humans perishing only in terms of spiritual knowledge but did not speak of hell as existing in some particular place. Zhang also cited this sutra in explaining that the Buddhist teaching of Emptiness *(Xukong;* in Sanskrit *Śunyātā)* lacked the power to destroy things.[66] For Zhang, Buddhism lacked the ability to do what it claimed, that is, to destroy hell or to release souls from hell. This convinced him that Buddhism was deceiving people.

VI

The *Refutation* devoted an entire chapter to criticizing the Buddhist practice of chanting mantras. Mantras consist of sacred texts whose oral repetition is thought by Buddhists to bestow a spiritual power. The monk Jie illustrated his work on this point with examples drawn from the Tang and Qing dynasties.[67] In the first year of the Shunzhi emperor (1644), there was a monk from Hubei province named Shalan, whose chanting was said to make a pot levitate. Jie also spoke of a monk from Sanyin named Wang Jun[lü], whose chanting was able to transform a small bowl of fruit into a cornucopia.

Zhang was very critical of the chanting of mantras and believed it was another form of Buddhist deception. For example, Jie stated that Xiao Yu, the palace steward of Emperor Taizong of the Tang dynasty, believed in the effectiveness of mantra chanting in protecting life and in staving off death, and yet Zhang noted that the chanting of these monks from the west had not been effective in preventing their own deaths.[68] Moreover, in 644, when Emperor Taizong attempted to invade Korea in order to punish the regicide of the usurping Korean court minister Chuan Gaisuwen, the emperor asked the "Buddhist monks from the west" (i.e., from central Asia?) and his palace steward to chant mantras in order to secure calm waters on the Eastern Sea so that the imperial fleet could transport its troops safely to Korea.[69] However, Zhang claimed that after sixty days the chanting had still been ineffective.[70] He regarded the claims that chanting could move mountains and hold back the sea to be baseless and exaggerated talk.[71]

Zhang noted that in the first year of the Shunzhi emperor "Indian monks" *(Fan seng)* came to China.[72] In this and the previous example from Emperor Taizong's time, when Zhang spoke of "Western monks," Zhang emphasized the foreign origin of the Buddhist monks. In fact, given the decline and extinction of Buddhism in India by A.D. 1400, it could not have been "Indian monks" who came to China in 1644. Rather, these monks were probably from regions on the western borders of China (possibly Tibetans or Mongols) and may have entered China at the time of the fluid political situation when the Manchus conquered the Ming. Nevertheless, his point was to emphasize the alien origins of Buddhism. Although the Lord of Heaven missionaries were also said by Zhang to have come from the West—actually the "Far West"—Zhang believed that the Heavenly Teaching melded with and confirmed the indigenous Literati Teaching of China in a way that Buddhism did not. When these so-called Indian monks came to China in 1644, the Yellow River was flooding or threatening to do so. According to Zhang, the Shunzhi emperor questioned why the monks did not chant mantras to hold back the raging Yellow River. Since holding back a river would seem to be easier than holding back a sea, Zhang used this instance to cast further doubt on the efficacy of chanting mantras.[73]

The disagreements between the Buddhists and Christian literati in the *Refutation* were sometimes based on misunderstandings as well as intellectual predispositions. Jie's disagreement with Xu Guangqi's presentation of Christianity appears to have been based on a misunderstanding of God's forgiveness. Jie falsely assumed that the Christian conception of hell was similar to the Buddhist hell in being a place of transition. Jie believed that the Lord of Heaven's forgiveness was offered to people in hell and that, after receiving this grace, they were released from hell.[74] This belief led Jie to compare Christian grace to a situation in which a onetime general amnesty had been offered and all criminals had been released from jail. Since such a teaching took no account of the inevitability of later criminal acts and the filling up of jails again after the amnesty had been offered, Jie regarded the Christian teaching of forgiveness as illogical.

Jie's misunderstanding was shaped by Chinese culture and apparently by the Festival of Departed Spirits (Yulan [pen] hui; Ullambana in Sanskrit), often referred to as All Souls' Day. This festival was a blending of Buddhism with Chinese ancestral worship and Daoism.[75] This blending was reflected in the sutra teaching of Mulian (Maudgalyayana) that was commonly recited on the day of the festival by monks. Mulian was an exemplary model of filial piety, who, with the assistance of the Buddha, endured many hardships in order to rescue his mother from hell.[76] This festival became immensely popular in China and even literati participated in the ceremonies for feeding hungry ghosts of deceased ancestors up to seven generations in the past.

There is a resemblance between the Chinese Festival of Departed Spirits and the Catholic All Souls' Day held on 2 November as a day of prayer and solemn services, including requiem masses, for the souls in Purgatory. However, the apparent similarity between these two festivals is lessened by the fact that Christian judgment is based on only one cycle of birth-and-death and God's judgment follows at the end. By contrast, Buddhist reincarnation causes the consequences of one's karma to be subject to continual reevaluation, particularly since hell is not the result of a final judgment, but rather a continuing phase of existence of the soul. As Zhang pointed out, Jie misunderstood that God's forgiveness was not limited to those living at a particular point in time, but was available to all generations.[77]

Jie believed that the efficacy of the Tathāgata words *(Zhen yan)* (i.e., words of Truth) in Buddhist chanting would release the souls from hell and cause them to be reborn in the Western Paradise of Amitabha Buddha. The Western Paradise, though similar in its pleasures to the Christian heaven, was, like the Buddhist hell, a stage of reincarnation and a transitory rather than eternal abode.

Zhang rightly sensed that the essential ingredient of Jie's argument about being released from hell involved the Buddhist notion of illusion. One could transcend an existence in hell by recognizing that its illusory nature was a manifestation of the Mind-Only. To make his point, Jie used the phrase "holding on to an illusory hell."[78] A recognition of the illusory nature of hell enabled one to escape from it, because it was a prison created by one's own mind. Zhang responded to this argument by scoffing: "Is the elaborate construction of the ten princes who rule over the Ten Hells all built on an illusion?"[79] Furthermore, Zhang asked, if hell were unreal, where then were the sinners in hell supposed to be? The argument is disappointing as a point in an intellectual debate, but as a statement of cultural disposition, it is more significant. Jie's argument was simply not credible to Zhang because Jie's Mind-Only epistemology was irreconcilable with Zhang's realistic Confucian epistemology.

VII

The conclusion of the *Refutation* deals with the differing reverence appropriate to the Buddha and the Lord of Heaven. Jie raised the point by criticizing Xu Guangqi for slandering the Buddha, Dharma (Truth) and Sangha (community of followers) out of ignorance.[80] For Jie, it would have been as appropriate for a common person *(shuren)* to compare himself to the Buddha as for the Son of Heaven (the Chinese emperor) to compare himself to the Lord of Heaven. Hong's rebuttal presented an argument that was not only utterly Confucian, but also melded with Christian monotheism. In stating that the Lord of Heaven and Earth is one and not plural in number, Hong argued from the nature of things. A family should have only one father and a nation should have only one ruler; any other situation creates immorality and chaos. Confucianism demanded a unified hierarchical structure in terms of authority and legitimacy. Christian monotheism complemented these demands, whereas Buddhism did not. Hong's rebuttal was an example of how Xu's proposal to "supplement Confucianism and displace Buddhism" was further developed and carried to a deeper level of meaning by later Chinese Christians.

The intensity of Zhang's negative feelings toward Buddhism is revealed in some of his comparisons. In response to Jie's point that it was slanderous for the common people to compare themselves to the Buddha, Zhang responded with biting irony. He conceded that, although most of the common people could not be compared to the Buddha, there was a category of people who could be so compared.[81] This category included the followers of the six famous princes in Chinese history who rebelled against lawful authority. The list of princes is fascinating in its diversity, though it is clear that Zhang viewed these princes as seditious threats to law and morality.

The first of these princes was Huo Shuchu of the Zhou dynasty, brother of King Wu, who revolted at the time of the ascension of his nephew to the throne as King Cheng in 1115 B.C. The second included the rebels of the Seven Kingdoms, who revolted against the Han emperor Jing in 154 B.C. The third on this list was the crown prince Li Chengqian, the neurotic Turkophile whose homoerotic feelings for a boy dancer led him to seek revenge over the boy's assassination by rebelling against his father, the Tang emperor Taizong, in 643. The last three princes on Zhang's list all come from the Ming royal family, whose early representatives cultivated a tradition of rebellion and usurpation. They included Zhu Gaoxu, who unsuccessfully attempted in 1426 to overthrow his nephew the Xuande emperor; Zhu Zhifan, who rebelled in 1510; and Zhu Chenhao, who rebelled in 1519. Since, in the Confucian view of history, the failures of these princes confirmed that their attempts were not blessed by the Mandate of Heaven, all six of these princes have been condemned as immoral subverters of rightful authority. By associating these rebels with the Buddha, Zhang showed that he viewed the Buddhists as not just another religion, but as subversive threats to Chinese culture, law, and truth. This was a very traditional Confucian perspective and the remarkable aspect of it was that Zhang was one of a minority of late-seventeenth-century literati who did not see Christianity in this same seditious light.

Zhang wrote the following poem on the Lord of Heaven's judgment of individuals at death:

The good and evil deeds of people,
merit the keenest attention.
If there were no final judgment,
good deeds would be efforts in vain.
How can one comprehend that the majestic Lord
does not lose sight of even the smallest element?
Whether He is judging something large or small,
neither form nor spirit can escape Him.
Since His commandments are already given,
our hour of reckoning is not far off.
Those various Buddhist and Daoist demons,
will tempt us and work their spells.
Once we fall into their clutches,
there is eternal woe without end.
This is why the ancient sages,
were careful from morning until night.[82]

CHAPTER 6

In the Eastern Sea and in the Western Sea
Sages Arise Who Are Identical in Thinking

When I was young, I too had dreams of examination success and official glory, perhaps at the court in Beijing. I passed the licentiate exam and worked hard in competing for the provincial examination. But eventually, I tired of the memorization and cramming because it became an exercise in empty words. I turned my back on the world and sought meaning in the Buddha. I studied the sutras and chanted, but I found that there was something illogical about the way the monks reasoned and I could not be a monk. Finally one day I encountered Zhu Ji'nan. Master Zhu was a very learned scholar, and he was the one who first taught me about the Heavenly Teaching. I became a diligent student, received instruction from the Western scholars, and was baptized. There was tremendous opposition to my doing so, but I closed my ears to the criticism. Some of my former friends hated me for doing this and turned their backs on me, saying that the so-called scholar Zhang was completely rejecting the truths of our land for the teaching of the Western barbarians. But I am convinced that only by adopting the Heavenly Teaching can I return to the ways of the ancients and become a true scholar. Confucius honored Heaven, and I too honor Heaven. Confucius and Mencius attacked false teachings, and I too attack the false teachings of Buddhism and Daoism. This is the True Way and I will not turn back.[1]

I

Although Zhang's attempts to inculturate Christianity into Chinese literati culture have been little noted in China, his work as a historian has been recognized.[2] History is the field of knowledge in which Chinese literati have excelled, and Zhang's achievements in this field confirm just how typical his activities as a literatus were. His *History*, whose full title is *Supplements to the History of the Comprehensive Mirror Topically Arranged (Tongjian jishi benmo buhoubian)*, was a massive work of scholarship. Yet the work appears to contain little or no mention of the Lord of Heaven Teaching, and the reasons for the omission are not difficult to surmise. First of all, the parameters of traditional Chinese historical writing were strict and narrow. For Zhang to have introduced an apologetic argument for Christianity into such a historical work would have made the work so controversial as to deny it the orthodox status that he sought and achieved.

What appears to us as a glaring—or even deceptive—omission of his deepest beliefs from the *History* would have been viewed very differently by Zhang. He saw himself as a very orthodox literatus whose acceptance of the Lord of Heaven Teaching reinforced his orthodoxy. For this reason, the term "conversion" would have been entirely too radical to describe how Zhang viewed the adoption of this teaching from the West. Nevertheless, to those familiar with Zhang's thinking, it is clear that his *History* contains one of the pillars of his argument for the inculturation of Christianity into China, namely, his criticism of Buddhism and Daoism.

Zhang's *History* belongs to the third major type of general history *(tongshi)* to be used in traditional China. This type involves the narration of events in chronological order according to topics *(jishi benmo)*. Prior to the Song dynasty (960–1279), the two major forms of writing general history in China had been the annals-biography form *(jizhuan)* and the annals-chronicle form *(biannian)*. The annals-biography form had been introduced by the famous Han historian Sima Qian (ca. 183–85 B.C.), with his vivid portraits of Han dynasty figures in his *Records of the Grand Historian (Shiji)*.[3] The next major advancement in the writing of history was made in the Song dynasty by Sima Guang (1019–1086), the well-known scholar-official and prominent conservative political opponent of Wang Anshi's reforms. Sima is believed by some to be the greatest of Chinese historians and this judgment is based on his compilation of the most ambitious individual work in Chinese history.[4] His *Comprehensive Mirror for Aid in Government (Zizhi tongjian)* (1085) in 294 *juan* attempted to cover in chronicle form the 1,363-year period between 403 B.C. and the founding of the Song dynasty in A.D. 960. When the long draft was presented to Sima by his assistants, it is said to have filled two entire rooms of his house.[5] He used over three hundred sources, including Dynastic Histories (*zhengshi*) and Veritable Records (*shilu*). The *Comprehensive Mirror* was such a ground-breaking and seminal work of history that it inspired later Chinese historians to adapt its contents to new forms.

One of the most serious deficiencies of the *Comprehensive Mirror*, particularly from the perspective of contemporary Western historians, is its focus on isolated events without an attempt to develop some pattern of causal connections.[6] An attempt to rectify part of this deficiency and to organize events into more coherent connections was made by the scholar-official Yuan Shu (1131–1205).[7] Yuan sought to rearrange the *Comprehensive Mirror* into separate topics and to deal with each topic by arranging events in a chronological sequence. To this end, he extracted material on 239 topics and organized them under separate headings. He did not alter the extracts from Sima's work nor did he rework the materials into a more unified treatment. Nevertheless, Yuan's changes were substantial enough to introduce a third major style of writing history. This new style emphasized the sequence of events in history and brought together previously dispersed information into meaningful new patterns, though Yuan and most writers of this third style of history for the most part only rearranged existing works without adding new materials or interpretations.[8]

Zhang's *History* (1690) was written as a supplement to the historical work by Yuan Shu. Zhang's research was so extensive and his manuscript became so massive in length—fifty *juan*; or over 1,700 sheets—that printing was not feasible.[9] Consequently, the *History* became a very rare work. In the wake of the Taiping Rebellion (1851–1864), a number of old families in Jiangsu province had to sell their collections of old books. It was in this manner that a manuscript of Zhang's *History* came into the hands of a prominent official named Ding Richang (1823–1882), who assembled a famous rare book collection.[10] Ding commissioned the scholar Mo Youzhi (1811–1871) to make an annotated catalogue of the collection between 1867 and 1869. Among the works that Mo examined was Zhang's *History*, and subsequently Mo published an outline of the work's contents.[11] Around 1945 the Hangzhou Christian historian Fang Hao discovered a copy of the first seven chapters of Zhang's *History* in the Beitang collection in Beijing.[12]

Zhang's *History* continued a theme found in his other works, namely, the criticism of Buddhism and Daoism. The *History* differed from Zhang's other works in that it was, first, organized as a history and, second, far longer and more detailed. But the *History* was by no means peripheral to Zhang's attempt to blend Christianity with Confucianism. Fang Hao used the classical imagery of the warp and the woof (i.e., intersecting threads) of weaving, that is, two symbiotic and essential ingredients, to explain the importance of the *History* in Zhang's thinking. While the historical content of the *History* represented the warp, the philosophic ideas of all the orthodox literati represented the woof of Zhang's thinking.[13] It is clear that Zhang's detailed study in compiling the *History* provided him with the numerous instances from the past that he used in his other works to support his arguments for blending Christianity and Confucianism. It was his preparation of the *History* that gave his views a detailed historical perspective that is unique among Chinese Christian literati.

To sustain his thesis that Buddhists and Daoists had brought disorder to the nation and destruction to the family, Zhang compiled an extensive collection of quotations from the Dynastic Histories, to which he appended clarifying quotations from minor officials and literati. There is a two-part parallel structure to the *History* in which Zhang duplicated these criticisms for both Buddhism and Daoism. Not only are the falsehoods of Buddhism and its followers attacked, but lists of rulers and magistrates who advanced the calamities of Buddhism as well as lists of sages and worthies who attacked Buddhism are also included. Similarly, not only are the errors of Laozi and the Daoists attacked, but lists of those rulers and ministers who promoted the calamity of the Dao by cultivating Daoist immortality are presented as well as lists of sages and worthies who attacked Daoism.

As in his other works, Zhang's attitude toward Buddhism was far harsher than toward Daoism. This is reflected in the fact that of the fifty *juan,* the first forty-one are devoted to Buddhism, whereas only the last nine deal with Daoism. Whereas five *juan* are devoted to distinguishing the similarities and differences between Buddhists and literati, only two *juan* are devoted to distinguishing the Daoists from the literati. For Zhang, Buddhists involved primarily adherents of the Chan sect, and Daoists were mainly seekers of the elixir of longevity or immortality. Although there was nothing new about a literatus attacking Buddhism and Daoism, it was quite unusual to use an orthodox historical form to lay the groundwork for inculturating Christianity into Chinese culture.

Had it not been for his *History*, Zhang's recognition as a scholar in standard Chinese sources would have been totally eclipsed. His main claim to recognition in such works as a Hangzhou local history or Chinese historiographies derives from his *History*.[14] Zhang's other works that attempt to inculturate Christianity into Chinese culture are not included in these listings, because it was typical to omit references to most forms of religious affiliation in official biographies. Unlike Confucianism, which was considered part of one's official career, Buddhism, Daoism, and Christianity were regarded as belonging to a more private sphere.[15]

Zhang's *History* reveals that his attempt to reconcile Confucianism and Christianity became even more radical as his life progressed. This was not because his ideas themselves were becoming more radical, but because the intellectual environment around him was becoming less receptive to these ideas. In the span of Zhang's own lifetime, the Chinese cultural climate toward borrowing from foreign teachings had gone from being syncretic and experimental to being close-minded and unreceptive. Certainly by 1690 when he completed his *History*, Zhang was clearly aware of this growing hostility. Consequently, he wrote a work of history that attempted to be impeccably orthodox in style and content and built the whole work around a critique of Buddhism and Daoism. And yet it is surely one of the more notable oversights of Chinese historians that this recognized and orthodox history contained some of Zhang's primary arguments for why Christianity should be recognized as supplementing and even surpassing the teaching of Confucius.

Rather than being peripheral to his other works, Zhang's *History* could be viewed as a type of cultural Trojan horse for facilitating the inculturation of Christianity into China. And yet Zhang would probably have been offended by the deceit implied in the image of a Trojan horse. If he had wished to conceal his views on the compatability of Confucianism and Christianity, he could have omitted discussing their compatability in his other writings. Aware of the growing hostility of fellow literati and of the tenuous status of the Lord of Heaven Teaching at the Manchu court in Beijing, Zhang chose to proceed in a way that befit the dignity of the scholar that he was— with discretion and erudition.

II

The Chinese literati are often portrayed as a class whose creative vitality began to ebb in the Ming dynasty (1368–1644), so that by the mid-Qing they had rigidified in their thinking and functioned more as impediments than as promoters of learning. Zhang Xing-yao does not fit this pattern. One could argue that Zhang's creativity, flexibility, and willingness to adopt foreign elements represented a tiny minority of Confucian literati and an exception to the predominant pattern. However, the fact that he expressed so many typical literati views and that he viewed himself as being utterly true to the literati tradition suggests that he cannot so easily be dismissed as an aberration whose views are without significance for the class of literati as a whole.

In part 3 of the *Similarities,* Zhang made some of his most radical statements. In the preface to this section he summarized his view of why his adoption of the Heavenly Teaching was appropriate to Chinese history. Since the time of the legendary sages Yao and Shun, China had accumulated a great totality of achievement that was all attributable to Confucius.[16] However, the programs of the famous Han Confucian scholar Dong Zhongshu (ca. 179–104 B.C.) broke with the True Way as defined in the writings of Confucius.[17] Moreover, Zhang dated the development of Daoism and Buddhism from Dong's time. One could dispute Zhang's dating on the chronological grounds that Daoism predated Dong whereas Buddhism in China postdated Dong, but Zhang appears to be viewing them from a much longer perspective of development. His treatment of these two teachings is nearly always in conjunction—the teachings of "the two masters Buddha and Laozi" *(ershi Shi Lao)*—because he felt that they had a symbiotic relationship in which they resembled and stimulated one another. He said that during the Six Dynasties period (221–589) the arrival of the famous central Asian monk Kumārajīva (344–413) caused Buddhism to flourish in China and this, in turn, stimulated the Daoist studies of Laozi's *Way and the Power Classic (Dao de jing).*

Zhu Xi's criticism of Buddhism and Daoism as immoral teachings was one reason why Zhang admired Zhu and did not accept the Jesuit criticism of Song Neo-Confucianism. Zhu Xi particularly objected to Buddhism's cultivation of celibacy, because it detached people from cultivating the Five Human Relationships of ruler and subject, father and son, husband and wife, elder and younger, and friends. Zhang was particularly critical of the emphasis that Buddhism placed on the self as being the only thing worthy of cultivation.[18]

Zhang recognized that he was adding something to the teachings of Confucius. He saw that Confucius had limited himself to concentrating on the human experience between birth and death, that Confucius had not dealt with the notion of an immortal soul (*linghun*), and that Confucius had lacked the power of judgment to reward or punish people in heaven or hell. Consequently, Zhang saw himself as diverging from Confucius to the extent that the Heavenly Teaching supplemented and transcended the limitations of the Sage. Nevertheless, Zhang remained in his mind a true follower of the Sage, who was simply "changing the string [of his lute] or shifting the course [of his carriage]" (*gaitong yizhe*). This was a metaphorical way of saying that he was making a limited change in policy or a slight adjustment in course of action.[19]

The literati tradition placed great emphasis on the transmission of the True Way (*Zheng Dao*) as a vital, living force. However, the transmission of the Truth conveyed by Confucius was believed to have, in its most essential form, lapsed after Mencius (371?–289? B.C.), whereas the Truth of the Lord of Heaven had been transmitted without interruption down to today through the succession of popes.[20] Zhang was referring to the idea of apostolic succession expressed in Matthew 16:18–19 by which Jesus transferred his authority (i.e., the authority of Heaven) to his disciple Peter, who then passed it down in a form that eventually became institutionalized as the papacy. And yet Zhang's understanding of apostolic succession and the papacy was clearly based on an idealized and distinctly Roman Catholic view whose historical reality was less pristine. If the Jesuits had told Zhang of the behavior of many of the late medieval and Renaissance Holy Fathers, he would have been scandalized. And one could scarcely have expected the members of a society that had constituted the pope's right arm in the Counter Reformation to have given Zhang an objective explanation of the Protestants' reinterpretation of apostolic succession.

One of the most intriguing ways in which Zhang claimed that the Heavenly Teaching transcended the Literati Teaching was in the greater recognition that Christianity gave to women. Zhang explains how it was believed by the ancient Chinese that women were more difficult to change than men and that the sages and worthies who lived with women found it difficult to transform their wills.[21] As a result, Confucius drew few instructive examples of women from the Four Books and Five Classics, and these works offered very limited practical guidance to women who were seeking instruction on moral cultivation.

By contrast, Zhang noted that the Heavenly Teaching did not neglect women with regard to baptism. Furthermore, eminent women, such as Mary Magdalene of the gospels and Agatha, a martyr of Sicily ca. 250 whose persecutors severed the breasts from her body, were set forth as examples of sainthood. (The Sicilian Intorcetta was probably the source of this story about Saint Agatha.) Zhang noted that from time to time a pope officially proclaimed a festival in honor of a female saint. Later in part 3, Zhang returned briefly to the Heavenly Teaching's treatment of women, but there the emphasis was on the overall egalitarian nature of Christianity. He stated that there were no restrictions with regard to whether one were educated or ignorant, male or female and that in this regard the Heavenly Teaching surpassed the Literati Teaching.[22] However, in referring to the Lord of Heaven, Zhang was less inclined to use the term "Great Father-Mother" or "Great Parent" (Da Fumu;) than Yang Tingyun was.[23] This term occurs only once in the *Similarities*[24] and was less important than purely male designations for God such as the "Lord of Heaven Holy Father (Tianzhu Shengfu).[25]

Zhang was aware of the biblical account of Adam and Eve in which an impure woman brought down the punishment of God upon mankind, though his interpretation of the event did not lead him to condemn women so much as to place responsibility for sinning on the whole human race.[26] Zhang presented the account in the context of explaining how the Heavenly Teaching surpassed the Literati Teaching in clarifying the difference between good and evil spirits. Confucius had failed to understand this distinction, and his lack of understanding had created confusion among the literati. Chinese society had long made some distinction between different types of spirits, such as *shen* (benevolent spirits) and *gui* (demonic ghosts).[27] However, Zhang believed that the Heavenly Teaching surpassed the Literati Teaching in clearly distinguishing spirits as *shen*, which he interpreted as "angels" *(tianshen)*, and *gui* as "evil spirits" *(xiegui)*.[28] The origins of this distinction were traced by Zhang to the creation of the world, in which there was some sort of opposition among spirits. Consequently, the Lord of Heaven had expelled certain spirits from Heaven as a form of punishment.

Zhang explained the Lord of Heaven's creation of the first male and female (Adam and Eve), who were placed in the Earthly Paradise (Ditang). An angel was sent down to command them not to eat the forbidden fruit of the Tree of Good and Evil. The woman was encouraged by the demon *(gui)* to eat of the fruit so that their knowledge of good and evil would be equal to the Lord of Heaven's. When the man was led by the woman to eat the forbidden fruit, they were both expelled from the Earthly Paradise, and their sin was transmitted to their human descendants. Zhang explained that the Lord of Heaven was later incarnated in human form in order to restore the damage done by this primal man and woman and to redeem human sins by giving people a new path to follow.[29] Zhang noted that the details of this account were recorded in a book (Genesis 2–3) of which "our Chinese people" *(wo Zhongguo ren)*, unlike the adherents of the "Moslem religion" *(Huihuijiao)*, were unaware. As a result of all this, Zhang explained, the angels resided in heaven, while the demons lived in hell, though sometimes the Lord of Heaven caused the angels to descend to earth in order to issue warnings to people. Human souls, which were indestructible, also resided in heaven and hell, though their positions were different from angels and demons.

Zhang believed that the Heavenly Teaching surpassed the Literati Teaching in its power to deal with disease and death. He explained how humans had lost the freedom from these twin blights when the primal male and female were expelled from the Earthly Paradise for violating the Lord of Heaven's commands.[30] Whereas Confucius regarded illness and death as inevitable to the human condition (*Analects* VII.34 and IX.11), the Western History *(Xi shi)* (i.e., the Bible) recorded that the incarnated Lord of Heaven during a three-year period healed people who were lame, blind, deaf, dumb, and suffering from leprosy. Moreover, only the Lord of Heaven had the ability to command the afterlife *(fuhuo)*.

III

Zhang devoted a great deal of effort in the first two parts of the *Similarities* to showing how the teachings of Confucius and Mencius were superior to the teachings of the Buddha and Laozi. In part 3 he showed how the Literati Teaching fell short of the Heavenly Teaching. Confucius and Mencius were easily absolved of responsibility for failing to know the Heavenly Teaching, because at the time when they lived, the Lord of Heaven had not yet descended to earth in incarnated form to reveal the full teaching.[31] Zhang stated that this knowledge of the full teaching was unknown in China until the "Western teachers" *(Xi shi)* (i.e., missionaries) brought it to China. In another work, Zhang indicated that he was aware of Christian missionaries who had preceded the Jesuits and specifically mentioned the Nestorian Christians who had come to China during the Tang dynasty as well as the Franciscans who later came to Canton.[32] One of the most important parts of this teaching was the notion of an afterlife. Life is short, but the afterlife is eternal, and Zhang believed that those who strived after the petty profits of today would inherit an endless calamity. He argued that the only way to protect oneself from "falling into an eternal fire" *(lun yu yonghuo)* was to keep the Lord of Heaven in mind in one's daily thoughts and actions.[33]

The soul and the afterlife were closely linked in Zhang's mind. Confucius had not denied the existence of a soul and an afterlife, but neither had he emphasized them. From Zhang's perspective, Confucius could not have done so since the Lord of Heaven had not yet been incarnated to reveal the full teaching. Zhang realized that the idea of rewards in heaven and punishments in hell as a result of one's deeds in this life was not unknown in China, but it was not well understood. The Heavenly Teaching surpassed the Literati Teaching in showing how one might enter heaven and avoid hell.[34]

Zhang quoted from the *Doctrine of the Mean* (1.1) and the *Analects* (III.13 and XIV.37) to show that Confucius had a basic understanding that Heaven conferred upon humans a spiritual nature *(lingxing)*. However, later literati *(hou Ru)* did not understand this concept; they did not realize that the Lord of Heaven was the Great Father-Mother of people. Nor did they realize that the spiritual nature of human beings was indestructible and that good deeds and sins were the basis for being rewarded or punished by the Lord of Heaven.[35] Zhang explained that the Lord of Heaven was incarnated in order to bring this truth to the world and to teach people the Eight Blessings found in the Sermon on the Mount (Matthew 5:3–10).[36] Zhang did not list the Eight Blessings, but he clearly meant that Jesus blessed the poor, those who mourn, the meek, those who hunger and thirst for righteousness, the merciful, the pure in heart, the peacemakers, and those who are persecuted for righteousness' sake. The term "Eight Blessings" will strike the Western reader as a novel way of referring to the contents of the Sermon on the Mount. However, this sort of categorizing has a very Chinese ring to it and is probably an instance of how Christianity was Sinified.

Confucius was unable to teach the people about the soul and the afterlife. Zhang explained that Confucius had edited the Classics using subtle and powerful language with mysterious meaning, but he fell short of enlightening the people.[37] He presented Confucius' death as a matter of fate whereas, by contrast, the death of the Lord of Heaven was said to be something that the incarnated Lord took upon himself in order to save mankind.[38] The incarnated Lord of Heaven sacrificed his life in order to appease the anger of God the Father (Tianzhu Shengfu) and to atone for the sins of mankind and give people an afterlife in Heaven. The love of the Lord of Heaven was so great that he sought to prevent people from falling into hell. In the over 1,700 years since the Lord of Heaven had been incarnated, the pope had acted on His authority, the scriptures had been collected and examined, and the bishops and priests had propagated good deeds throughout the world in order to save human souls.[39] In this manner, the Lord of Heaven Teaching was carried to China.

Zhang again acted as a Confucian prophetic voice in the wilderness who called the people to truth by contrasting the degeneration of teaching in his own day with that of previous times. He spoke of Hu (Yuan) Anding of the Song dynasty and Cao Yuechuan of the Ming dynasty as model teachers.[40] Master Hu's interpretation of the Classics clearly explained the School of Principle, and Master Cao's unveiling of the True Way acted as a lamp to guide people through the darkness. However, Zhang believed that teaching in his own day was much degenerated with both teachers and students lax and corrupt. The result was that the present representatives of the Literati Teaching were merely managing the records of literature and the arts. By contrast, the priests (siduo) of the Lord of Heaven Teaching were surpassing them in offering the Chinese people a way to transcend this sterile situation. However, one must first become an adherent of the teaching (fengjiaozhe) in order to receive the Lord of Heaven's compassion and to have one's sins washed away.[41] Zhang believed that since the time of the ancient Three Dynasties (Xia, Shang, and Zhou), which ended in the third century B.C., the Chinese people had not attained a comparable sensitivity to wrongdoing and striving toward goodness.[42] The laws of China emphasized fair punishment but lacked a sense of compassion, and, as a result, were spiritually destructive. For those who felt repentant for their sins, only praying to the Lord of Heaven for forgiveness would enable their souls to live even after their bodies had died.[43]

It was a fundamental belief of the literati that one of the characteristics of heterodox or false teachings was their inability to balance love and morality (benevolence and righteousness). One of the reasons Zhang believed that the Heavenly Teaching was orthodox and true was that, like the Literati Teaching, it balanced love of humanity with moral demands on the behavior of mankind. Not only did the Heavenly Teaching balance these two elements, but it surpassed the Literati Teaching in bestowing them. Zhang explained that what mattered in the Lord of Heaven Teaching was one's goodness or evil, regardless of whether one was of noble or humble status.[44]

In Chinese history, agriculture has always had a primary status, and Zhang dealt with this most precious commodity for human existence by reinterpreting a passage from the *Book of Odes*.[45] Whereas the traditional interpretation of this passage had been that the Prince of Millet (Hou Ji) had bestowed the grains (i.e., the art of husbandry) on the people, Zhang reinterpreted it to say that the Lord of Heaven was the ultimate source and creator of the five grains. Zhang went on to show how the Lord of Heaven surpassed both Confucius and the Buddha in the ability to generate food. The *Analects* (XV.1) described how the provisions of Confucius and his disciples became exhausted in the state of Chen and how his disciples became so ill that they could not stand. By contrast, Zhang spoke of how the Bible recorded the incident of the Lord of Heaven creating food in the miracle of the loaves and fishes.[46]

Confucius' efforts in editing the Classics and preparing them for publication fell short of fully enlightening the people. Zhang believed that Confucius was surpassed in his efforts by the Lord of Heaven, whose suffering and sacrifice was made in order to offer people a release from their sins, an escape from hell, and eternal life in heaven. The Lord of Heaven's love was so great that he refused to abandon those who were cast off in society, whether wives and daughters, the ignorant, the blind, or the terminally ill. How could Confucius' effort of editing the Classics possibly be compared to this?[47]

IV

For Intorcetta, Zhang was a scholarly pillar of the Hangzhou church in the late seventeenth century. Although the intellectual achievements of China Jesuits were remarkable, their knowledge of Chinese culture was rarely comparable to that of a first-rate Chinese scholar. Intorcetta in particular was far more of an administrator than a scholar by nature. Consequently, when the Chinese Rites and Term Controversy threatened to destroy the work of the Jesuits in China, Intorcetta turned to Zhang to compose a scholarly defense of the Jesuit position.

The Chinese Rites and Term Controversy involved two different aspects: the meaning of Chinese rites to ancestors and Confucius, and the validity of using indigenous Chinese names for God. The Jesuits themselves were divided over whether ancient Chinese terms, such as Shangdi (Lord-on-High), were too tainted by pagan associations to be acceptable for Christians. However, they were nearly unanimous in arguing that most rites to ancestors did not violate the monotheistic nature of the Christian God, because these rites were more civil and social than religious in nature. However, there were Franciscans, Dominicans, and secular priests in China who took far less accommodating positions toward the Chinese rites. They argued that Chinese rites to ancestors and Confucius as well as native Chinese terminology for God violated the teachings of Christianity. The controversy had been building since the beginning of the seventeenth century, when Fr. Ricci had formulated an accommodating position toward the Chinese rites that most Jesuits had accepted. Conflicting rulings from Rome intensified the debate. In 1656 Fr. Martini had secured from Pope Alexander VII a ruling favorable to the Jesuit position, but this decision was not conclusive.[48] Debate continued, and in 1693 the vicar apostolic of Fujian, Charles Maigrot, issued a mandate containing seven articles, four of which dealt with the rites to Confucius and deceased ancestors.[49] Maigrot was a member of the Missions étrangères of Paris, an intensely anti-Jesuit society, and his mandate disputed the validity of Martini's explanation of Chinese rites, which had been the basis of the pro-Jesuit 1656 ruling. Maigrot's mandate asked the Holy See to reconsider the matter and to issue a new ruling. This mandate was a challenge to all Jesuits in China, and Intorcetta in neighboring Zhejiang province would have been keenly aware of the dangers. As an administrator seeking to organize a response to Maigrot's challenge, Intorcetta turned to Zhang.

Long buried in the Jesuit archives in Rome is a fourteen-page essay by Zhang Xingyao entitled "A Discussion of Sacrificial Rites" *(Sidian shuo).*[50] A Portuguese inscription on the cover page states that the work was written by a scholar of Hangzhou at the command of Fr. Intorcetta.[51] Zhang's authorship is clearly identified in the Chinese text, though the work is undated. We can only estimate that it was written sometime between Zhang's baptism in 1678 and Intorcetta's death in 1696. It is a work only mildly defensive and yet it is clearly attempting to explain that there are different types of sacrificial rites, some of which are objectional from a Confucian-Christian point of view. But the practice of certain rites to ancestors was presented by Zhang as a Confucian-Christian moral obligation for Chinese.

The line of reasoning in this brief essay once again confirms Zhang's orthodox outlook as a Confucian literatus. For him, the Chinese meaning of the rites was embodied preeminently in the *Book of Rites (Li ji).* Drawing upon passages mainly from the *Book of Rites,* Zhang explained Chinese sacrificial rites by referring, in traditional Chinese style, to the ancients. He stated that the sacrificial rites to the ancient kings had two aspects—making petitions *(qi)* for blessings and making recompense *(bao)* for benefits received.[52] Zhang believed that both the petitioning and the recompensing were directed toward the Lord-on-High (Shangdi). In his mind, this view was confirmed in the Six Classics (the *Book of Changes,* the *Book of Odes,* the *Book of Documents,* the *Book of Rites,* the *Spring and Autumn Annals,* and the *Rites of Zhou*).

In the first two pages of his essay, Zhang listed a number of specific sacrifices made by the emperor or officials to the Lord-on-High, drawing his examples primarily from the *Book of Rites* but also from the *Book of Poetry.* On New Year's Day of the Chinese lunar calendar (which falls in late January or early February of our Gregorian calendar), the son of Heaven petitioned the Lord-on-High for a good harvest of grain.[53] On the second day of spring, the emperor petitioned the Lord-on-High for the birth of a son. Zhang also discussed the *lei* sacrifice whereby a commander who was mobilizing troops petitioned the Lord for victory.[54] Zhang also mentioned that, on the second day of summer, the emperor made a sacrifice to the Lord-on-High for rain. This was called the *yu* sacrifice.[55] Zhang emphasized that these sacrifices were all directed at the transcendent Lord-on-High and not at some immanent force within the universe.[56]

In addition to sacrifices to the Lord-on-High, Zhang described four other types of sacrificial rites prevalent in China. The first of these four sacrificial rites involved "shrines to spirits" (shenci). This type of sacrifice was not directed toward the Lord-on-High, but rather toward the souls of deceased humans who had made outstanding contributions to serving the people. Again drawing from the Book of Rites, Zhang stated that in antiquity sacrifices were offered to three types of such individuals: (1) those who strengthened the state, (2) those who boldly confronted great calamity, and (3) those who defended the people against great misfortunes.[57] These individuals included sage kings, distinguished scholars, filial sons, and loyal officials. Although their bodies died, their souls ascended to heaven and became spirits.[58]

There was a connection between these spirits and a system of belief about the souls of human ancestors that had already been established in Chinese culture by the time of the Zhou dynasty (ca. 1050–221 B.C.).[59] Just as the demonic gui spirits of the deceased could inhabit animals, plants, mountains, streams, and oceans, so too could the benevolent shen spirits embody the wind, clouds, thunder, rain, mountains, sea, and rivers, as Zhang noted.[60] But for the most part, Zhang was concerned with the figures of Chinese antiquity who became gods, such as Guan Yu (died A.D. 219), the famous warrior associated with the last days of the Han dynasty. Guan's "peach garden oath" with Liu Bei and Zhang Fei has been immortalized in the novel Romance of the Three Kingdoms (Sanguo yanyi), and Guan is often portrayed with a scowling red face and a long beard. Zhang noted that the Ming Wanli emperor canonized Guan Yu as the god of war in 1594.[61]

Zhang proceeded to cite a number of figures from Chinese history drawn from twenty historical works, some of which are quite obscure. The unusual merit of these figures was remembered with sacrifices. However, the sacrifices to the spirits of such meritorious individuals proliferated wildly. During the Tang dynasty Di Renjie (629–700), who was a loyal minister to Empress Wu and was posthumously ennobled with the title of Duke of Liang, was sent as imperial ambassador and governor to the region of Henan. There he found in the states of Wu and Chu over 1,700 shrines to gods, most of which he closed on moral grounds.[62] But he destroyed them in a way that preserved their positive historical features.[63] Of the 1,700 shrines, only four were left intact. These four involved sacrifices to the Xia dynasty founder Yu and three figures from the Spring and Autumn period (722–481 B.C.), namely, Gong Bai, Wu Yuan, and Ji Zha.[64] What Zhang criticized most about these sacrifices to gods were the self-seeking attempts by curates of these shrines to manipulate the sacrifices through fraudulent divination in order to increase their profits.

Zhang praised the closing of such spirit shrines by the Duke of Liang, because their sacrifices did not embody the original meaning of sacrifice that had been established by the ancient kings.[65] Whereas the Lord-on-High created "heavenly spirits" (i.e., angels) *(tianshen)* to guide things, humans created earthly spirits or gods who were bogus in terms of functioning as true spirits. Zhang stated that these gods took forms as various as deceased people, river spirits, a golden dragon, and the Four Deva-kings who stand guard at the entrance to Buddhist temples. Belief in these gods had led people to think that they had the authority to control fortune and misfortune, and this belief fostered attempts to determine the future through fraudulent forms of divination.[66] But Zhang rejected all of this and quoted from the *Book of Documents* to say that only the Lord-on-High had the power to bestow blessings on those who did good and misfortune on those who did evil.[67]

Zhang addressed an important issue of the Rites Controversy when he stated that those who seek to be complete followers of the Lord *(Zhu)* need to disassociate themselves from worldly deception of the sort connected with the sacrificial rites to spirits (gods). Although many people confused the rites of these spirit shrines with the sacrifices of the ancients, Zhang stated that these shrines to spirits were not part of the way of the ancient kings.

The second of the four sacrificial rites that Zhang discussed involved shrines that were established to honor living persons *(shengci)*. These shrines were usually dedicated to an official whose meritorious service had gained him great popularity among the local populace. Zhang gave an instance drawn from the Daoist work *Zhuangzi*. When Master Gengsang Chu, who lived in the Weilei Mountains, began to practice the Daoist way of Laozi, the lives of the people of that area began to improve with abundant harvests.[68] When Master Gengsang's powers were recognized by the people (much to his annoyance, because the powers of a Daoist sage depend upon mystery and concealment), the people proposed that they turn over their altars of soil and grain to him and make Gengsang the object of their ancestral worship by having him impersonate their deceased ancestors in the ancestral ritual. Zhang regarded this as an attempt to create a "shrine to living people."

Zhang was critical of these "shrines to living people" because they encouraged people to ingratiate themselves in seeking to please the objects of the shrine and because the results of establishing such shrines were not positive. Moreover, he noted a fickle element in such shrines and gave as an example the shrine that was built for the Duke of Liang in Weizhou, where the Duke had served. Later, the greed and cruelty of his son forced the people to doubt the validity of having established a shrine to the father, and so they began to attack the Duke of Liang.

The third of the four sacrificial rites that Zhang described involved shrines established as a form of gratitude for benefits received *(luwei)*.[69] Like the shrines to living persons *(shengci)*, but unlike the shrines to humans who had made notable contributions *(shenci)*, these *luwei* were established during the lifetime of the persons being honored. Zhang was particularly harsh in his criticism of these shrines and for two reasons. First of all, they fostered an enormous degree of flattery (as opposed to sincere reverence) in an effort to secure the favor of living people in positions of power. Second, the rites were ill-founded because they made an ultimate judgment about the people being honored that only the Lord-on-High had the omniscience to make.

To illustrate how ill-founded such shrines were, Zhang mentioned several famous instances of notable figures who were honored with shrines in their lifetimes but whose reputations did not survive their deaths. For example, Zhang referred to Wang Dun (died A.D. 324), a prominent military commander and official of the Eastern Jin dynasty, who after receiving great honors became haughty and challenged the imperial throne with impunity.[70] Zhang noted that, after Wang Dun died, he suffered the punishment of a rebel, that is, his tomb was opened and he was decapitated.[71]

Zhang also cited the example of Li Linfu (died 752), a member of the Tang imperial family, whose cunning and flattery led him to become one of the most powerful figures in the government. After nineteen years of such power, he died and was soon accused of a crime that led to his coffin being opened and desecrated.[72]

Zhang noted that the followers of the Buddha and Laozi were particularly prone toward establishing these sorts of shrines to honor eminent persons during their lifetimes.[73] These followers were said to often place such shrines before the image of the Buddha. However, Zhang argued that this was all ill-founded because the Buddha lacked the ability to judge the goodness and evil of individuals. This power belonged solely to the Lord-on-High.

Of the four sacrificial rites that he described, Zhang favored only those associated with the ancestral hall (jiamiao). His rejection of the shrines to spirits, shrines to living people, and shrines to evoke blessings and give thanks to living people was based on reasoning that cannot easily be distinguished as either Confucian or Christian. This is because Zhang had fused the two teachings in his own thinking. He found confirmation for these views in both Confucianism and Christianity. But Zhang was aware that the ancestral halls were being criticized by some Europeans as a form of reverence too close to the reverence reserved for the Lord-on-High, and he had heard (perhaps from Intorcetta) the arguments that baptized Chinese should abstain from ancestral rites.

Zhang's essay was an attempt to refute the European arguments critical of Chinese ancestral rites. Viewing these four types of sacrificial rituals with the eye of an insider deeply familiar with the history and classical literature of his own culture, Zhang saw distinctions that Europeans less familiar with Chinese culture (even Jesuits who were longtime residents in China) could not see. Of course, one could argue conversely that Zhang's knowledge of Christianity was incomplete or had been incompletely explained by the Jesuits. But given that Europeans were attempting to establish Christianity in China, Zhang's views deserved a certain credibility and at least a hearing. The fact that his manuscript was buried in the Jesuit archives in Rome for three centuries shows that this did not happen until now.

Although Zhang agreed that the other three types of rituals should be rejected, he realized that for a baptized Christian to be authentically Chinese, the reverence of the ancestral hall *must* be retained. Here we see that Zhang dealt with one of the core issues of Chinese Christians, namely, how to retain the practice of ancestral rites while embracing this teaching from the Far West. Although it is widely believed that the problem of ancestral rites was not solved in China, Zhang indicated that, as with so many other areas of conflict between the Literati Teaching and the Teaching from the Far West, he had found a personally satisfying resolution to the conflict.

Zhang used an impeccably Confucian argument to justify the validity and importance of the ancestral hall, namely, that it dated from the highest antiquity. He quoted the passage from the *Book of Rites* that states: "The king built seven ancestral halls for himself, with a raised altar and excavated surrounding area for each hall."[74] With these halls and altars, the king's reverence extended to nine generations of ancestors and descendants. According to the *Book of Rites,* a lesser number of ancestral halls, altars, and generations were delegated to a feudal lord (five halls involving seven generations), a great officer (three halls involving five generations), an officer of a high ruler (two halls involving three generations), and an officer of one department (one hall to honor his parents). Zhang also quoted the *Book of Rites* to state that the building of an ancestral hall should be a gentleman's first concern when establishing buildings on a site.[75] Zhang noted that Confucius quoted the *Book of Rites* to state that sages distinguished between close and distant ancestors in building their ancestral halls and taught people to remember their origins by tracing their ancestors back to antiquity.[76]

As a historian, Zhang was very conscious of the chronological development of ancestral halls. Whereas they had been cultivated in the Zhou dynasty, the Legalist policies of the Qin dynasty (221–206 B.C.) suppressed the ancestral rites. In the Han dynasty (206 B.C.– A.D. 220), Zhang claimed, men of high position often established ancestral halls in cemeteries, though these were relatively few in number. It was in the Wei (220–264) and Jin (265–419) dynasties that reverence for ancestors was reestablished in the halls *(miao)* and was later written into law. In the Tang dynasty ancestral halls spread to such a degree that every honorable official had a hall where his ancestors were honored each new year with a sacrifice.[77] In the Song dynasty (960–1279), the ancestral halls proliferated in tandem with gentry clans whose clan regulations became quite extensive.[78]

Zhang believed that ancestral halls had "four benefits" *(si shan)*.[79] The first benefit involved a cultivation of reverence for one's parents that transcended their deaths. It required not only performing certain rites at specified times and seasons in the ancestral hall but also serving the ancestors through recalling and contemplating their appearance.[80] This process was quite specific in the form it took and was far from being a formality, because inner feelings were more important than outward observances. Zhang illustrated this process by quoting from the *Book of Rites:*

During the preparatory fasting, the mourner thinks of his departed ones in terms of where they sat and moved, how they smiled, their intentions, their joys, and their favorite pleasures. On the third day of this fasting, one will see the objects of his fasting. On the day of the sacrifice when he enters the chamber of the ancestral hall, he will seem to see [the deceased] in the place [where the deceased spirit tablet is]. After moving about [and performing certain rites] and as he is going out the door, his reverence will certainly cause him to hear the sound of movements, and he will sigh as he seems to hear the sound of the deceased sighing.[81]

The tone of this passage is one of remembrance and reverence rather than worship, and clearly Zhang cited it in order to rebut criticisms made by certain Europeans against the Chinese rites. And yet the passage could also be interpreted as an attempt to evoke the spirit of the deceased, and this ambiguity fostered the Rites Controversy debate.

The second benefit of the ancestral hall was that it influenced people to recognize how their present existence depended on close relatives and ancestors.[82] Dependence on kin was an important value that the historically minded Confucian culture sought to cultivate. The third benefit of the ancestral hall was that it enabled one to better organize one's consciousness of the ancestors. The proliferation of the number of ancestors with the passage of time and generations created a bewildering collection of ancestors to remember. In the ancestral hall the tablets—literally, "clay images of people" *(du zhi ren)*—were used to organize the ancestors by generations so that they could be honored properly. Those ancestors who received the greatest reverence were the most recent (because their proximity fostered more distinct memories) and the oldest (because of their role as founders of the family). The fourth benefit involved a more social realm in which ancestral halls reinforced a consciousness of the extended family or clan. Through the development of clan regulations that were recognized by the Chinese state as having the force of law, clan elders were able to control (through the use of rewards and punishments) those family members who were rebellious and who broke the rules of the clan.

At the conclusion of "A Discussion of Sacrificial Rites," Zhang defended the importance of ancestral reverence. Any Chinese Christians who did not establish ancestral halls and revere their ancestors would be harshly criticized by other Chinese for lacking proper respect for their fathers.[83] One must remember that, in China, lack of filial respect was considered abominable, unnatural behavior. It was a criminal act that evoked the harshest condemnation. Zhang's implication is clear: it was not possible for Christians in China to abstain from practicing ancestral rites. One unfamiliar with Zhang's thinking might accuse him of simply developing a rationalization that would permit a practical compromise by which Chinese Christians could practice two contradictory beliefs, namely, belief in the monotheistic God and ancestral worship. But Zhang's thinking was far too intellectually consistent and his beliefs were too sincere to allow for such cynical expedience. We may not regard Zhang's resolution of these contradictory beliefs to be acceptable, but Zhang apparently did.

By clearly explaining what the ancestral hall involved and how ancestral reverence did not violate the true worship of the Lord-on-High, Zhang attempted to make it possible for Chinese Christians to worship their ancestors while adhering to Christianity. In fact, Zhang did not merely seek to allow Chinese Christians to honor their ancestors. He went one step further and stated that those who did not attend to the souls *(hun)* of their ancestors would be punished in hell while those who did would be rewarded by heaven. Clearly, Zhang was blending ancestral reverence with the biblical commandment to honor one's father and mother (Exodus 20:12) to which all Christians are bound. Consequently, Zhang's essay transformed ancestral reverence from a human option into a divine obligation.

In this and other writings, Zhang gave new applications and interpretations to basic Christian teachings. These new meanings are clear in the last page of Zhang's essay where—for at least a second time in his writings—he portrayed the Lord-on-High in the image of a parent. He stated that we honor and revere the Lord-on-High because He is the "Great Father and Mother" *(Da Fumu)* of all people.[84] Through our personal spiritual cultivation we can move toward the good and away from evil. By performing acts of ancestral reverence, such as ritual libations to ancestors, we can attain blessings and avoid calamities. In the next-to-last statement, Zhang wrote that we need to love others as ourselves and feel sympathy for those who are suffering misfortune. Jesus said that loving others as ourselves was the second greatest commandment (Mark 12:3). But this was only Zhang's penultimate statement. In his very last statement Zhang wrote that filial thoughts and love and harmony toward close relatives cannot be surpassed. In searching for a Chinese image that would convey the reverence due to God, Zhang could think of no greater human reverence that what Chinese felt toward their parents.

V

Apart from the continual minor revisions to the *Similarities,* the last work to which Zhang devoted himself was *Clearly Distinguishing the Heavenly Teaching [from Heterodoxy] (Tianjiao mingbian).* This was a collaborative work whose idea was first conceived by Ding Yuntai (styled Lü'an) of Jiyang, then part of Ji'nan prefecture in Shandong province, five hundred miles (eight hundred kilometers) north of Hangzhou.[85] Ding belonged to a distinguished family of longtime Christians. It is unclear whether Ding suggested the idea for *Clearly Distinguishing* in a personal visit or in writing, but the fact that he did so indicates that Zhang was not totally isolated from contacts beyond Zhejiang province.

There was an active Christian community in Ji'nan that had been served by unique cooperation between the Jesuits and a Franciscan. From 1650 to 1665 the Franciscan Antonio Caballero a Santa Maria (Li Andang) worked out of the Eastern Church in Ji'nan, and from about 1660 to 1665 the Jesuit Jean Valat (Wang Ruwang) worked out of the Western Church. One of the outstanding Christian literati at Ji'nan was Shang Huqing (styled Weitang), who changed his name, after becoming a Christian, to Shang Shiji.[86] Shang passed the provincial examination *(juren)* in 1639, six years after Zhang's birth, and served in several official posts. He assisted Caballero in writing Chinese works on Christianity.[87] There are numerous similarities between Zhang's writings and those coauthored by Caballero and Shang, including the lack of a sharp distinction between God and Jesus. There is some evidence that Shang read an early version of Zhang's *Similarities.*[88]

Zhang's aim in *Clearly Distinguishing* was to simplify and reduce the content of the Heavenly Teaching to ten chapters *(juan).*[89] The preface to *Clearly Distinguishing* was dated in the lunar month covering late June and early July of 1711 and showed that Zhang's understanding of the Heavenly Teaching had continued to evolve in terms of specifics. The Lord of Heaven is uniquely referred to with a fusing of His usual name with the ancient Chinese name for God to form "Lord of Heaven Lord-on-High" (Tianzhu Shangdi). He is said to have been incarnated in the country of Judea (Rudeya) in the reign of Emperor Yuan of the Han dynasty, that is, in 47 B.C. After suffering and dying, He was said to have been resurrected *(fuhuo)*, after which He resided for forty days on earth, commanding his disciples to write the Four Gospels and establishing the papacy.[90] There are slight inaccuracies and exaggerations in Zhang's account, particularly when he claimed that for a thousand years the morality of the Western nations had been unified in harmony and their customs had been pure. The source of this inaccuracy might have been the Jesuits themselves, for example, Fr. Aleni, whose *Dialogues about the West (Xifang wenda)* exaggerated European harmony and morality.

Still, most of Zhang's facts are correct, if not always precise. He spoke of how in the Tang dynasty a missionary from the West by the name of Aloben brought Nestorian Christianity to China and how this incident had been confirmed by the discovery early in the seventeenth century of the Nestorian Tablet *(Jingjiao bei)*. Zhang claimed that the Buddhists appropriated the Nestorian teaching. Although this may sound outrageous, it appears that at the time of the great anti-Buddhist persecution of 845, Nestorian Christians also suffered, and the religion could have gone underground and merged with some school of Buddhism.[91] Zhang was also aware that Western missionaries of the Franciscan order *(Fangjige xiansheng)* arrived in Canton during the reign of the Wanli emperor (reigned 1573–1619). Finally, the Jesuits arrived, and Zhang does make one rare reference to a specific Jesuit by name—Mister Ricci of the Far West *(Li Xitai xiansheng)*.

Unlike his reference to the Franciscans, Zhang did not refer to the Jesuits by the name of their religious order, because to have done so would have diminished the sense of identity that he was trying to establish between the Chinese literati and the Western literati (i.e., the Jesuits). Zhang emphasized this identity by quoting from the Neo-Confucian philosopher Lu Xiangshan (Jiuyuan) (1139–1193) of Jiangxi province, who had engaged in a famous debate with Zhu Xi at Goose Lake. Zhang quoted Lu as saying: "In the Eastern Sea and in the Western Sea sages arise who are identical in thinking."[92] This quote exactly expressed the point he was trying to make in regard to the Jesuits and the literati.

In the preface to *Clearly Distinguishing*, Zhang gave a brief biographical note describing himself as a restless seeker of truth. Dissatisfaction with studying for the provincial examination *(juren)* led him to turn to Buddhism. After becoming dissatisfied with the teaching of the Buddha, he met the learned Zhu Ji'nan, who introduced him to the Heavenly Teaching.[93] This meeting led Zhang eventually to his baptism and to his ostracism by friends and acquaintances for having betrayed the Literati Teaching. But Zhang defended himself and was convinced that the Heavenly Teaching and Literati Teaching were paths leading to the same Truth and that he, not those who spurned him, was restoring and completing the True Way of antiquity.

Zhang was troubled and decided to walk. He walked through Qiantang Gate and immediately saw the West Lake. The mist was lifting and the lake stretched smooth like a mirror. The lake had always soothed him. He passed the Sheng Yin Monastery and went along Su Avenue, where Golden Sand Bay stretched before Thunder Peak Pagoda. The haze still hid the sun. What was troubling him was the growing hostility of literati friends to his work and beliefs.

It was now thirty-five years since he had first committed himself in writing to defending the Lord of Heaven Teaching. He had not taken such a decisive step because he had been overawed by the Western scholars who had lived in Hangzhou since before he was born, though he had to concede that some of them were very impressive and possessed a learning that in some ways surpassed the Chinese literati. But Father Intorcetta had died eleven years ago, and the present Western scholars in Hangzhou were not the equal of Fathers Intorcetta and Martini. Still, they believed some surprising things that we sometimes find hard to understand. No, he had taken this step thirty-five years ago because he was convinced that the teaching about the Lord of Heaven was true, and it was true because it continued and completed what the ancients had believed. Zhang had embraced the Lord of Heaven Teaching because he was convinced that this was the only way to recover what had been lost of the teachings of China's ancients and the only way to know the Truth.

In 1672 he had been filled with hope and conviction when he wrote the preface for his work that tried to reveal all the connections between China's ancient teachings and this new teaching from the Far

West. But he had convinced few of his fellow literati. It is true that he had a small circle of followers, mostly in Zhejiang, and that he had close associates like Hong Ji, and he had his son Youling. But beyond that, the literati were not only unresponsive, but it seemed as if things were becoming more difficult. The news from Beijing of the incredibly stupid and offensive acts of the envoy from Rome named Tournon had even alienated the emperor, who had previously been so supportive of the missionaries.

Zhang spotted a favorite tavern and decided to stop for a bowl of Longjing tea. The warm tea soothed his stomach. He watched some countrywomen piling into a boat to take them on their pilgrimage out to a monastery in the lake. The women had round white faces with high cheekbones and they combed their hair high. Most of them wore blue or green, but two or three younger women wore bright red skirts. Following behind the women came their husbands, carrying umbrellas and dry clothing.

Zhang's thoughts returned to his problem. It was clear that there was nothing else to do but continue with his work showing the similarities between the Lord of Heaven Teaching and the teaching of China's ancients. He would search for more examples from his historical notes. He had always felt that the key to solving the problem of convincing people lay in history. He would speak with Hong, who might have some new insights. He might even be ready to publish the *Similarities* next year, if the atmosphere improved. He would not give up. How could he? Never as long as he lived would he forget what had happened on the day of his baptism. He had waited a long time before taking that final step. Father Intorcetta had heaved a great sigh of relief when Zhang told him that he was ready to go through with it. But the event had touched him in a way he could never have imagined before the moment when the drops of water touched his head. The fragrance he sensed at that moment filled his head and moved his soul. Because of what happened that day and because of the way he was, he could not turn back.

Zhang was ready to go back. He would stop on the way and buy a new inkstone, one that was just right for expressing a new idea that he had. As he passed one of the tea shops, a highly painted woman leaned out and called to him. He smiled and looked away. The scents from the noodle and dumpling shops were making him hungry. He began to walk at a faster pace. He was going home. He had work to do.[94]

CHAPTER 7

At the End

Zhang wrote:

> The time of your death,
> is so sudden that it cannot be known.
> The good and evil of your life,
> at this point cannot be altered.
> Wife and children all encircle you,
> as their love and longing seek to hold you,
> but sickness and pain oppress your body,
> while the fear and dread are unbearable.
> If the Lord does not protect you,
> you will surely be bound by Satan.
> Move toward the good and away from evil,
> guarding against danger hour by hour.
> Do not indulge the desires of your flesh,
> nor depart from thoughts of the Way.
> Time is a galloping colt,
> and it you must urgently heed.[1]

By the end of his life, Zhang's attempts to convince fellow literati of his ideas were meeting with increasing resistance. Not only was the cultural and political climate becoming more hostile, but the talents of the Jesuits who resided in Hangzhou after Intorcetta's death in 1696 were clearly of a more modest stature than predecessors like Martini or Intorcetta. Whereas Hangzhou in the early seventeenth century had been a mission center that guided even the missionaries at Beijing, by the end of the century it had become a transient base for missionaries who were passing through. The Jesuits who did reside in Hangzhou were there for such a short time that they failed to develop long-term relationships with the Chinese Christian community.

The Portuguese Father Joao Baptista (Guo Ruowang, 1654–1714), for example, directed the rebuilding of the fire-damaged Church of the Savior, which was completed in 1699.[2] The work was hastened by a monetary contribution from the Kangxi emperor made during the Kangxi emperor's southern tour in 1699, when he sent a personal representative to visit the two Christian churches at Hangzhou and Nanjing.[3] The short-lived French Father Philibert Geneix (Yan Wuben, 1667–1699) resided only briefly in Hangzhou, though he was already suffering from the illness that would shortly take his life.[4] The Sicilian Father Laurifice returned to Hangzhou between 1697 and 1700 and served as rector.[5] The French Father Jean-Charles de Brossia (Li [alias Xi] Shengxue, 1660–1704) resided at Hangzhou from 1702 to 1704.[6] The Franciscans appear to have sensed a missionary vacuum in Hangzhou and began arriving there in 1702 to establish a Franciscan residence.[7]

The Italian Jesuit Agostini Barelli (Ai Siding, 1656–1711) arrived in Hangzhou in 1702, six years after the death of Intorcetta, and although he remained in Hangzhou for nearly nine years, little is recorded of his achievements.[8] According to Fr. Barelli, the Christians in Hangzhou as of November 1705 numbered 400 men and 550 women.[9] When the Kangxi emperor passed through Hangzhou in 1707, Barelli and two French Jesuits—Jean-Alexis de Gollet (Guo Zhongchuan, 1664–1741) and Cyr Contancin (Gong Dangxin, 1670–1732)—were summoned to appear before the throne. They were joined by three members of the Missions étrangères of Paris and several Dominicans. Only the three Jesuits agreed to abide by the emperor's conditions to obtain a license (piao) to remain in China. These conditions consisted of accepting Fr. Ricci's accommodative interpretations of the Chinese rites and committing to remain in China for the rest of their lives. When he died in January of 1711, Barelli was buried in Dafangjing.[10] It was during Fr. Barelli's residence that the ill-founded attempt of the Jesuit opponents to establish an alternate Christian base in Hangzhou collapsed. The attempt had begun in 1698 when the Dominican Father Astudillo had paid 150 taels (ounces of silver) to purchase a residence in Hangzhou for the Franciscans.[11] In 1705 the bitter opponent of the Jesuits, the papal legate (and soon-to-be cardinal) de Tournon, acquired this site and named Monseigneur Mezzafalce as the administrator of the vicariat. However, shortly afterward, Tournon was expelled from China by the Kangxi emperor, and in 1723 the Franciscan chapel was converted into a Chinese ancestral temple *(zu tang)*. [12]

Barelli was replaced by the Alsatian Jesuit Romain Hinderer (De Ma'nuo, 1668–1744), who arrived in Hangzhou in 1711. Fr. Hinderer was a courageous martyr-priest, but—either because of his own nature or the historical circumstances—he fit less into the Riccian mold of a Jesuit scholar than into the popular image of a pastor to the people. He did work with the Jesuit Fathers de Mailla and Régis to draw maps of Fujian, Henan, Jiangsu, and Zhejiang provinces, but his primary contribution was to serve the established Christian communities in Zhejiang and Jiangsu provinces with inexhaustible energy. [13] The confessions, communions, baptisms, and last rites that he administered numbered in the thousands, and the count was reported to Europe in the widely read German publication *Der Neue Welt-Bott*. [14] Hinderer's scholarly interests were applied to composing a new method of assisting at the mass *(Yu misa gongcheng)*, which used allegories to make the mass more meaningful. [15] This new form of presenting the mass became tremendously popular, and Hinderer's work was reprinted in Chinese prayerbooks into the twentieth century. Since the demands of administering to so many Christians throughout two provinces forced the priest into a life of perpetual travel, in which he spent only part of his time in Hangzhou, Fr. Hinderer's contact with the now elderly Zhang would have been very limited.

In terms of numbers, the Hangzhou church in Hinderer's time had not yet declined. In the years from 1718 to 1720 there were more than one thousand Christians in Hangzhou, which is twice as many as the five hundred recorded in the annual letter of 1678–1679. [16] Although Fr. Hinderer was the sole missionary in Hangzhou at this time, he was assisted by thirty catechists who had been trained in the Jesuit college. In his letter of 27 September 1719, Fr. Hinderer gave an accounting of the previous year's progress. [17] Between 1 September 1718 and 1719, Hinderer baptized 228 people (25 men, 36 young men, 51 infant boys, 30 married women, 32 unmarried women, and 54 infant girls). In addition, Hinderer had heard 1,615 confessions and distributed the host to 1,230 communicants. Of the twelve times that he administered the last rites, one wonders if one was for Master Zhang.

Even if one allows for the fact that these numbers were expanded by the inclusion of churches in the towns surrounding Hangzhou, the number of 228 for one year compares favorably with the twenty baptisms in Hangzhou itself for the two-year period of 1678 and 1679.[18] And yet the nature of the converts was changing. Whereas the twenty baptisms of 1678 and 1679 had involved literati like Zhang, Hinderer was baptizing people of less distinguished status.

In spite of these sizable numbers, Hinderer was presiding over a church that was clearly under siege. He notes in 1719 that not a single eminent gentleman was supporting the church and that the provincial governor despised Christians. Nevertheless, the Hangzhou church enjoyed a period of peace in the twelve months between September 1718 and September 1719, a peace that we now know was about to end. Although the letters published in *Der Neue Welt-Bott* were often edited, we can obtain some idea of Hinderer's method by the account he wrote of a young woman, a non-Christian, who was overcome by a poltergeist and nearly choked to death. Fr. Hinderer helped her and she became a Christian, but he could not save her from dying, though she did so in faith as a Christian.[19] The outcome of this incident could hardly have appeared to the non-Christian population of Hangzhou as a triumph.

The passing of the Kangxi emperor in 1722 and the accession to the throne of the Yongzheng emperor proved to be very bad news for Christianity. The Yongzheng emperor's animosity toward the Jesuits was first aroused when the Portuguese Father J. Mourao (Mu Jingyuan, 1681–1726) supported a competing heir in a succession struggle and was condemned to death. Ultimately, however, the emperor's hostile attitude toward Christianity was based on the threat posed by the missionaries and the foreign authority of Rome to the political stability of China.[20] In 1724 the Yongzheng emperor initiated an anti-Christian persecution that forced Hinderer to go into hiding in Zhejiang province.[21] By the mid-1720s the Christian community in Hangzhou had become a martyrs' church. Fr. Hinderer was attacked by a group of hostile Chinese, who threw him into a river and left him for dead. Fortunately, he was rescued by the faithful.[22] Although the culprits were apprehended and sentenced to punishment by the authorities, the Christian community was condemned to continued martyrdom. Eventually, Hinderer was expelled from Hangzhou. By 1730 he had appealed to Li Wei, the governor-general of Zhejiang, to be allowed to delay his departure on the grounds of advanced age and illness, but Li appointed an official to escort him to Macao.[23]

With Hinderer's departure, the Christian community in Hangzhou went underground and the Church of the Savior fell vacant. Li memorialized the throne saying that he had inspected the site and found it unsuitable for a Buddhist temple, but he recommended that it be converted into a temple to the Goddess of Sailors, the Celestial Empress (Tianhou), and this conversion took place in 1731.[24] The women's chapel had been converted into a Buddhist temple in 1730, and one wonders if most non-Christian Chinese saw a significant difference between a chapel dedicated to the Virgin Mary and a temple dedicated to the female bodhisattva of mercy, Guanyin.[25] At Li's recommendation, the Yongzheng emperor issued an edict expelling the missionaries from Zhejiang and Jiangsu provinces. This edict, along with an explanation of the reasons for the expulsion, were inscribed on a stone tablet and placed outside the door of the church for all to see.[26] Although Catholic missionaries returned to Hangzhou in 1839 at the time of the Opium War, the Church of the Savior was not restored to them until 1862.[27] One suspects that it was at this time that the new name of Immaculate Conception Church was adopted.

II

By 1731 Zhang was very probably dead, and it does not appear that his disciples carried on his endeavors. Viewed from one perspective, Zhang represented the culmination of a remarkably creative movement that dated from Ricci and the Three Pillars. This movement was initiated by the Jesuit missionaries who established a series of missions along a 1200-mile (1900-kilometer) track from Canton in the south to Beijing in the north. Numerous literati were attracted to this Lord of Heaven Teaching and many—predominantly, but not exclusively, from the lower gentry—adopted this teaching and made creative attempts to inculturate Christianity into traditional Chinese culture. However, shortly after 1700 this movement receded into obscurity.

It is possible that Zhang's influence spread beyond his small circle of disciples in his own lifetime. There is some evidence that the

French Jesuit Joachim Bouvet (Bo Jin), who lived at the court in Beijing in close proximity to the Kangxi emperor from 1688 to 1693 and from 1699 until dying in 1730, read some of Zhang's writings. However, Bouvet drew conclusions that were vastly different from those of Zhang. Bouvet's Chinese work *An Examination of the Ancient and Modern [Chinese] Worship of Heaven; The Essentials of the Heavenly Learning (Gujin jing Tian jian Tianxue benyi)* (1701–1707) appears to have borrowed from Zhang's *Similarities*.[28] For example, there are numerous parallels between the passages from classical texts cited by Zhang in part 1 of his *Similarities* and those cited by Bouvet in his *Examination*. The presence of a copy of the *Similarities* in the old Jesuit collection of the Beitang Library in Beijing indicates that Bouvet could have had access to the work. However, Bouvet believed that the oldest parts of the Chinese Classics were not historical texts meant to be taken literally but rather were filled with mythic and allegorical truths that could be extracted only by figurative interpretation.[29]

Because of Bouvet's emphasis on a figurative interpretation, his theories eventually became known as "Figurism." Bouvet believed that when the Classics were interpreted in this way, they foreshadowed the truths of Christian revelation even before the historical incarnation of Christ. Although Bouvet's ideas were shared by a very small circle of Jesuits, most missionaries regarded his views as not only extreme, but also dangerous to the mission. Certainly any claim that the three oldest dynasties (Xia, Shang, and Zhou) were merely legendary would have been most offensive to the Chinese, who not only revered the antiquity of these dynasties, but also prided themselves on their knowledge of history. Consequently, Bouvet's superiors forbade him to disseminate his writings and even to discuss them with the Chinese. Only recently have his manuscripts begun to be reexamined. Even if Bouvet was influenced by Zhang's works, Bouvet's condemnation to silence reinforces the sense that this particular phase of inculturation of Christianity into Chinese culture was coming to an end early in the eighteenth century.

The open intellectual climate of the late Ming had been fostered, in part, by the disintegrating political structure of the dynasty and by its lack of control of the literati. By 1700 this climate had given way to a strong Manchu court that closely supervised the literati. Furthermore, the Manchu rulers became particularly suspicious of subversive organizations with religious underpinnings, of which Christianity was seen as an example. The Chinese Rites Controversy reinforced the view of Christianity as a subversive organization controlled from abroad (Rome). Moreover, the intense factional in-fighting among the missionaries diminished them in the eyes of the Chinese throne. Finally, the intellectual climate of the early Qing saw a revival of a rigid Neo-Confucian orthodoxy. All of these forces contributed to make Zhang the last in a line and the end of an era.

If the history of Christianity in China had ended in the eighteenth century, there would be nothing more to add, but the revival of a postcolonialist indigenous Chinese church in the last half of the twentieth century shows that the inculturation of Christianity in Chinese culture has resumed. Indeed, it may never have stopped. What earlier appeared as periods of suspension of the inculturation process may only have been phases of ebb and flow or even surface quiescence accompanied by underground growth. In his historical survey of the Catholic Church in Zhejiang province published in 1936, the late Father Fang Hao, who was himself a Zhejiang native, spoke of the history of the church as one of continuous development divided into three phases: (1) seventeenth-century growth, (2) eighteenth-century decline that was well under way by the time of the death of the Kangxi emperor in 1722, and (3) a revival in the nineteenth and twentieth centuries.[30] Fr. Fang presented statistics showing not only that the number of Catholics in Zhejiang grew from 6,332 in 1885 to 90,013 in 1935, but also that there were significant signs of progress in inculturation in the growing proportion of Chinese over foreign clergy.[31]

A parallel to a more recent phase of inculturation may be useful. Recent studies indicate that when the Catholic Church revived in 1979 after thirty years of repression by a hostile, atheistic government and persecution by the Red Guards and others, there were at least as many practicing Catholics in China (three million by conservative estimate) as there had been prior to the Communist takeover in 1949.[32] If one compares Fr. Fang's statistics with recent figures for Zhejiang province, we see that while the number of priests between 1935 and 1989 declined from 116 to 40, the number of Catholics increased from 90,013 to 160,000.[33] What makes these numbers so amazing is that most China scholars had regarded Chinese Christianity to have been practically exterminated by the end of the Cultural Revolution in the early 1970s.[34]

Part of the cause of this surprising phenomenon is that the Communist government, by forcing Chinese Christians to terminate all ties with foreign Christians and foreign support, unwittingly aided the inculturation process. Although the papacy's series of rulings of the early eighteenth century forbidding Chinese Christians to practice their ancestral and Confucian rites was an enormous setback for the process of inculturating Christianity in China, this setback proved to be far more temporary than most scholars even today recognize. It was temporary not merely because, as is often thought, Rome reversed itself on the Chinese rites in 1939, but because—in the view of one scholar—the Chinese Catholic Church over time has resolved the conflict between Christianity and Chinese culture.[35] Catholicism, although foreign in origin, is now viewed by many Chinese as fully in harmony with the reverence for familial obligations that forms the core of China's historical heritage.[36] In many Catholic villages today, ties to Catholicism are received more as part of the heritage of their ancestors than as a foreign teaching.

There are certainly differences between the mid-twentieth-century phase of the inculturation of Christianity in China and the phase of the late seventeenth and early eighteenth centuries in which Zhang lived. But it is strikingly relevant that many in the Chinese church have come to believe that the main sign of the authority of one's faith is the sanctity that is revealed through self-sacrifice and martyrdom. It might be an exaggeration to say that Zhang was a martyr, but one would be well within the facts to say that he offered his life and scholarship in support of his beliefs and, in the process, suffered the loss of esteem of his fellow literati and possibly a loss of status as well as material rewards. Zhang became an isolated figure, leading a small circle of followers against a tide of growing hostility and, given the anti-Christian policies emanating out of Beijing, even danger. He would have had to have been a man of great hope not to have died in despair.

Today things look quite different. Not only has the Dafangjing cemetery been restored as a historical monument, but, more significantly, the Church of the Savior has been restored as a Catholic church in which Christians of Hangzhou worship. Looked at from the perspective in which the inculturation of Christianity into China has been a process of continual ebb and flow that has at times slowed but never fully ceased, one could say that Zhang was not the last in a movement but rather one of the founders of Chinese Christianity.

Whichever he was, one suspects that Zhang would have been willing to submit to the eventual judgment of history, whose study he so loved, and to the judgment of his God, to whom he was so devoted.

———————————————

Zhang wrote:

> Great and wide is Heaven,
> its round form can be seen.
> If you say that Heaven is just air,
> how then can you distinguish between its being round or square?
> Heaven surely exists,
> the literati refer to it as the Lord's home.
> And that is where all good people go,
> having joy eternal without end.
> It enables the saints to meet with blessings,
> and its great bliss surpasses all.
> What hope is there for mere mortals,
> whose eyes are blinded by the desires of the world and whose
> minds are disordered?
> They have ignorant doubts about [Heaven's] existing.
> They are merely preoccupied with the earthly cemetery on
> Beimang Mountain.[37]
> Move your life toward the good and away from evil,
> and at the end, you will soar like a bird up to Heaven.[38]

———————————————

APPENDIX

List of Painted Images in the Church of the Savior, Hangzhou (1678–1692), and Correspondences with Zhang Xingyao's Eulogies

The correspondences between Zhang Xingyao's thirty-eight "Inscriptions in Praise of the Sage Teaching" *(Shengjiao zanming)* and the seventy-two paintings produced and hung in the Hangzhou church from 1678 to 1692 are indicated by the roman and arabic numerals placed below in the column on the right. These numerals follow the order of the eight parts into which Zhang divided his eulogies. All of the correspondences appear certain, except for one. Zhang's eulogy of the "Holy Mother presenting Jesus at the Lord's Temple" (VI.2) may or may not match the image portraying the circumcision of Christ (no. 41). This uncertainty is indicated by a question mark. Unless otherwise noted, most paintings were two to two and one-half meters on each side.

The author's explanatory insertions are in brackets.

[The images in this section were placed beside the main altar, except for the images of Saint Francis Borgia and the three martyrs of Japan, which were placed beside the two side altars.]

1. Sacred Image of the Savior (main altar) (3.5 meters × 3.5 meters)
2. Genealogy of Christ, from Abraham to Christ (6 meters × 5 meters)
3. Saint Ignatius of Loyola (1491–1556), founder of the Society of Jesus
   IV.4
4. Saint Francis Xavier (1506–1552), pioneering Jesuit missionary to East Asia
   IV.3
5. Aloysius [Luigi] Gonzaga (1568–1591), pious member of an eminent family who renounced his inheritance to become a Jesuit
6. Saint Stanislaus Kostka (1550–1568), devout religious and patron of Poland
7. Saint Francis Borgia (1510–1572), third general of the Society of Jesus
   VIII.1
8. The Three Martyrs of Japan (three Japanese Jesuit lay brothers crucified at Nagasaki on 5 February 1597)
   VIII.2
   (a) Paolo Miki, S.J.
   (b) Giacomo Kisai, S.J.
   (c) Giovanni Soan di Gotò, S.J.

[The Four Evangelists:]
9. Saint John
10. Saint Matthew
11. Saint Luke
12. Saint Mark

13. The Annunciation of the Birth of Christ (Luke 1:26-38)
14. The Immaculate Conception of the Virgin Mary
15. The Nativity of Christ (Luke 2:1-14)
16. The Nativity of the Virgin Mary
17. Saint Gregory (540-604), Pope Gregory I (the Great) III.1
18. Saint Ambrose (339-397), bishop of Milan III.2
19. Saint Augustine (354-430), church father III.3
20. Saint Jerome (345-419 or 420), church father III.4

[The images in the next section were placed at the sides of the two side altars.]

21. Saint Peter (side altar) (3 meters × 3 meters) I.1
22. Saint Paul (side altar) (3 meters × 3 meters) I.2
23. The Archangel Michael V.1
24. Guardian Angel V.2
25. Saint Joseph, husband of the Virgin Mary (Matthew 1:18-25) VI.4
26. Saint Joachim, father of the Virgin Mary VI.5
27. Saint John, the favorite disciple of Jesus
28. John the Baptist, who baptized Christ (Matthew 3:1-17; Mark 1:2-11; Luke 3:1-21; and John 1:19-34) VI.7
29. Saint Silvester, who baptized Emperor Constantine IV.5
30. The presentation of the Virgin Mary at the Temple VI.1
31. Saint Helena (255-330), Roman empress and mother of Emperor Constantine
32. Saint Rosalia (died 1160), patroness of Palermo and object of legend and cultic worship
33. Saint Catherine of Siena (1347-1380)
34. Saint Theresa of Avila (1515-1582)

[The images of the next section were placed at the side of the front of the church in the choir.]

35. The entrance of Christ into Jersusalem with palms (Matthew 21:1-11; and John 12:12-15)
36. The Last Supper (Matthew 26:20-35; Mark 14:17-26; and Luke 22:14-28)

37. The Resurrection of Christ (Matthew 28:1-10; and Luke 24:1-12)
38. The descent of the Holy Spirit (Acts 2:1-4)
39. The ascension of Christ to Heaven (Luke 24:51; and Acts 1:9-11)
40. The Assumption (ascent of the Virgin Mary into Heaven)
41. The Circumcision of Christ (Luke 2:21)   VI.2[?]
42. The Adoration of Christ by the Three Magi (Matthew 2:1-12)

[The next four images were placed at the entrance to the church.]

(The Four Last Things:)
43. Death   VII.1
44. Judgment   VII.2
45. Heaven   VII.4
46. Hell   VII.3

[The images in the next section were placed on the upper part of the side walls of the church, extending from the altar rail to the front of the choir.]

47. Saint Andrew, the apostle   I.3
48. Saint James the Greater, the apostle   I.4
49. Saint Philip, the apostle   I.6
50. Saint James the Lesser, the apostle   I.5
51. Saint Thomas, the apostle   I.7
52. Saint Bartholomew, the apostle   I.8
53. Saint Simon, the apostle   I.11
54. Saint Jude Thaddeus, the apostle   I.12
55. Saint Matthew, the apostle   I.9
56. Saint Barnabus, missionary   I.10
57. Saint Stephen, first Christian martyr (Acts 6:1-8:2)   II.1
58. Saint Lawrence (died 258?), Roman martyr   II.2
59. Saint Dominic (ca. 1170-1221), founder of the Dominican order   IV.2
60. Saint Francis of Assisi (1182-1226), founder of the Franciscan order
       IV.1
61. The Visitation of the Virgin Mary to Saint Elizabeth (Luke 1:39-45)
       VI.3
62. Jesus at twelve years of age is found by his parents in the temple with
the doctors (Luke 2:41-51)   VI.6

[The images in the next section were placed on the lower part of the side walls of the main part of the church. They each measured 1 meter × 2.5 meters.]

63. Feast of the Holy Innocents
64. The miracle of Christ healing the paralytic (Matthew 9:2)

65. Saint Mary Magdalene, who with her tears washes the feet of Christ (Luke 7:36–50)
66. Christ, who frees the adulterous woman from death by stoning and pardons her from sin (John 8:3–11)
67. The miracle of the man blind from birth who receives eyesight from Christ (John 9:1–41)
68. The miracle of the multiplication of the bread with which Christ sated the hunger of the crowd (Matthew 14:14–21; and Mark 1:23–26)
69. The miracle of Christ, who drives away the demon in the man possessed by the devil (Mark 1:23–26)
70. The miracle of Christ, who gives hearing and speech to a man who was deaf and mute (Mark 7:32–37)
71. The miracle of Christ raising Lazarus from the dead (John 11:17–44)
72. The miracle of Christ raising the son of a widow from the dead (Luke 7:11–16)

[The artistic medium of the seraphs below apparently differed from the seventy-two images above.]

73–77. Large seraph (highest order of angels)
78–84. Large seraph (highest order of angels)—continued

NOTES

INTRODUCTION

1. Jacques Gernet, *Chine et christianisme, action et réaction* (Paris, 1982), pp. 322-333.

2. Erik Zürcher, *Bouddhisme, Christianisme et société chinoise* (Paris, 1990), pp. 11-37.

3. See N. Standaert, "Inculturation and Chinese-Christian Contacts in the Late Ming and Early Qing," *Ching Feng* 34 (4) (December 1991): 1-16.

4. Zhang Xingyao, *Shengjiao zanming*, manuscript in the Bibliothèque nationale, Paris, ms. chinois 7067.

CHAPTER I

1. This imaginative reconstruction of Father Martini's first encounter with the Manchus in Wenzhou in 1645 is based on his own description, published in certain later editions of his popular history of the Manchu conquest of China. See M. Martini, *De bello Tartarico historia* in the Latin version appended to Martini's *Novus atlas Sinensis* (Amsterdam, 1655), pp. 18–19. Also see Fang Hao, *Zhongguo Tianzhujiao shi renwu zhuan* (Biographies of historical personages in the Chinese Catholic Church), 3 vols. (Hong Kong, 1970-1973), 2, p. 115; J. J. L. Duyvendak, "Early Chinese Studies in Holland," *T'oung Pao* 32 (1936): 322, 326-328; G. Melis, "Martino Martini's Travels in China," in *Martino Martini, Geografo, Cartografo, Storico, Teologo*, edited by G. Melis (Trent, 1983), p. 429; Louis (Aloys) Pfister, S.J., *Notices biographiques et bibliographiques sur les Jésuites de l'ancienne mission de Chine, 1552 à 1773*, 2 vols. (Shanghai, 1932-1934) p. 257; and L. Struve, *The Southern Ming, 1644-1662* (New Haven, 1984), pp. 60-61, 75-94.

2. A. C. Moule, *Quinsai with Other Notes on Marco Polo* (Cambridge, England, 1957), p. 13.

3. *Shang you Tiantang, xia you Su Hang.*

4. See *The Travels of Marco Polo*, translated by Ronald Latham (Baltimore, 1958). Polo's description of Hangzhou, which he called "Kinsai" (Quinsai), is found on pages 184-201.

5. Jacques Gernet, *Daily Life in China on the Eve of the Mongol Invasion, 1250-1276*, translated from the French by H. M. Wright (Stanford, 1962), pp. 38-39.

6. Ibid., p. 113.

7. Ibid., p. 123.

8. Ibid., pp. 133-135.

9. Polo, *Travels,* pp. 215-216; Gernet, *Daily Life,* pp. 96-97.

10. A. C. Moule, *Quinsai,* pp. 22, 36.

11. Joseph Dehergne, S.J., *Répertoire des Jésuites de Chine de 1552 à 1800* (Rome, 1973), pp. 49-50; N. Standaert, *Yang Tingyun, Confucian and Christian in Late Ming China* (Leiden, 1988), p. 54. For a brief history of the Catholic church in Zhejiang province, see Fang Hao, "Zhejiang Tianzhujiao lüeshi" (A brief history of the Catholic Church in Zhejiang province), in *Guofeng yuekan* 8 (9-10) (1936): 62-75, reprinted in *Wocun zazhi* (Hangzhou) 5 (6) (1937): 335-350.

12. Pfister, *Notices biographiques,* p. 54.

13. Arthur Hummel, ed., *Eminent Chinese of the Ch'ing Period (1644-1912)* (Washington, D.C., 1943), p. 453.

14. Dehergne, *Répertoire,* p. 49; L. Carrington Goodrich and Chaoying Fang, eds., *Dictionary of Ming Biography, 1368-1644,* 2 vols. (New York, 1976), p. 32.

15. Pasquale d'Elia, S.J., *Fonti Ricciane,* 3 vols. (Rome, 1942-1949), 1, p. 290; Pfister, *Notices biographiques,* p. 47; Dehergne, *Répertoire,* p. 89.

16. Joseph Sebes, S.J., "Martino Martini's Role in the Controversy of the Chinese Rites," in *Martino Martini, Geografo, Cartografo, Storico, Teologo,* edited by G. Melis, p. 472.

17. Dehergne, *Répertoire,* pp. 50, 89, 274; and Fang Hao, "Hangzhou Dafangjing Tianzhujiao gu mu zhi yange" (The development of the old Catholic cemetery at Dafangjing at Hangzhou), originally published in *Wocun zazhi* 4 (8) (1936): 469-473; reprinted in *Fang Hao liushi zidinggao* (The Collected works of Marius Fang Hao, revised and edited by the author on his sixtieth birthday) (Taipei, 1969), p. 1945.

18. d'Elia, *Fonti Ricciane,* 2, p. 308 (number 712).

19. In comparison with other seventeenth-century Chinese converts, far more information is available on the Three Pillars. Informative entries on Xu Guangqi, Li Zhizao, and Yang Tingyun; are found in Fang Hao, *Zhongguo Tianzhujiao shi* 1, pp. 99-138; and Hummel, *Eminent Chinese,* pp. 316, 452-454, 894-895. Willard J. Peterson has written an article "Why Did They Become Christians?" in *East Meets West: The Jesuits in China, 1582-1773,* edited by Charles E. Ronan, S.J., and Bonnie B. C. Ho (Chicago, 1988), pp. 129-152. Some of Xu's writings have recently been republished in China in *Xu Guangqiji,* edited by Wang Zhongmin (Shanghai, 1963; reprinted 1984). N. Standaert has published an intellectual biography on Yang Tingyun cited above. Numerous references to the Three Pillars appear in other works dealing with the early-seventeenth-century China Mission.

20. Peterson, "Why Did They Become Christians?" p. 139.

21. Standaert, *Yang Tingyun,* p. 53.

22. The story of Yang's conversion is told in Peterson, "Why Did They Become Christians?" pp. 130-134, and in greater detail in Standaert, *Yang Tingyun,* pp. 53-60.

23. Fang Hao, "Zhejiang Tianzhujiao lüeshi," pp. 341-344.

24. Ibid., pp. 337, 344-346.

25. Xu Zongze, *Ming-Qing jian Yesuhuishi yizhu tiyao* (A summary of Jesuit translations made in the late Ming and early Qing periods) (Taipei, 1958), pp. 473-478.

26. Paul Brunner, S.J., *L'euchologe de la Mission de Chine, editio princeps 1628 et développements jusqu'à nos jours* (Münster, Westfallen, Germany, 1964), p. 15.

27. These lists of Christian works printed in China are incomplete. A manuscript of the lists is preserved in the Bibliothèque nationale, Paris (ms. chinois 7046: VII, IX, and X).

28. Dehergne, *Répertoire,* p. 154.

29. Ibid., p. 223.

30. Ibid., p. 102.

31. Zhu Zongyuan (styled Weicheng) wrote several works on Christianity, including *Da ke wen* (A dialogue on Christianity) and *Zhengshi lüeshuo* (A summary account of saving the world). See Fang Hao, *Zhongguo Tianzhujiao shi* 1, pp. 91-98; and idem, *Fang Hao liushi zidinggao,* pp. 227-233.

32. Antonius de Gouvea, *Asia Extrema* (1644), cited in Fang Hao, *Zhongguo Tianzhujiao shi* 2, p. 29; and idem, *Fang Hao liushi zidinggao,* p. 228.

33. Dehergne, *Répertoire,* p. 76.

34. Brunner, *L'euchologe,* pp. 36-37.

35. Pfister, *Notices biographiques,* p. 108. Cf. Fang Hao, who traces the founding of a seminary in Hangzhou to the efforts of Fr. Aleni in the 1620s in the article "Shiqi shiji shi de Hangzhou xiuyuan shiye" (The operation of educational academies during the seventeenth century in Hangzhou), *Wocun zazhi* 4 (9) (1936): 538.

36. Dehergne, *Répertoire,* p. 95.

37. Ibid., p. 218.

38. D. E. Mungello, *Curious Land: Jesuit Accommodation and the Origins of Sinology* (Stuttgart, 1985), p. 138.

39. Xu Zongze has reinforced this impression of Martini's extensive travels by saying that he traveled "to each of the provinces, to Beijing and to the Great Wall" during the years 1644-1645 (*Ming-Qing jian Yesuhuishi yizhu,* p. 384). Ma Yong later disputed Fr. Xu's claim on the grounds that, with the Manchu conquest creating chaos in northern China during 1644-1645, Martini would have been unable to have traveled extensively in northern China during that time. See Ma Yong, "Jindai Ouzhou Hanxuejia de xianqu Maerdini" (Martini—pioneer of modern European sinolo-

gy), *Lishi yanjiu* 6 (1980): 157. Ma further states that during the period 1644–1645 the Manchu armies were attacking Nanjing and Martini was trying to evade them by returning from Nanjing to Hangzhou. G. Melis claims that Martini visited seven of the fifteen provinces of Ming China, namely, Beizhili, Shandong, Nanjing, Zhejiang, Fujian, Jiangxi, and Guangdong. See G. Melis, "Martino Martini's Travels in China," p. 431.

40. Dehergne, *Répertoire,* p. 166.

41. For information on Martini's itineraries, see G. Melis, "Martino Martini's Travels in China," pp. 421–444.

42. The fall of Beijing to the Manchus is treated in detail in Frederic Wakeman, Jr., *The Great Enterprise,* 2 vols. (Berkeley, 1985), 1, pp. 225–318.

43. Martini, *Novus atlas Sinensis,* p. 133. The phrases quoted are from Martini's *Atlas,* as translated in Melis' "Martino Martini's Travels in China," pp. 434–439.

44. Martini, *Atlas,* p. 136, cited in Melis, "Travels," p. 435.

45. Martini, *Atlas,* p. 136, cited in Melis, "Travels," p. 435.

46. Martini, *Atlas,* p. 91, cited in Melis, "Travels," p. 436.

47. Martini, *Atlas*, p. 92.

48. Ibid.

49. Ibid., p. 94, cited in Melis, "Travels," p. 437.

50. Martini, *Atlas,* pp. 32, 98.

51. Ibid., p. 103.

52. Ibid., p. 106.

53. Martini, *Atlas,* p. 106, cited in Melis, "Travels," p. 438.

54. Martini, *Atlas,* p. 101.

55. Several of these heroic activities attributed to Martini have been questioned, in particular by the Chinese scholar Ma Yong in his article "Jindai Ouzhou Hanxuejia de xiaqu Maerdini," p. 159.

56. Melis, "Travels," p. 427.

57. Xie Guozhen, *Nan Ming shilüe* (A brief history of the Southern Ming) (Shanghai, 1957), pp. 88–91.

58. Melis, "Travels," pp. 429–430; Ma Yong, "Jindai Ouzhou Hanxuejia," p. 159.

59. Martini's encounter with the Manchus in Wenzhou is summarized in D. E. Mungello, *Curious Land,* pp. 106–107. The account did not appear in the first edition of *De bello Tartarico historia* (Antwerp, 1654) nor in the French translation of that edition (Paris, 1654). J. J. L. Duyvendak in his article "Early Chinese Studies in Holland," p. 328n, surmises that Jacobus Golius of Leiden persuaded Martini to insert the account into *De bello Tartarico historia.* The account did appear in a later Latin edition (Amsterdam, 1655), pp. 126–128, and in the Latin edition appended to Martini's *Atlas.*

60. Sebes, "Martino Martini's Role in the Controversy of the Chinese Rites," in *Martino Martini, Geografo, Cartografo, Storico, Teologo,* pp. 477–478.

61. Melis, "Travels," p. 432.

62. See Melis' chronology of Martini's travels between Europe and China in *Martino Martini, Geografo, Cartografo, Storico, Teologo,* p. 569. Martini's journey throughout Europe from 1653 to 1657 is described in Mungello, *Curious Land,* pp. 108–109.

63. Fang Hao, *Zhongguo Tianzhujiao shi* 2, pp. 118–119; Pfister, *Notices biographiques,* p. 108.

64. Standaert, *Yang Tingyun,* pp. 66–68.

65. Fang Hao, *Zhongguo Tianzhujiao shi* 2, pp. 117–118; Standaert, *Yang Tingyun,* p. 103; Moule, *Quinsai,* p. 15.

66. Pamela Crossley, "The Tong in Two Worlds: Cultural Identities in Liaodong and Nurgan during the 13th–17th Centuries," *Ch'ing-shih Wen-t'i* 4 (9) (1983): 40–41.

67. Hummel, *Eminent Chinese,* pp. 792–794, 797.

68. Gertraude Roth, "The Manchu-Chinese Relationship, 1618–1636," in *From Ming to Ch'ing: Conquest, Region, and Continuity in Seventeenth-Century China,* edited by Jonathan D. Spence and John E. Wills, Jr. (New Haven, 1979), p. 13.

69. Hummel, *Eminent Chinese,* p. 797.

70. Fang Hao, *Zhongguo Tianzhujiao shi* 2, pp. 49; Hummel, *Eminent Chinese,* pp. 792–797.

71. Fang Hao, *Zhongguo Tianzhujiao shi* 2, pp. 49–50.

72. Ibid., p. 50.

73. Joseph Dehergne, S.J., "Les chrétientés de Chine de la période Ming (1581–1650)," *Monumenta Serica* 16 (1957): 15.

74. Fr. Fang claims that the church that Martini built was just west of the Tianshui Bridge (*Zhongguo Tianzhujiao shi* 2, p. 117). However, Fr. Dehergne located a list of churches in China from ca. 1664 in manuscript 640 of the Chinese library of Zikawei that places this church south of the Tianshui Bridge and just inside Beiguan Gate. See Dehergne, "Les chrétientés de Chine," pp. 117, 118.

75. Fang, *Zhongguo Tianzhujiao shi* 2, p. 115; Pfister, *Notices biographiques,* p. 259.

76. Fang, *Zhongguo Tianzhujiao shi* 2, p. 50.

77. This account of Martini's death was recorded by Fr. P. Couplet in a letter dated 26 April 1684 at Paris written to the Berlin court physician and proto-Sinologist Christian Mentzel. The letter is preserved as manuscript no. 299 of the Hunter Collection in the Special Collections Department of the Glasgow University Library. The proto-Sinologist T. S. Bayer reproduced this passage from Couplet's letter in the preface to his *Museum*

Sinicum (St. Petersburg, 1730). This preface has been translated by K. Lundbæk in *T. S. Bayer (1694-1738), Pioneer Sinologist* (London, 1986), pp. 54-55.

78. Pfister, *Notices biographiques,* p. 259; Dehergne, "Les chrétientés de Chine," p. 18; Fang, *Zhongguo Tianzhujiao shi* 2, p. 116.

79. *Litterae Annuae 1678-1679,* Archivum Romanum Societatis Iesu (ARSI), Jap. Sin. 117, f. 171r; Joseph Dehergne, S.J., "La Chine centrale vers 1700," 2, "Les vicariats apostoliques de la côte. Étude de géographie missionnaire," *Archivum Historicum Societatis Iesu* 30 (1961): 313.

80. Dehergne, "La Chine centrale vers 1700," 2, pp. 313, 314. The name Zhaoshi tang (Church of Serving [God] Openly) was also sometimes used for this Hangzhou church, but Pelliot believed this was a generic name applied to many Christian churches. See P. Pelliot, "Une liasse d'anciens imprimés chinois des Jésuites retrouvée à Upsal," *Toung Pao* 29 (1932): 115-116.

81. Charles le Gobien, S.J., *Histoire de l'édit de l'empereur de la Chine, en faveur de la Religion Chrestienne* (Paris, 1698), p. 65.

82. For this and the information that follows, I am indebted to T. Kaori Kitao of Swarthmore College, the art historian, who kindly responded to my written inquiries.

83. The Gesù was probably adopted from the earliest facade of this type, which was the Santa Maria Novella (1456) in Florence built by Leon Battista Alberti. See Leonard von Matt and Franco Barelli, *Rom, Kunst und Kultur der 'Ewigen Stadt' in mehr als 1000 Bildern* (Cologne, 1977), pp. 270-271.

84. Nikolaus Presver, *An Outline of European Architecture,* 7th edition (Middlesex, England, 1963), pp. 232-237.

85. Much of the information that follows is drawn from a detailed late seventeenth-century description of the Hangzhou church in Father le Gobien's *Histoire,* pp. 65-68. Le Gobien, who never traveled to China, notes (pp. 96-97) that his description of the Church of the Savior is based upon the eyewitness account of the Jesuit Father Claude de Visdelou (Liu Ying, 1656-1737). Fr. Visdelou first visited Hangzhou in 1687, soon after arriving in China at the port of Ningbo. Although the interior decoration of the Hangzhou church was completed by then, it is unclear whether his eyewitness account was based on his visit in 1687 or a later visit. It is known that he was in nearby Suzhou in 1691 and perhaps visited Hangzhou again at that time.

86. Le Gobien, *Histoire,* p. 65.

87. The women's chapel, usually called the *Templum Beatae Virginis* (Chapel of the Blessed Virgin), is referred to in the letter from Fr. A. Thomas dated 7 October 1685, ARSI, Jap. Sin. 150, f. 102r-102v, and in *Litterae Annuae 1680,* ARSI, Jap. Sin. 116, f. 269v. The women's chapel is

also referred to as the church of *Virginis Dei* (Virgin of God) in the *Litterae Annuae 1678–1679*, ARSI, Jap. Sin. 117, f. 171r. In addition, Fr. le Gobien states that the women's church was dedicated to the Holy Virgin (*Histoire*, p. 70). The dormitory and library of this college are mentioned in the Chinese biography of Intorcetta, "Taixi Yin Juesi xiansheng xinglüe" (A biography of Master Intorcetta from the Far West), pp. 5b–6a. The manuscript of this unpublished work is preserved in the Bibliothèque nationale, Paris (ms. chinois 1096).

88. Fang Hao, "Shiqi shiji shi de Hangzhou xiuyuan shiye," p. 538.

89. A letter from Fr. A. Thomas dated at Hangzhou, 7 October 1685, refers to the Blessed Virgin Church being adjacent to the seminary. ARSI, Jap. Sin. 150, f. 102v.

90. Le Gobien, *Histoire*, pp. 70–71.

91. Martini's portraits are preserved in the Museo Provinciale d'Arte in the Buonconsiglio Castle of Trent. The seventeenth-century portrait measures 91.5 cm. × 66 cm. and the eighteenth-century portrait 30 cm. × 23.5 cm. Color reproductions of these oil paintings may be found in Melis, ed., *Martino Martini, Geografo, Cartografo, Storico, Teologo*, pp. 582–583.

92. In this imaginative reconstruction, Zhang's initial glimpse of Martini at the construction site of the Church of the Savior (Hangzhou) in 1661 is hypothetical, although Martini's role in the construction was as much a fact as the neighbors' fears about the baleful geomantic effects of the construction.

CHAPTER 2

1. In this imaginative reconstruction, Zhang's visit to the Jesuit cemetery at Dafangjing to attend the reinterment ceremony of Martini is hypothetical, although the ceremony did occur in April of 1679.

2. The information about Intorcetta's fraternal rank in his family and the tensions that his call to the priesthood created with his two older brothers with regard to his filial obligations is taken from an anonymous thirteen-page (6½ double Chinese pages) Chinese biography of Intorcetta entitled "Taixi Yin Juesi xiansheng xinglüe" (hereafter cited as TYJXX), Bibliothèque nationale, Paris, ms. chinois 1096.

3. Fr. Francesco Intorcetta was also a Jesuit. Both of P. Intorcetta's brothers had died by 1683. See Intorcetta's letter to his brother Francesco, in Carmelo Capizzi, "La decorazione pittorica di una chiesa in China nella seconda metà del seicento. Una littera inedita del P. Prospero Intorcetta S.I.," *Studi e ricerche sull'Oriente cristiano* 12 (1989): 16.

4. TYJXX, p. 1a.

5. TYJXX, p. 1b.

6. Abel Rémusat, *Nouveaux mélanges asiatiques*, 2 vols. (Paris, 1829), 2, p.

229; Carlos Sommervogel, S.J., *Bibliothèque de la Compagnie de Jésus*, 12 vols. (Brussels and Paris, 1890-1932), 4, col. 640; Pfister, *Notices biographiques*, p. 321; Dehergne, *Répertoire*, p. 129.

7. Rémusat, *Mélanges* 2, p. 229, and Sommervogel, *Bibliothèque* 4, col. 640, claim that, in addition to Intorcetta and Martini, there were fifteen Jesuits in the group that accompanied Martini to China, but Pfister, *Notices bibliographiques*, p. 258 and Fang Hao, *Zhongguo Tianzhujiao shi* 2, p. 115, claim sixteen.

8. Robert Streit, O.M.I., *Bibliotheca Missionum* (Freiburg, 1929), 5, p. 808.

9. A. da Silva Rego, "Patronato Real," *New Catholic Encyclopedia* 10, p. 1114.

10. Pfister, *Notices bibliographiques*, p. 258. Intorcetta's Chinese biography claims that nine out of a group of ten died on this journey, but we know of at least two who survived—Martini and Intorcetta himself.

11. TYJXX, p. 1b.

12. TYJXX, p. 2a; Pfister, *Notices bibliographiques*, p. 321.

13. C. R. Boxer, "Some Sino-European Xylographic Works, 1662-1718," *Journal of the Royal Asiatic Society (of Great Britain and Ireland)*, 1947, pp. 199-202.

14. A detailed discussion of this collaborative Jesuit effort of translating the Confucian Four Books is presented in Mungello, *Curious Land*, pp. 247-299.

15. TYJXX, p. 2a.

16. TYJXX, p. 2b.

17. Intorcetta's role in producing the first European translation of the Four Books is discussed in two articles by Sicilian scholars: (1) Vincenzo di Giovanni, "In To Çe Kio-ssé ouvero il Primo Traduttore europeo di Confucio," *Archivo storico Siciliano* (Palermo), 1 (1873?): 35-48; and (2) Paolo Beonio-Brocchieri, "Prospero Intorcetta," in *Scienziati siciliani gesuiti in Cina nel secolo XVII: Atti del convegno a cura di alcide luini* (Palmero, 1983), pp. 171-182.

18. C. R. Boxer concludes that Paul was the printer of *Sinarum scientia politico-moralis* on the basis of a remark made in Domingo Fernandez Navarrete's *Controversias antiguas y modernas de la Mission de la Gran China* (Madrid, 1679), p. 61 (Boxer, "Some Sino-European Xylographic Works, 1662-1718," p. 199).

19. TYJXX, p. 2b; R. Streit, *Bibliotheca Missionum* 5, p. 836.

20. Domingo Fernandez Navarrete, *Tratados historicos, politicos, ethicos, y religiosos de la monarchia de China* (Madrid, 1676). For a detailed treatment of Fr. Navarette's role at the Canton meeting, see J. S. Cummins, *A question of Rites: Friar Domingo Navarrete and the Jesuits in China* (Aldershot, England, 1993), p. 142-214.

21. Pfister, *Notices bibliographiques,* p. 322; Dehergne, "Les chrétientés de Chine," p. 129.

22. TYJXX, pp. 2b–3a.

23. TYJXX, p. 3a.

24. TYJXX, pp. 3a–3b.

25. Litterae Annuae Vice Provinciae Sinicae, 1677–1680. ARSI, Jap. Sin. 116, f. 240v.

26. TYJXX, p. 3b; Pfister, *Notices bibliographiques,* p. 323. Fang Hao claims that the seminary had already been established by Fr. M. Dias (the junior). See Fr. Fang's article "Shiqi shiji shi de Hangzhou xiuyuan shiye," pp. 537–538.

27. TYJXX, pp. 3b–4a.

28. P. Intorcetta, *Compendiosa narratio de statu Missionis Chinensis, 1581–1669* (Rome, 1672), 16 pp. The original manuscript was composed in Italian. This *Compendiosa narrazione dello stato della Missione Cinese, 1581–1669,* was dedicated to the cardinals of Sacrae Congregationis de Propaganda Fide in April of 1671 and is preserved in the Biblioteca Nazionale di Napoli, ms. 9.

29. In addition to the translations of two of the Four Books, Intorcetta may also have carried to Europe at this time an introduction that, after considerable revision, eventually was published as the first part of the "Proëmialis Declaratio" of *Confucius Sinarum philosophus.* See K. Lundbæk, "The First European Translations of Chinese Historical and Philosophical Works," in *China and Europe,* edited by Thomas H. C. Lee (Hong Kong, 1991), p. 38. Mr. Lundbæk believes that Intorcetta was the author of the "Essay on the Chinese Script," which was originally part of the introductory materials in manuscript to *Confucius Sinarum philosophus* but which was omitted from the published work. See K. Lundbæk, *The Traditional History of the Chinese Script, from a Seventeenth Century Jesuit Manuscript* (Aarhus, 1988), pp. 42–45. The seventeen pages of this manuscript are reproduced in facsimile in this work.

30. Pfister, *Notices bibliographiques,* p. 326. The *Yesuhui lie* (Rules of the Society of Jesus), attributed to Intorcetta, is preserved in two *juan* of thirty-six and fifty-four double leaves. The manuscript is written on Chinese draft paper with intersecting horizontal and vertical lines that create boxes for individual characters. Each sheet consists of 450 boxes divided into eighteen horizontal and twenty-five vertical boxes; many of the sheets are nearly filled with characters. The manuscript is preserved in the Bibliothèque nationale, Paris, as ms. chinois 7445.

31. "Excerpta ex responsione P. Prosperi Intorcetta ad P. Navarrete (Ord. S. Domin.)," 68 pages, Fonds Brothier 104, ff. 39–72, since 1990 preserved in the Archives françaises de la Compagnie de Jesus, Vanves, France.

32. Sommervogel, *Bibliothèque* 4, col. 640; Pfister, *Notices bibliographiques,* p. 323.

33. Pfister, *Notices bibliographiques,* p. 323; Dehergne, *Répertoire,* p. 129. I note that Fr. Dehergne does not include Intorcetta among his list of "Visitors of Japan and of China" found in the appendix of his *Répertoire,* pp. 321–323, even though he clearly states on p. 129 that Intorcetta was visitor during the years 1676–1684 and was "again named visitor" *(de nouveau nommé visiteur)* on 10 January 1698 by Rome.

34. See Evelyn Sakakida Rawski, *Education and Popular Literacy in Ch'ing China* (Ann Arbor, 1979).

35. Zhang Xingyao, *Shengjiao zanming* (Inscriptions in praise of the Sage Teaching [i.e. Christianity]), 36 inscriptions in an undated manuscript. Copy in the Bibliothèque nationale, Paris, ms. chinois 7067.

36. See the letter of Father Intorcetta to his brother, Father Francesco Intorcetta, dated 18 August 1683 at Hangzhou, ARSI, Jap. Sin. 163, f. 223r–224v. This letter has been published with annotations in Carmelo Capizzi, "Decorazione pittorica," 3–21.

37. Ibid., pp. 12, 19. Intorcetta measured these paintings in palm *(palma)* lengths, an inexact measurement equal to approximately 25 centimeters. The large painting measured 14 palms × 14 palms which is approximately equivalent to 3.5 × 3.5 meters.

38. Intorcetta's letter of 18 August 1683, in ibid., p. 21, and le Gobien, *Histoire,* p. 66.

39. Intorcetta's letter of 18 August 1683, in Capizzi, "Decorazione pittorica," p. 19.

40. Le Gobien, *Histoire,* p. 67.

41. Intorcetta's letter of 18 August 1683, in Capizzi, "Decorazione pittorica," p. 21.

42. Some of the best information on the Jesuit cemetery in Hangzhou (Dafangjing) has been supplied by the late Fr. Fang Hao, who was a native of Hangzhou. See his "Hangzhou Dafangjing Tianzhujiao gu mu zhi yan'ge" and his "Zhejiang Tianzhujiao lüeshi." Also see Xu Mingde, "Yidali Hanxuejia Wei Kuangguo mudi kao" (An investigation of the grave of the Italian sinologist Wei Kuangguo [M. Martini]), *Lishi yanjiu* 1981 (4): 183–187, revised as "Shiqi shiji Yidali Hanxuejia Wei Kuangguo mudi kao" (An investigation of the grave of the seventeenth-century Italian sinologist Wei Kuangguo), *Sino-Western Cultural Relations Journal* 11 (1989): 1–10.

43. Xu Mingde in his article "Shiqi," p. 4, explains the origin of the name Fangjingnan by saying that the cemetery lay southeast *(nan)* of the spring *(fangjing).* Cf. Fang Hao, "Hangzhou Dafangjing," p. 1940.

44. Fang Hao, "Hangzhou Dafangjing" (1969) p. 1940; Xu Mingde, "Shiqi," p. 4.

45. Fang Hao, "Hangzhou Dafangjing" (1969), p. 1940.

46. Xu Mingde, "Shiqi," p. 5.

47. Hanghui gonglu (road) is also known as Hangyu gonglu. See ibid., p. 4.

48. Joseph Needham, *Science and Civilisation in China*, 7 volumes in progress (Cambridge, England, 1954-), 4, part 1, p. 244.

49. The vegetation of Dafangjing has not always been well cared for. In or shortly before 1936 Fr. Fang visited the cemetery and noted the jungle-like conditions. See his "Hangzhou Dafangjing," p. 1940.

50. No fence is mentioned by a visitor to the Dafangjing cemetery in 1890. See G. E. Moule, "A Roman Catholic Cemetery near Hangzhou," *The Chinese Recorder* 21 (11) (November 1890): 509-512.

51. The Dafangjing church is referred to as a "chapel" *(Sacellum)* in the 1680 *Litterae Annuae*, ARSI, Jap. Sin. 116, f. 269v. It is called the "new Temple of the Savior" *(novum Salvatoris Templum)* in the 1678-1679 *Litterae Annuae*, ARSI, Jap. Sin. 117, f. 171r.

52. The Jesuit *Litterae Annuae* of 1680, ARSI, Jap. Sin. 116, f. 269v, states that it was a "chapel together with a sepulcher" *(Sacellum iuxta sepulturam)*.

53. One European example of such a modest chapel with crypt below the altar in dimensions similar to the Dafangjing chapel would be the Chapel of Pope Leo X (ca. 1514) in Rome, whose facade was designed by Michelangelo. (I am indebted for this information to T. Kaori Kitao.) The lateral dimensions of this Roman chapel are approximately three meters in height and approximately five meters in width. These dimensions are only slightly smaller than those of the Dafangjing chapel.

54. David S. Nivison, "Aspects of Traditional Chinese Biography," *Journal of Asian Studies* 21 (1962): 459.

55. The inscriptions on the two stele that list the names of nine Jesuits buried within the chapel are reproduced in Xu Mingde, "Shiqi," pp. 5-7.

56. I was unable to gain access to the interior of the Dafangjing chapel, and so my description of the interior is drawn from published accounts. Fang, in "Hangzhou Dafangjing" (p. 1940), gives the lateral dimensions of the square chapel as two *zhang* (twenty-three and one-half feet or slightly more than seven meters). A *zhang* is a traditional Chinese measurement that varied slightly by region but generally contained eleven and three-fourths feet or slightly more than three and one-half meters. Xu in his article "Shiqi," p. 5, repeats Fr. Fang's measurement and adds that the total surface area of the Dafangjing chapel would be approximately forty square meters.

57. G. E. Moule, "Cemetery," p. 510.

58. Fang Hao, "Hangzhou Dafangjing" (1969), pp. 1940, 1944.

59. Ibid., p. 1945.

60. D. G. Mirams, *A Brief History of Chinese Architecture* (Shanghai, 1940), pp. 86–89.

61. Liang Ssu-ch'ang, *A Pictorial History of Chinese Architecture*, edited by Wilma Fairbank (Cambridge, Mass., 1984), pp. 191–192; Michèle Pirazzoli-t'Serstevens, *Living Architecture in Chinese*, translated by Robert Allen (New York, 1971), plate 126.

62. Nivison, "Biography," p. 459. The stone inscribed with Martini's name at Dafangjing lacks the brief laudatory biography and formal poem in praise of the deceased that were typical of the *shendao bei*, but biographical information on Martini is included on one of the tablets in front of the chapel.

63. James L. Watson, ed., *Death Ritual in Late Imperial and Modern China* (Berkeley, 1988), pp. 14–15.

64. See Needham, *Science and Civilisation*, 2, pp. 139–154; 5, part 3, pp. 8–11 et passim.

65. Ibid., 5, part 3, p. 206.

66. Ibid., pp. 224–229.

67. Litterae Annuae 1678–1679, ARSI, Jap. Sin. 117, f. 170r–171v.

68. Fang Hao, *Zhongguo Tianzhujiao shi* 2, p. 116.

69. Ibid., pp. 116–117.

70. *Litterae Annuae* 1678–1679, ARSI, Jap. Sin. 117, f. 170v.

71. Fang Hao, *Zhongguo Tianzhujiao shi* 2, pp. 135–136, states only that the three brothers were "deeply superstitious" *(mixin ji shen)*.

72. TYJXX, p. 4a; Lo-shu Fu, *A Documentary Chronicle of Sino-Western Relations (1644–1820)*, p. 93.

73. John W. Witek, S.J., *Controversial Ideas in China and in Europe: A Biography of Jean-François Foucquet, S.J. (1665–1741)* (Rome, 1982), pp. 41–46.

74. Jonathan D. Spence, *Ts'ao Yin and the K'ang-hsi Emperor* (New Haven, 1966), pp. 134–138.

75. Ibid., p. 124.

76. Ibid., pp. 137–138.

77. The Kangxi emperor's visit to Hangzhou is recorded in *Qing shi biannian* (The annals of Qing history), edited by Lin Fujun and Shi Song, 3 volumes (Beijing, 1988), 2, pp. 581–582.

78. The record of Intorcetta's first encounter with the Kangxi emperor is found in *Xichao dingan* and is reproduced in Fang Hao, *Zhongguo Tianzhujiao shi* 2, pp. 136–139.

79. TYJXX, p. 4b.

80. Zhao Chang is also referred to as Pursama and Parsama. See Antonio Sisto Rosso, O.F.M., *Apostolic Legations to China of the Eighteenth Century* (South Pasadena, 1948), p. 161.

81. For the important role that Zhao Chang played as an imperial mes-

senger, see J. S. Sebes, S.J., *The Jesuits and the Sino-Russian Treaty of Nerchinsk* (Rome, 1961), pp. 177, 299.

82. TYJXX, p. 4b.

83. Fang Hao, *Zhongguo Tianzhujiao shi* 2, p. 138.

84. Ibid., pp. 138–139.

85. TYJXX, p. 4b.

86. Dehergne, "La Chine centrale vers 1700," p. 313.

87. This petition (recorded in *Xichao dingan*) and consequent responses leading up to the Toleration Edict of 1692 were inscribed on a stele that was erected in the front courtyard of the Nantang (South Church) in Beijing. The Chinese text of this stele and a French translation appear in the article by Willem A. Grootaers, C.I.C.M., "Les deux steles de l'église du Nant'ang à Pekin," *Neue Zeitschrift für Missionswissenschaft* 6 (1950): 246–255 plus Chinese text.

88. Dehergne, "La Chine centrale vers 1700," p. 307.

89. Songgotu is referred to as "Sosan" (third son) in Jesuit accounts. He was a member of the Manchu Plain Yellow Banner. See his biography by Fang Chao-ying in Hummel, *Eminent Chinese,* pp. 663–666. Songgotu's important role in helping to secure the Toleration Edict of 1692 is described in John W. Witek, S.J., "Understanding the Chinese: A Comparison of Matteo Ricci and the French Jesuit Mathematicians Sent by Louis XIV," in *East Meets West: The Jesuits in China, 1582–1773,* edited by Charles E. Ronan, S.J., and Bonnie B. C. Oh (Chicago, 1988), pp. 89–93.

90. Rosso, *Apostolic Legations,* p. 128.

91. Ibid., pp. 128–129.

92. Hummel, *Eminent Chinese,* p. 271.

93. Fang Hao, *Zhongguo Tianzhujiao shi* 2, p. 139; Hummel, *Eminent Chinese,* p. 271.

94. Fang Hao, *Zhongguo Tianzhujiao shi* 2, p. 140; Charles O. Hucker, *A Dictionary of Official Titles in Imperial China* (Stanford, 1985), p. 346.

95. An English translation of this memorial appears in A. H. Rowbotham, *Missionary and Mandarin: The Jesuits at the Court of China* (Berkeley, 1942), p. 110.

96. K. S. Latourette, *A History of Christian Missions in China* (London, 1929), pp. 126–127.

97. Rowbotham, *Missionary and Mandarin,* p. 111.

98. L. C. Arlington, *In Search of Old Peking* (Beiping, 1935), p. 45.

99. Fang Hao, *Zhongguo Tianzhujiao shi* 2, p. 141.

100. *Zhengjiao fengbao,* quoted in ibid., p. 141.

101. TYJXX, p. 5b. The Changchunyuan (Palace of Eternal Spring) was located outside of Xizhi Gate in the village of Haidian. See Fu Lo-shu, *Documentary Chronicle,* pp. 112, 483 n. 334.

102. Fang Hao, *Zhongguo Tianzhujiao shi* 2, p. 142.
103. Ibid., p. 136.
104. TYJXX, pp. 5b-6a.
105. TYJXX, p. 6b.
106. TYJXX, p. 7a.
107. In this imaginative reconstruction, the description of Father Intorcetta baptizing the foundlings who had been gathered from the streets by catechists is hypothetical insofar as it applied to Hangzhou. However, the Jesuit Father F. Nöel did describe such a practice as occurring in Beijing in a letter of 1703. See *Der Neue Welt-Bott* (number 83), 1 (4), p. 17. This letter was originally published in the Jesuit collection *Lettres édifiantes et curieuses* (Paris, 1706), 6, 68f.

CHAPTER 3

1. In this imaginative reconstruction, the description of Zhang's decision to be baptized is hypothetical, although the circumstantial evidence is that Father Intorcetta performed the baptism, which occurred in 1678.

2. The entry for Zhang Xingyao in the most commonly consulted biographical dictionary for premodern China, the *Zhongguo renming dacidian* (Shanghai, 1921), p. 944, confuses Zhang Xingyao with an almost exact contemporary (*zi:* Zizhao) whose name *(xing* and *ming)* differs only slightly in the third character *yao.* These two slightly variant forms of *yao* (see the glossary for the distinction between *yao*[1] for our Zhang and *yao*[2] for the other Zhang) are often treated as interchangeable. The *Zhongguo renming dacidian* uses this variant form of yao to unknowingly give the name for the other Zhang, but lists the hometown (Qiantang district) of our Zhang. It goes on to list an additional *ming* (personal name) Taigui and *zi* (style) Dizhong for the other Zhang. The encyclopedic dictionary *Zhongwen dacidian* (Taipei, 1962-1968), no. 10026.674, duplicates this confusion.

Actually, the other Zhang Xingyao (*zi:* Zizhao) was from Wuqiang district in the northeastern part of former Zhili province (present-day Hebei province), which contained Beijing. The biography for the other Zhang is correctly given in the *Da Qing jifu xianzhe zhuan*, edited by Xu Zhichang (Tianjin, date?), 10/30/26a-26b, and in the local history *Wuqiang-xian xinshi* 8, p. 401. He was the son of a regional defense commander and was selected in 1658 as a graduate for preeminence *(bagong)*, one of one or two students selected every twelfth year from each literati school throughout the realm to be sent to the capital. As perhaps the eldest son of a prominent family, this other Zhang appears to have bypassed the official examinations, although his brother Zhang Xingfa attained the *juren* degree in 1701 and his brother Zhang Xinwei attained the highest degree of *jinshi* in 1703. At Beijing Zhang was admitted to the National University (Taixue), administered by the Imperial Academy (Guozi jian), where he was trained in the techniques of research and editing. He then became one of twenty or more drafters for the Grand Secretariat (Neige), a post that carried the official rank of 7b. See Charles O. Hucker, *A Dictionary of Official Titles in Imperial China* (Stanford, 1985), no. 1618 (pp. 193–194) and no. 4193 (p. 346).

By some irony, this other Zhang was appointed prefect of the city of Ningbo (rank 4a) in Zhejiang province, nearly two hundred miles (three hundred and twenty kilometers) east of Hangzhou where our Zhang lived. As prefect, he was noted for his judicious distribution of rice to relieve the people in the aftermath of a flood in 1690 and also for measures to counter a drought and famine in 1693. It was his service in Ningbo that enabled him to receive an entry in the *Zhejiang tongzhi* (Zhejiang province gazetteer), a mark of status not accorded to our Zhang. Given the proximity of Ningbo to Hangzhou, it is likely that our Zhang knew of this other Zhang. The other Zhang is said to have sacrificed to his ancestors in his family village in 1706, and so his lifespan closely paralleled that of our Zhang, who died shortly after 1715.

3. Fang Hao, *Zhongguo Tianzhujiao shi* 2, p. 103.

4. A family history entitled *Jiaxue yuanliu* says that Zhang Fuyan was exposed to the teaching of a Yang Yiyuan (see ibid.). Fang Hao suggests that this Yiyuan could be another form of Yang Tingyun's pen name Qiyuan. However, this suggestion has not been confirmed by Mr. Standaert, the leading contemporary scholar on Yang Tingyun. Although the chronology would have allowed for such contact, we cannot be certain that Zhang Xingyao's father had contact with Yang Tingyun.

5. *Jiaxue yuanliu,* cited in ibid.

6. Ibid., pp. 100, 103.

7. Ibid., p. 103.

8. Zhang Xingyao, *Tianjiao mingbian* (TJMB), preface, reprinted in Xu Zongze, *Ming-Qing jian Yesuhuishi yizhu,* p. 123. Also see Fang Hao, *Fang Hao liushi zidinggao,* p. 233.

9. Zhang Xingyao, *Tianzhujiao Rujiao tongyi kao* 1, p. 1b. (This work will be cited hereafter as TRTYK, based on the abbreviated version of the title, *Tian Ru tongyi kao.*) There are several versions in manuscript of this work, and they reveal slight variations. Extant copies are preserved in the Xujiahui (Zikawei) Library, Shanghai, and in the Bibliothèque nationale, Paris, Département des manuscrits orientaux (ms. chinois 7171). The TRTYK is divided into three parts, whose differences indicate that the parts were, to a certain extent, written separately. A comparison of the manuscripts in Shanghai and Paris reveals that part 1 *(Tianjiao he Ru)* has three prefaces (1672 [Shanghai], 1702 [Paris], and 1715 [Shanghai and Paris]). Of the three parts, part 1 appears to have evolved over the longest period. Part 2 *(Tianjiao bu Ru)* has one preface, written in or shortly after 1705 (Shanghai

and Paris), whereas part 3 *(Tianjiao chao Ru)* contains one undated preface (Shanghai and Paris). A discovery of other manuscript versions could reveal additional prefaces and further information about the long evolution of this work. A copy of the TRTYK was also found by Feng Zanzhang in 1947 in the Beitang Library, though I have been unable to ascertain if this copy is still extant because the Beitang collection remains sealed off within the National Library of China (Zhongguo guojia tushuguan) in Beijing. See Feng Zanzhang, "Beiping Beitang tushuguan zanbian Zhongwen shanben shu mu (si): yibian gongjiao shanben shu mu," *Shangzhi bianyiguan guankan* 2 (4–5) (1947): 365. Feng lists the TRTYK under the classification number 1910 and notes that the work consists of a manuscript of seventy-six leaves bound in one volume. Unless otherwise noted, all consequent note references refer to the Xujiahui version.

10. Litterae Annuae Vice Provinciae Sinensis Anni 1678–1679, ARSI, Jap. Sin. 117, f. 170r.

11. T'ung-tsu Ch'u, *Local Government in China under the Ch'ing* (Cambridge, Mass., 1962), p. 18.

12. TJMB, preface, reprinted in Xu Zongze, *Ming-Qing jian Yesuhuishi yizhu,* p. 123.

13. Ping-ti Ho, *The Ladder of Success in Imperial China* (New York, 1962), p. xi.

14. Lynn A. Struve, "Ambivalence and Action: Some Frustrated Scholars of the K'ang-hsi Period," in *From Ming to Ch'ing* (New Haven, 1979), p. 342.

15. Ibid., p. 324f.

16. TRTYK 2, pp. 28a–28b.

17. Many of the *Litterae Annuae* are preserved in the Jesuit Archives in Rome. The most extensive list of the *Litterae Annuae* from China is found in the two-part article by J. Dehergne, S.J., entitled "Les Lettres annuelles des missions jésuites de Chine au temps de Ming (1581–1644)," *Archivum Historicum Societatis Iesu* 49 (1980): 379–392; and "Lettres annuelles et sources complémentaires des missions jésuites de Chine (suite)," *Archivum Historicum Societatis Iesu* 51 (1982): 247–284. A useful introduction to Jesuit sources on China is found in P. A. Rule's article "Jesuit Sources," in *Essays on the Sources for Chinese History,* edited by D. D. Leslie et al. (Columbia, South Carolina, 1975), pp. 176–187. An excellent description of the Jesuit *Litterae Annuae* is found in N. Standaert's *Yang Tingyun,* pp. 74–76. Also see M. H. Rienstra, ed., *Jesuit Letters from China, 1583–1584* (Minneapolis, 1986).

18. *Litterae Annuae V. Provinciae Sinensis Anni 1678–1679.* ARSI, Jap. Sin. 117, f. 161r–182r, 182r–198r.

19. *Qiantang-xian zhi* (first edition 1609; 1718 edition) in 36 *juan; Hangzhou-fu zhi,* originally compiled by Shao Jinhan (1784), reedited by Gong Jiajun in 178 *juan* (1922).

20. Frederick D. Cloud, *Hangchow, the "City of Heaven"* (Shanghai, 1906; reprinted Taipei, 1971), p. 8.

21. Nancy Lee Swann, "Seven Intimate Library Owners," *Harvard Journal of Asiatic Studies* 1 (1936): 389.

22. A photograph of the old Qiantang Gate and city wall is found in Cloud, *Hangchow,* facing page 1, and is reproduced in fig. 15.

23. *Litterae Annuae,* ARSI, Jap. Sin. 117, f. 171v.

24. Ibid., f. 170r.

25. TRTYK, 1, p. 4a et passim.

26. Confucius' statement appears in *Lunyu* VII.1: "I have 'transmitted what was taught to me without making up anything of my own.' I have been faithful to and loved the Ancients" (*The Analects of Confucius,* translated by Arthur Waley [London, 1938], p. 123).

27. Zhang Xingyao and Hong Ji, *Pi lüeshuo tiao bo,* Bibliothèque nationale, Paris, ms. chinois 7107, f. 7b.

28. J. D. Young translates *xian Ru* as "original Confucianism." See his *Confucianism and Christianity, the First Encounter* (Hong Kong, 1983), pp. 28, 132n.

29. Li Madou [Ricci], *Tianzhu shiyi,* 2 *juan* (1603), 1, pp. 16b–22b. For the English translation of these passages, see M. Ricci, S.J., *The True Meaning of the Lord of Heaven,* translated by Douglas Lancashire and Peter Hu Kuo Chen, S.J., edited by E. J. Malatesta, S.J. (St. Louis, 1985), pp. 113–131. The *Tianzhu shiyi* was later reprinted in the famous collection of Christian literature edited by Li Zhizao *Tianxue chuhan,* 52 *juan* (1628; reprinted in Taipei, 1965, in 6 volumes), 1, pp. 351–635.

30. The term "Neo-Confucianism" had its first recorded appearance in the eighteenth century in the French form of *"neo-confuceens"* in volume 2 (1777) of *Mémoires concernant l'histoire . . . des Chinois, par les missionnaires de Pékin,* by the China missionary and Jesuit Jean-Joseph-Marie Amiot (Qian Deming, 1718–1793). See K. Lundbæk, "Notes sur l'image du néo-confucianisme dans la littérature européene du XVIIe à la fin du XIXe siècle," in *Actes du IIIe colloque international de sinologie de Chantilly* (Paris, 1983), pp. 131–176.

31. Standaert, *Yang Tingyun,* pp. 210–219.

32. Private correspondence from Mr. Lundbæk dated 11 September 1991.

33. See Mungello, "The Reconciliation of Neo-Confucianism with Christianity in the Writing of Joseph de Prémare, S.J.," *Philosophy East and West* 26 (1976): 389–410. Also see Knud Lundbæk, *Joseph de Prémare (1666–1736), S.J.: Chinese Philology and Figurism* (Aarhus, 1991).

34. TRTYK 1, p. 5a.

35. TRTYK 1, p. 5a.

36. TRTYK 1, p. 5b.

37. TRTYK 1, p. 1a.

38. The *geyi* method was discontinued with the arrival of the learned Buddhist monk Kumārajīva in China in 401 and with the increasing sophistication of the knowledge of Buddhism by Chinese translators. See K. K. S. Ch'en, *Buddhism in China* (Princeton, 1964), pp. 62-69. See also A. F. Wright, *Buddhism in Chinese History* (Stanford, 1959), pp. 37-38; and E. Zürcher, *The Buddhist Conquest of China* (Leiden, 1959), pp. 33-34, 184.

39. TRTYK 1, p. 1b.

40. Zhang Xingyao, *Tianjiao mingbian*, 1711 preface, reprinted in Xu Zongze, *Ming-Qing jian Yesuhuishi yizhu*, p. 123.

41. TRTYK 1, pp. 1b-2a.

42. See Standaert, *Yang Tingyun*, p. 53-60.

43. Fang Hao, *Fang Hao liushi zidinggao*, p. 233.

44. The mirror in Christianity is a very rich image. It was enriched by Christian borrowing from Platonism and Neoplatonism, which saw the mirror as a changeable likeness of eternity. Nicolas of Cusa believed that all creation was the mirror of God. In Christianity, a mirror signified truth, self-knowledge, and wisdom. See J. Bouvet, *Vorschlag einer wissenschaftlichen Akademie für China: Briefe des Chinamissionars J. Bouvet S.J. an G. W. Leibniz*, edited by Claudia von Collani (Stuttgart, 1989), pp. 49n-50n.

45. See the entry on *"Arkandisciplin"* in *Lexikon für Theologie und Kirche*, edited by Josef Höfer and Karl Rahner, 2d edition (Freiburg, 1986), 1, cols. 863-864. I am grateful to Ms. von Collani for bringing this entry to my attention.

46. The Jesuit account of the Passion of Christ was first written by the Spanish Jesuit Didace de Pantoja (Pang Diwo, 1571-1610), who was a companion of Ricci's in Beijing. Fr. Pantoja's Passion account *Pangzi yi quan* first appeared in 1608-1610 in Beijing. The Portuguese Jesuit M. Dias (the younger) slightly revised the Passion account for the prayerbook edition of 1628. The account is found in [*Tianzhu*] *Shengjiao rike* (1665 edition), Bibliothèque nationale, Paris, mss. chinois 7353-7354, coedited by Guo Zhujing (L. Cattaneo), Fei Qigui (G. Ferreira), Yang Manuo (Em. Diaz), Fu Fanji (F. Furtado), and Fei Lede (R. de Figueiredo); reviewed by Li Leisi (L. Buglio) and Nan Huairen (F. Verbiest), 3 *juan* (1665 edition), 3, pp. 1a-18a.

47. Harrie Vanderstappen, S.V.D., "Chinese Art and the Jesuits in Peking," in *East Meets West: The Jesuits in China, 1582-1773*, edited by Charles E. Ronan, S.J., and Bonnie B. C. Oh. (Chicago, 1988), p. 106.

48. Li Zubo et al., *Tianxue chuan'gai* (Beijing, 1664), pp. 4a-4b.

49. For a perceptive and balanced account of Yang Guangxian's attack on Christianity, see John D. Young, *Confucianism and Christianity, the First Encounter* (Hong Kong, 1983), pp. 77-96.

50. See Mungello, "Die Schrift T'ien-hsüeh ch'uan-kai als eine Zwischenformulierung der jesuitische Anpassungsmethode im 17. Jahrhundert," *China Mission Studies (1550-1800) Bulletin* 4 (1982): 24-39.

51. The three illustrations (numbers 28, 42, and 43 out of a collection of forty-eight) appear in Yang Guangxian, *Budeyi* (1965), reprinted in *Tianzhujiao dongchuan wenxian xubian,* edited by Wu Xiangxiang (Taipei, 1966), 3, 1136, 1138, and 1140.

52. Vanderstappen, "Art and the Jesuits," pp. 106–107.

53. Young, *Confucianism and Christianity,* p. 85.

54. Standaert, *Yang Tingyun,* pp. 142–143. In his *Tianzhu shiyi* 2, pp. 69a–69b, Ricci only briefly refers to Adam's corruption of human nature. His description is vague, and he avoids using the term "original sin" *(yuanzui).* An English translation of this passage may be found in Ricci, *The True Meaning of the Lord of Heaven,* p. 447.

55. TRTYK 3, pp. 6b–7a.

56. See Zhang Xingyao, *Shengjiao zanming,* Bibliothèque nationale, Paris, ms. chinois 7067, pp. 9a, 10a.

57. TRTYK 2, p. 33b.

58. TRTYK 3, p. 15b.

59. TRTYK 3, p. 20a

60. TRTYK 3, pp. 20a–20b.

61. TRTYK 3, p. 9a.

62. TRTYK 3, p. 16b.

63. Young, *Confucianism and Christianity,* pp. 102–103.

64. For the negative reaction of the powerful eunuch Ma Tang to the crucifix, see M. Ricci's *China in the Sixteenth Century: The Journals of Matthew Ricci,* edited by N. Trigault; translated by L. J. Gallagher (New York, 1953), p. 365. Also see J. D. Spence, *The Memory Palace of Matteo Ricci* (New York, 1984), pp. 246–247.

65. In this imaginative reconstruction, the description of Fr. Intorcetta's reaction is hypothetical but is based on an actual fire that occurred in 1692 as described in his Chinese biography, TYJXX, pp. 5b–6a.

CHAPTER 4

1. This imaginative reconstruction of Zhang's conversation with his old friend Ji Jiongfan in the summer of 1705 is based on a description by Zhang in his preface to part 2 of *Similarities* (TRTYK), pp. 1–2a.

2. The names of sixty-eight disciples who assisted Zhang in compiling his *History* are listed in an introductory section to that work. See Fang Hao, *Zhongguo Tianzhujiao shi* 2, p. 102.

3. Of the thirty-seven disciples in Zhejiang province, seven resided in Hangzhou, five in Renhe, fourteen in Qiantang, seven in Yuhang; and one each in Jiaxing, Haining, Cixi, and Pingyang. Many of the disciples had the comparatively rare surname of Min, including the Hangzhou native Min Pei (styled Mingke). This Min Pei may be identical to the Hangzhou gentleman styled Yu Cang who attained the highest official degree *(jinshi)*

at the time of the Kangxi emperor (reigned 1661–1722). Cf. Fang Hao, *Zhongguo Tianzhujiao shi* 2, p. 102; and *Zhongguo renming dacidian*, p. 1211.

4. Master Ding Yuntai (styled Lü'an) is mentioned in Fang Hao, *Zhongguo Tianzhujiao shi* 2, p. 100; and Xu Zongze, *Ming-Qing jian Yesuhuishi yizhu*, p. 121. His home village was in the Jiyang district, which was part of Ji'nan prefecture.

5. TRTYK 1, p. 2a. The full title of Zhang's *History* is *Tongjian jishi benmo buhoubian* (Supplements to the history of the *Comprehensive Mirror* topically arranged).

6. See the index of Chinese classical texts in the English translation of *Tianzhu shiyi:* Matteo Ricci, S.J., *The True Meaning of the Lord of Heaven*, pp. 483–485.

7. Zhu Xi more than anyone else was responsible for creating the category of the Four Books by grouping four separate works together and writing commentaries on them as follows: (1) *Daxue zhangju* (The Great Learning divided into chapters and sentences) (1189), (2) *Zhongyong zhangju* (The Doctrine of the Mean divided into chapters and sentences) (1189), (3) *Lunyu jizhu* (Collected commentary on the Analects) (1177), and (4) *Mengzi jizhu* (Collected commentary on the Mencius) (1177). Zhu Xi's grouping of these four books together under the title *Sishu jizhu* (Collected commentary on the Four Books) and his commentaries on them elevated them to classical status. This elevation was officially recognized in 1313, when the Four Books became the basis of the official examinations. They retained that status until the abolition of the examination system in 1905. See Wing-tsit Chan's article on the *Sishu zhangju jizhu* in *A Sung Bibliography (Bibliographie des Sung)*, edited by Yves Hervouet (Hong Kong, 1978), pp. 44–45.

8. See Mungello, *Curious Land*, pp. 261–271.

9. The *Shujing* and the *Shijing* have been translated with parallel Chinese-English texts by two different scholars. See James Legge, trans., *The Chinese Classics*, 5 vols. (Oxford, 1893), vol. 3 (The Shoo King or the Book of Historical Documents), and vol. 4 (The She King or Book of Poetry). Also see Bernard Karlgren, "The Book of Documents," *Bulletin of the Museum of Far Eastern Antiquities (BMFEA)* (Stockholm), 22 (1950): 1–81, with glosses in *BMFEA* 20 (1948): 39–315, and 21 (1949): 63–206; and *The Book of Odes: Chinese Text, Transcription and Translation* (Stockholm, 1950), originally published in *BMFEA* 16 (1944) and 17 (1945). The glosses appear in *BMFEA* 14 (1942): 71–247; 16 (1944): 55–169; and 18 (1946): 1–198. "Glosses on the Book of Odes" and "Glosses on the Book of Documents" have been reprinted as separate volumes by *BMFEA*. Legge's translation is based on the New Text *(Xinwen)* version of fifty chapters. (Legge subdivides four of these original chapters into three parts each to produce the fifty-eight chapter divisions found in his translation.) Karlgren's translation follows the Old Text *(Guwen)* version of twenty-eight chapters. The Old Text

version omits twenty-two of the New Text's fifty chapters on the now widely accepted grounds that they are forgeries dating from the third or fourth century A.D. See S. Durant's article on *Ching* (Classics) in the *Indiana Companion to Traditional Chinese Literature,* edited by W. H. Nienhauser, Jr. (Bloomington, 1986), pp. 311–312.

10. K. C. Chang, *Early Chinese Civilization* (New Haven, 1976), p. 151.

11. Nienhauser, *Indiana Companion,* p. 311.

12. J. R. Hightower, *Topics in Chinese Literature* (Cambridge, Mass., 1950), pp. 2–3; B. Watson, *Early Chinese Literature* (New York, 1962), pp. 21–23; Nienhauser, *Indiana Companion,* p. 311.

13. Wu-chi Liu, *An Introduction to Chinese Literature* (Bloomington, 1966), p. 11.

14. Watson, *Early Chinese Literature,* pp. 27–31.

15. In his *Similarities,* Zhang drew fifty-three citations from the forged chapters of the *Documents,* fifty citations from the authentic chapters, and three citations from chapters that I have been unable to trace.

16. Hightower, *Topics,* p. 3; Watson, *Early Chinese Literature,* p. 203; and Liu, *Introduction to Chinese Literature,* p. 11.

17. Nienhauser, *Indiana Companion,* p. 312.

18. TRTYK 1, pp. 6a–12b.

19. TRTYK 1, pp. 12b–15b.

20. TRTYK 1, pp. 19a–20b.

21. TRTYK 1, pp. 20b–21b, 24a–25b.

22. TRTYK 1, pp. 22b–23b.

23. TRTYK 1, pp. 26b–27b.

24. Hou Wailu et al., *Zhongguo sixiang tongshi* (A comprehensive intellectual history of China) (Beijing, 1960), vol. 4, part 2, pp. 1222–1223. Cf. Thomas H. C. Lee, "Christianity and Chinese Intellectuals: From the Chinese Point of View," in *China and Europe: Images and Influences in Sixteenth to Eighteenth Centuries,* edited by Thomas H. C. Lee (Hong Kong, 1991), pp. 5, 22.

25. In regard to part 1 of TRTYK, the preface of 1672 is found only in the Zikawei Library (Shanghai) manuscript, whereas the preface dated 1702 is found only in the Bibliothèque nationale (Paris) manuscript. The 1715 preface is found in both of these manuscripts.

26. The preface to part 2 of TRTYK in both the Shanghai and Paris manuscripts is undated but refers in the opening line to the summer of 1705, indicating that it was probably written in or shortly after 1705.

27. TRTYK 2, p. 1a.

28. TRTYK 2, p. 1b.

29. TRTYK 2, p. 2a.

30. TRTYK 2, p. 2b, cited from the "Tang gao" (Announcement of Tang) in the *Shujing.* See *Shisan jing zhu shu* (Notes and commentary on the

Thirteen Classics), photolithographic edition based on *Shisan jing zhu shu jiaokanji*, compiled by Ruan Yuan and originally printed in 1806, 2 vols. (Beijing, 1980), p. 162, top.

31. Zhang cited *Lunyu* II.24, III.13, IV.8, VI.20, VII.34, and XI.11 in TRTYK 2, p. 4b.

32. Zhang cited *Lunyu* I.8 and XV.29 in TRTYK 2, p. 6a.

33. TRTYK 2, pp. 7a–8a.

34. See the discussion of *The Scholars* in C. T. Hsia, *The Classic Chinese Novel: A Critical Introduction* (Bloomington, 1980), pp. 203–244. Also see Paul S. Ropp, *Dissent in Early Modern China: Ju-lin wai-shih and Ch'ing Social Criticism* (Ann Arbor, 1981).

35. TRTYK 2, pp. 6a–7a.

36. Charles O. Hucker, A *Dictionary of Official Titles in Imperial China* (Stanford, 1985), p. 528.

37. TRTYK 2, p. 7a.

38. TRTYK 2, p. 8a.

39. *Lunyu* XIV.6.

40. William Frederick Mayers, *The Chinese Reader's Manual* (Shanghai, 1874; reprinted Taipei, 1978), p. 169.

41. TRTYK 2, p. 9a.

42. TRTYK 2, p. 9b.

43. *Lunyu* XV.11.

44. *Mengzi* 7a.40, cited in TRTYK 2, pp. 10a–10b.

45. TRTYK 2, p. 17a.

46. TRTYK 2, p. 17b.

47. TRTYK 2, p. 18a.

48. TRTYK 2, p. 11a.

49. TRTYK 2, p. 12a.

50. Cf. Laurence G. Thompson, *Chinese Religion,* 4th edition (Belmont, Calif., 1989), p. 11.

51. *Mengzi* 6a.4.

52. TRTYK 2, pp. 15a–16b.

53. TRTYK 2, p. 12a.

54. Confucius' statement about "overcoming the self" is found in *Lunyu* XL.1. Zhu Xi's commentary on *Lunyu* VI is found in his *Sishu jizhu,* p. 10b, quoted in TRTYK 2, p. 12b.

55. TRTYK 2, pp. 15a–15b.

56. *Lunyu* XV.8.

57. *Mengzi* 6a.10.

58. *Lunyu* XVIII.1, cited in TRTYK 2, p. 13a.

59. TRTYK 2, pp. 15b–16a.

60. TRTYK 2, p. 14a.

61. TRTYK 2, p. 16b.

62. Zhang, *Tianjiao mingbian*, preface, cited in Xu Zongze, *Ming-Qing jian Yesuhuishi yizhu*, p. 122.

63. *Xu Guangqi xinglüe* (A summary of the deeds of Xu Guangqi), manuscript preserved in the Bibliothèque nationale, Paris, ms. chinois 1023. Published in *Xu Wending gong shishi sanbai nian jinian wen huibian* (A literary collection in commemoration of the three hundredth anniversary of the death of Xu Wending) (Shanghai, 1933), pp. 3–8. The obscurity of this manuscript is shown by its absence from such standard Jesuit sources as Pfister's list of works by Couplet. See Pfister, *Notices biographiques*, pp. 310–313.

64. Zhang Xingyao, *Shengjiao zanming*, manuscript in the Bibliothèque nationale, Paris, ms. chinois 7067.

65. I am indebted to Paul W. Kroll, professor of Chinese at the University of Colorado at Boulder, for his assistance in identifying the poetic form of Zhang's thirty-eight inscriptions.

66. Zhang, *Shengjiao zanming*, f. 1a.

67. Gao Yizhi (A. Vignone), *Shengjiao xingshi* (Jiangzhou, Shanxi, 1629).

68. TRTYK 2, p. 18b.

69. TRTYK 2, pp. 18b–19b.

70. TRTYK 2, p. 20b.

71. TRTYK 2, pp. 21a–21b.

72. Z. D. Sung, *The Text of the Yi King* (Shanghai, 1935), p. 126.

73. TRTYK 2, pp. 26a–26b.

74. TRTYK 2, p. 26b.

75. TRTYK 2, p. 22a.

76. TRTYK 2, p. 23a.

77. TRTYK 2, pp. 23a, 23b.

78. Zhang quoted from the *Shijing*, Mao 254 (Legge, *Classics* 3, ii.X.8) as follows: "Great Heaven is intelligent, And is with you in all your goings. Great Heaven is clear-seeing, And is with you in your wanderings and indulgences" (Legge, *Classics* 4, p. 503). Karlgren translated the passage as "Great Heaven is called intelligent, it observes your goings; great Heaven is called clear-seeing, it observes your sporting and extravagances" (Karlgren, *The Book of Odes* [Stockholm, 1950], p. 214).

79. TRTYK 2, p. 24a

80. TRTYK 2, pp. 24b–25a.

81. TRTYK 2, p. 25a.

82. The Hell of the Iron Bed *(Tiechuang diyu)* was one of the Eighteen Hells in Chinese folk religion. Presided over by the ruler Tie Jiaren, it was one of the hells visually portrayed in the famous Beijing Temple of Eighteen Hells (Shiba diyu miao), previously located in the eastern suburbs of Beijing, but destroyed after 1949. (See L. C. Arlington, *In Search of Old Peking* [Beijing, 1935], p. 263.) The Hell of the Iron Bed is described and illus-

trated in Anne Swann Goodrich, *Chinese Hells: The Peking Temple of Eighteen Hells and Chinese Conceptions of Hell* (Sankt Augustin, Germany, 1981), plate 18 and pp. 47–48.

83. This imaginative reconstruction of Zhang's dream of being in the Hell of the Flaming Iron Bed is hypothetical, but it concludes with a poem by Zhang on hell, one of the thirty-eight eulogies on Christianity by Zhang in his *Shengjiao zanming,* f. 11a.

CHAPTER 5

1. This prelude consists of an imaginative reconstruction featuring Master Zhang's recollection of his youthful reprimand by a Buddhist monk at the Sweet Dew of Immortality Monastery (Ganlusi). It is based on a description by Zhang in the *Refutation (Pi lüeshuo tiaobo)* (1689), coauthored by Zhang and Hong Ji, p. 35a.

2. The technical subject matter of *Taixi shuifa* (Western hydraulics) was dictated by the Jesuit S. de Ursis (Xiong Sanba) and transcribed by Xu Guangqi. The work was later edited by Li Zhizao and reprinted in the missionary collection *Tianxue chuhan,* 52 *juan* (1628; reprinted Taipei, 1965), 3, p. 1506. *Taixi shuifa* was also later included in Xu's *Nongzheng quanshu,* 60 *juan* (1625–1628), and eventually copied in this form into the *Siku quanshu.* See Hummel, *Eminent Chinese,* pp. 317–318.

3. *Pi lüeshuo tiaobo* (hereafter cited as PLSTB), Zhang preface, p. 1a.

4. PLSTB, Zhang preface, pp. 1a, 3b.

5. For a recent expression of the view that Chinese immanence and Christian creation are irreconcilable, see Jacques Gernet, *China and the Christian Impact* (Cambridge, England, 1982), pp. 198–199, 204, 208–213.

6. PLSTB, Zhang preface, p. 2a.

7. Hummel, *Eminent Chinese,* p. 317.

8. PLSTB, Hong preface, p. 2a. For information on the monk Master Jie of the Puren Monastery (Jieliu Xingce), see *Changzhao he zhi gao* (1904 edition), 41, p. 11a; *Wu deng quanshu,* 129 *juan,* 81, p. 344b; Chen Yuan, *Shishi yi nianlu* (Beijing, 1964), 20, p. 460; and Hasebe Yukei, *Min Shin Bukkyō shi kenkyū josetsu* (Taipei, 1979), pp. 68, 298. Jieliu Xingce's teacher, Ruoan Tongwen, is treated on page 34 of Hasebe's work. I am indebted to Mr. A. Dudink and Mr. N. Standaert, S.J., for their assistance in securing this information.

9. *Zhejiang Hangzhou-fu Tianzhutang kan shuban mulu* (A list of books engraved at the Lord of Heaven Church in Hangzhou prefecture, Zhejiang). Manuscript in the Bibliothèque nationale, Paris, ms. chinois 7046-X.

10. PLSTB, Zhang preface, p. 4a.

11. PLSTB, Hong preface, p. 1b.

12. PLSTB, introduction, p. 1a.

13. PLSTB, introduction, pp. 1a–2a.

14. PLSTB, introduction, p. 2b.

15. Each of the eight sections into which the *Refutation* is divided deals with a criticism of some particular Buddhist notion. These notions include (1) whether hell could simultaneously exist and not exist, (2) whether hell is created for a cruel purpose, (3) the power of the Buddhist teaching to effect one's release from hell, (4) assisting one's ascent to heaven, (5) whether *Tathāgata* words are efficacious, (6) the Storehouse Consciousness *(Karmavijñāna)* of changing manifestations, (7) rebirth into the Paradise of the West (i.e., Pure Land of Amitabha Buddha), and (8) whether comparing the common people to (Sakyamuni) Buddha represents a slander. The eight-part structure of the *Refutation* parallels the form of Xu Guangqi's *Pi wang,* which was reprinted in the *Refutation* as a preface, though the subject matter differs slightly. Xu's sections had dealt with his criticisms of the Buddhist notions of (1) breaking out of hell, (2) feeding mendicant monks, (3) forlorn souls at Blood Lake who lacked living descendants to offer sacrifices to them, (4) burning paper money for the dead, (5) chanting mantras, (6) transmigration, (7) chanting the name of (Amitabha) Buddha, and (8) the Chan sect.

16. Hong and Zhang both rebutted in sections 1, 2, 3, 5, and 8; only Hong rebutted in section 4; and Zhang alone rebutted in sections 6 and 7.

17. Because of the fundamental importance of *vijñāna* (consciousness) to the doctrine, it became known as the Vijñānavada or Yogācāra school.

18. Whereas some scholars, such as Hu Shi, have regarded the *Xi you ji* by Wu Cheng'en as a satirical fantasy, the recent translator Anthony C. Yu sees it as a serious allegorical work based on late Ming dynasty religious syncretism in which Confucianism, Buddhism, and Daoism are blended. See Yu's translation of Wu Ch'eng-en, *The Journey to the West,* 4 vol. (Chicago, 1977–1983). An abridged translation of *Xi you ji* can be found in Arthur Waley's *Monkey* (New York, 1943).

19. Garma C. C. Chang, *The Buddhist Teaching of Totality: The Philosophy of Hwa Yen Buddhism* (University Park, 1971), pp. 172–173, 183. In the seventh century, a disciple of Xuanzang carried the Mind-Only teaching to Japan, where it became known as the Hossō school. Although the Hossō school exerted only minor influence in Japan, it has retained a remarkable power to stimulate the imagination of Japanese. For example, the late novelist Yukio Mishima used the Mind-Only teaching in the dénouement of his magnificent tetralogy *The Sea of Fertility* (1968–1971).

20. Whereas the earlier Yogācāra school taught that the Storehouse was absolutely pure and detached from defilements and evil passions, the later Lankāvatāra taught that the ideas in the Storehouse were both pure and tainted. See D. T. Suzuki, *Studies in the Lankāvatāra Sūtra* (London, 1930), p. 182.

21. PLSTB, p. 1a.

22. I have interpreted *ju gu* and *zao gu* as being roughly equivalent to the second and third of Aristotle's Four Causes (material cause, formal cause, efficient cause, and final cause), although I concede that a Buddhologist could probably offer a more refined interpretation.

23. PLSTB, p. 1a.

24. There were notable exceptions to the dominant Confucianist realism, such as the idealistic philosophy of Wang Yangming (1472-1529), who was quite possibly influenced by Buddhism.

25. Wing-tsit Chan, *A Source Book in Chinese Philosophy* (Princeton, 1963), p. 373.

26. PLSTB, p. 1b. Xu Guangqi in his *Draft Memorial in Defense [of Christianity] (Bianxue shugao)* (1616), which was addressed to the emperor, spoke of Buddhism as a defiling force that had entered China 1,800 years previously. See his *Bianxue shugao*, reprinted in *Tianzhujiao dongchuan wenxian xubian* (Taipei, 1966), 1, p. 24.

27. PLSTB, pp. 2b-3a.

28. PLSTB, p. 3b.

29. PLSTB, pp. 3b-4b.

30. PLSTB, p. 5a.

31. *Hou shan ji* (14 *juan*), PLSTB, pp. 5a-5b.

32. Stephen F. Teiser, " 'Having Once Died and Returned to Life': Representations of Hell in Medieval China," *Harvard Journal of Asiatic Studies* 48 (1988): 436-437.

33. Goodrich, *Chinese Hells*, p. 68.

34. PLSTB, p. 6a.

35. PLSTB, pp. 6a-6b.

36. PLSTB, p. 7a.

37. PLSTB, p. 7a.

38. PLSTB, pp. 7b-9b.

39. PLSTB, p. 11b.

40. The *Refutation* returned briefly to the Mind-Only philosophy for the purpose of criticizing the Buddhist notion of the changing manifestations of *Karmavijñāna (Yeshi)* (Activity Consciousness). Whereas the Ālaya-vijñāna (Storehouse Consciousness) refers to consciousness in its undisturbed, native condition, *Karmavijñāna* refers to consciousness in its activated form (Suzuki, *Lankāvatāra Sūtra*, pp. 186-187). Jie argued that the guardian of hell and the ox-headed demons of hell were products of the changing manifestations of *Karmavijñāna* (PLSTB, p. 27a). In fact, Jie said that the totality of the infinite universe *(Dharmadhatu)* was a product of the mind, and hence the mind had the power to alter these things.

41. *Mengzi* VIa.1-6, in PLSTB, pp. 28a-28b.

42. PLSTB, p. 28b.

43. PLSTB, pp. 10a-10b.

44. Zhang drew from his knowledge of history to illustrate that benevolence without righteousness would be an indulgent, spoiled kind of benevolence akin to that shown by King Li Houzhu and Emperor Wu of the Liang dynasty. King Li was a ruler of the Southern Tang kingdom that was eventually destroyed by the founder of the Song dynasty, Song Taizu (reigned 960-975). Emperor Wu (reigned 502-549) was the founder of the Southern Liang dynasty. Both rulers were Buddhists, and Zhang claimed that their excess of benevolence and lack of righteousness led to the loss of their kingdoms. The other extreme was a lack of benevolence and excess of righteousness. Zhang illustrated this cruel righteousness with the example of Empress Wu Zetian (reigned 684-704) of the Tang dynasty. Empress Wu was also a Buddhist, and Zhang claimed that her rapacious underlings constructed instruments of punishment that resembled hell in their horror.

45. PLSTB, p. 11a.

46. Avici Hell is the last and deepest of the eight hot hells, where one suffers from intense scorching and is reborn to more suffering without interruption.

47. PLSTB, p. 12a.

48. Thompson, *Chinese Religion*, pp. 10-12.

49. E. Erkes, "The God of Death in Ancient China," *T'oung Pao* 35 (1940): 186-187.

50. Ibid., p. 188.

51. Ibid., pp. 194-195.

52. Ibid., p. 197.

53. Ibid., p. 205.

54. Ibid., p. 210.

55. Ibid., p. 190.

56. A. Goodrich, *Chinese Hells*, pp. 68-69; W. E. Soothill, *The Three Religions of China*, 2d edition (London, 1923), pp. 178-181.

57. Christian ideas might have come to China incorporated with Islam, or Islamic ideas on hell might have radiated both westward to influence Christian ideas of hell in Europe and eastward to shape ideas of hell in China. See J. J. Duyvendak, "A Chinese 'Divina Commedia,' " *T'oung Pao* 41 (1952): 258.

58. Duyvendak, "Divina Commedia," p. 281; Goodrich, *Chinese Hells*, p. 69. An Shigao's translation *Foshuo zuiye yingbao jiaohua diyu jing* appears in the Buddhist Tripitika *(Da zangjing)*. See *Taishō shinshū daizōkyō* (Tokyo, 1922-1936), 17, pp. 450-452.

59. See An Shigao, *Shiba nilijing*, in *Taishō shinshū daizōkyō* 17, pp. 528-530, cited in Duyvendak, "Divina Commedia," p. 288. An early variation on the compartmentalizing of Chinese hells involved eight primary hells, each of which had sixteen secondary hells *(Utsadas)*. In this system each of

the four sides of the primary hells had a doorway leading to four secondary hells. If one reckons that each of the primary hells had sixteen secondary hells, then this produced a total of 136 hells (8 times 16 equals 128, plus 8 equals 136). See W. E. Soothill and L. Hodous, *A Dictionary of Chinese Buddhist Terms* (London, 1937), p. 207; Goodrich, *Chinese Hells,* p. 70; Duyvendak, "Divina Commedia," pp. 259, 297. Later, popular Buddhism in China came to favor the system of eighteen hells over that of 136 hells, perhaps because the latter was too complex. (See Duyvendak, "Divina Commedia," p. 297.)

60. These ten hells are described in one of the most complete Chinese accounts of a journey into the other world. See Luo Maodeng, *Sanbao taijian xia xiyang yi* (1597). This work is described in some detail in Duyvendak, "Divina Commedia," pp. 262–312. Also see the description with illustrations of the Ten Courts of Hell in Wolfram Eberhard, *Guilt and Sin in Traditional China* (Berkeley, 1967), pp. 24–59.

61. Yang, *Religion in Chinese Society,* pp. 24–25.

62. Goodrich, *Chinese Hells,* pp. 71–78

63. PLSTB, p. 13a.

64. PLSTB, pp. 14b–15a.

65. Teiser, "Having Once Died," pp. 462–463.

66. PLSTB, p. 15b.

67. PLSTB, pp. 27a–27b. The monk Jie referred to the emperor Tang Taizong (reigned 627–649), who debated with the monks about the effectiveness of chanting.

68. PLSTB, pp. 24b–25a.

69. C. P. Fitzgerald describes this Korean campaign but does not mention the Buddhist monks chanting for calm seas. See his *Son of Heaven: A Biography of Li Shih-min, Founder of the T'ang Dynasty* (Cambridge, England, 1933), pp. 187–199.

70. Zhang indicated that his source for this information about Tang Taizong was the *Zizhi tongjian* (1084) by Sima Guang.

71. PLSTB, pp. 25a–25b. Zhang was certainly aware of the fact, though he did not discuss it in the *Refutation,* that Tang Taizong's fleet did eventually successfully cross the sea to Korea. However, this crossing apparently took place after the monks failed in securing calm water within sixty days.

72. PLSTB, p. 25b.

73. Zhang carried his criticism of mantra chanting closer to his own day in referring to immortals who make claims for magical powers. He spoke of a magician *(yaoren)* named Zhu Fangdan (honorary name Shuqing) who lived on Double Eyebrow Mountain (Ermei shan) in Huguang province during the reign of the Kangxi emperor (PLSTB, pp. 23b–24a). Zhu claimed to be an immortal *(shenxian),* and he developed mantras to save people from harm and published books to disseminate his teaching. But in

spite of his claims to being an immortal, Zhu died and the Buddhist bodhisattva blessings were lost.
74. PLSTB, p. 30a.
75. G. Schlegel, "Les termes bouddhiques *Yulan Pen* et *Yulan Po*," *T'oung
Pao*, series 2, 2 (1901): 146-148, 394-397.
76. An English translation by Eugene Eoyang of *Damuqianlian mingjian
jiu mu bianwen* (The Great Maudgalyayana rescues his mother from hell)
from the *Dunhuang bianwen* manuscript, Pelliot 2319, preserved in the Bibliothèque nationale, Paris, appears in the collection *Traditional Chinese Stories*, edited by Y. W. Ma and Joseph S. M. Lau (Boston, 1986), pp. 443-
462.
77. PLSTB, pp. 30a-30b.
78. PLSTB, pp. 30a, 30b.
79. PLSTB, p. 30b.
80. PLSTB, p. 32a.
81. PLSTB, p. 36b.
82. This postlude is not an imaginative reconstruction but rather a poem
by Zhang on Judgment from his *Shengjiao zanming*, p. 10b.

CHAPTER 6

1. Although this prelude is an imaginative reconstruction, Zhang's
description of how his frustration with the provincial examination led him
first to study Buddhism and eventually to adopt Christianity follows quite
closely his own description in his preface to *Tianjiao mingbian* (1711),
reprinted in Xu Zongze, *Ming-Qing jian Yesuhuishi yizhu*, p. 123.
2. See Jin Yufa, *Zhongguo shixue shi* (Shanghai, 1944), p. 199; Han Yu-
shan, *Elements of Chinese Historiography* (Hollywood, Calif., 1955), p. 56.
3. Endymion Wilkinson, *The History of Imperial China: A Research Guide*
(Cambridge, Mass., 1975), pp. 71-72; Han, *Elements*, pp. 49-57.
4. Rafe de Crespigny, "Universal Histories," in *Essays on the Sources for
Chinese History*, edited by D. D. Leslie, C. Mackerras and G. W. Wang
(Columbia, South Carolina, 1975), p. 65; E. G. Pulleyblank, "Chinese
Historical Criticism: Liu Chih-chi and Ssu-ma Kuang," in *Historians of
China and Japan*, edited by W. G. Beasley and E. G. Pulleyblank (London,
1961), pp. 152-158.
5. *Songchao shishi* (Basic Sinological Series), 3, pp. 40-41, cited in Pulleyblank, "Historical Criticism," pp. 155-156.
6. Pulleyblank, "Historical Criticism," pp. 158-159.
7. See Yuan Shu (styled Jizhong), *Tongjian jishi benmo* (Narratives from
beginning to end from the *Comprehensive Mirror for Aid in Government*) 42 juan
(1176). See the article by Aoyama Sadao in *A Sung Bibliography*, edited by
Y. Hervouet (Hong Kong, 1978), p. 85. Also see O. Franke, "Das *Tse tschi*

t'ung kien und das *T'ung kien kang-mu,* ihr Wesen, ihr Verhältnis zueinander und ihr Quellenwert," in *Sitzungsberichte der preussischen Akademie der Wissenschaften,* Phil.-Hist. Klasse Nr. 30 (Berlin, 1930), pp. 103–144. See especially, pp. 122–124.

8. Wilkinson, *History of Imperial China,* p. 72.

9. TRTYK 1, p. 2a.

10. Hummel, *Eminent Chinese,* p. 722.

11. Mo Youzhi, *Song Yuan jiu ben shujing yanlu,* 3 *juan* (1873), 3, pp. 4a–4b. For a description of Mo's work, see Hummel, *Eminent Chinese,* p. 582.

12. Chapters 1 through 7 of Zhang's *Tongjian jishi benmo buhoubian* consist of 149 leaves in two *ce,* catalogued under the number 1946. See Fang Hao, *Zhongguo Tianzhujiao shi* 2, pp. 101–102; and Fang, *Fang Hao liushi zidinggao,* p. 234.

13. Fang, *Fang Hao liushi zidinggao,* p. 238.

14. Zhang and his *History* are listed in the History section *(shibu)* of the Hangzhou local history *Hangzhou-fu zhi,* compiled by Shao Jinhan (1743–1796) et al. in 1784; edited by Gong Jiazun in 1888–1898, 178 *juan,* 87, p. 4a.

15. Standaert, *Yang Tingyun,* p. 212.

16. TRTYK 3, p. 1a. Regarding this and two other difficult passages, I would like to express my indebtedness to D. Bodde, professor emeritus of the University of Pennsylvania, for his kind assistance in translation.

17. In addition to the opening page of the preface to part 3 of the *Similarities,* Zhang discussed how Dong Zhongshu diverged from the thought of Confucius in his preface to the *Tianjiao mingbian* (1711), reprinted in Xu Zongze, *Ming-Qing jian Yesuhuishi yizhu,* p. 121.

18. TRTYK 3, p. 3a.

19. With thanks to Mr. Bodde for his translation assistance.

20. TRTYK 3, pp. 4a–5a.

21. TRTYK 3, pp. 5b–6a.

22. TRTYK 3, 16b.

23. Standaert, *Yang Tingyun,* pp. 116–121.

24. TRTYK 3, p. 16a.

25. TRTYK 3, p. 9a.

26. TRTYK 3, p. 14a.

27. Yang, *Religion in Chinese Society,* pp. 23–24.

28. TRTYK 3, p. 6a.

29. TRTYK 3, p. 7b.

30. TRTYK 3, pp. 8a–b.

31. TRTYK 3, p. 15b.

32. *Tianjiao mingbian,* preface, cited in Xu Zongze, *Ming-Qing jian Yesuhuishi yizhu,* p. 122.

33. TRTYK 3, p. 15b.

34. TRTYK 3, pp. 12b–13b.
35. TRTYK 3, p. 16a.
36. TRTYK 3, p. 16b.
37. TRTYK 3, p. 10a.
38. TRTYK 3, p. 10a.
39. TRTYK 3, p. 10b.
40. TRTYK 3, p. 11a.
41. TRTYK 3, p. 12a.
42. TRTYK 3, p. 17b.
43. TRTYK 3, pp. 18a–18b.
44. TRTYK 3, p. 11b.
45. *Shijing,* Mao 245 (Legge, trans., *The Chinese Classics* III.ii.I.6), cited in TRTYK 3, pp. 8b–9a.
46. Matthew 14:17–21, cited in TRTYK 3, p. 9a.
47. TRTYK 3, p. 10b.
48. George Minamiki, S.J., *The Chinese Rites Controversy* (Chicago, 1985), pp. 29–32.
49. Ibid., pp. 37–40.
50. Zhang Xingyao, *Sidian shuo* (hereafter cited SDS). Archivum Romanum Historicum Iesu, Japonica-Sinica I, 40/7a.
51. According to an unpublished catalog by Fr. A. Chan, S.J., on Chinese manuscripts in the Jesuit archives in Rome, the Portuguese passage reads: "Este he obra de un Letrado de Hoân cheu. A mandou o. P. Intorcetta."
52. SDS, p. 1a.
53. *Li ji, Yue ling* chapter. See *Shisan jing zhu shu* (Notes and commentary on the Thirteen Classics) (hereafter cited as SSJZS), a photolithographic edition based on *Shisan jing zhu shu jiaokanji,* compiled by Ruan Yuan and originally printed in 1806, 2 vols. (Beijing, 1980), p. 1356, middle.
54. *Li ji, Yue ling* chapter (SSJZS, p. 1333, top).
55. *Li ji, Yue ling* chapter (SSJZS, p. 1369, middle).
56. SDS, p. 1b.
57. *Li ji, Si fa* chapter (SSJZS, p. 1590, middle).
58. SDS, p. 2a.
59. Thompson, *Chinese Religion,* pp. 12–13, 20, 30.
60. SDS, p. 3a.
61. SDS, p. 3a.
62. SDS, p. 2b.
63. SDS, p. 4a.
64. SDS, p. 2b.
65. SDS. p. 3a.
66. SDS, p. 3b.
67. *Shu jing, Yin xun* chapter, SSJZS, p. 163, bottom (see Legge, trans.,

Book of Historical Documents IV.iv.8, in *Chinese Classics* 3, p. 198), cited in SDS, p. 3b.

68. *Zhuangzi,* chapter 23, cited in SDS, p. 4a. Shrines to living people *(shengci)* are briefly discussed in C. K. Yang, *Religion in Chinese Society* (Berkeley, 1961), pp. 173–175.

69. SDS, p. 4b.

70. SDS, p. 5a, indicates that his source was Sima Guang's *Zizhi tongjian,* the second year of the reign of the Taining emperor, Emperor Ming of the Jin, i.e., A.D. 324.

71. H. Giles, *A Chinese Biographical Dictionary* (Shanghai, 1898), pp. 846–847.

72. SDS, p. 5a, noted that Zhang's source was Sima Guang's *Zizhi tongjian,* the eleventh year of the reign of the Tianbao emperor (i.e., 752), Emperor Yuanzong (Xuanzong). Also see Giles, *Biographical Dictionary,* pp. 449–450.

73. SDS, p. 4b.

74. *Li ji, Ji fa* chapter, section 5 (SSJZS, p. 1589, top) (cf. Legge, *Chinese Classics* 2, p. 209), cited in SDS, p. 5a.

75. *Li ji, Chu li* chapter, part 2, section 7 (SSJZS, p. 1258, middle), cited in SDS, p. 5b.

76. *Li ji, Ji yi* chapter, section 28 (SSJZS, p. 1595, bottom).

77. SDS, p. 6a.

78. SDS, pp. 5b–6a.

79. SDS, p. 6a.

80. Zhang cites here from the *Chunqiu, Gongyang zhuan,* the commentary on year two of Duke Cheng.

81. *Li ji, Ji yi* chapter, section 3 (SSJZS, p. 1592, bottom); my translation slightly modifies that of Legge, *Chinese Classics* 2, p. 211.

82. SDS, p. 6b.

83. SDS, p. 7a.

84. SDS, p. 7b.

85. Xu Zongze, *Ming-Qing jian Yesuhuishi yizhu,* pp. 121, 123. See also Fang Hao, *Zhongguo Tianzhujiao shi* 2, p. 100; and Fang, *Fang Hao liushi zidanggao,* p. 234.

86. Fang Hao, *Zhongguo Tianzhujiao shi* 2, pp. 111–112; Fang, *Fang Hao liushi zidinggao,* pp. 234–235.

87. The works that Shang assisted Caballero in composing include *Tian Ru yin* (A comparison of the Heavenly and Literati teachings) (1664) and *Zhengxue liushi* (The touchstone of True Learning) (1698).

88. Fang, *Fang Hao liushi zidinggao,* pp. 234–235.

89. TJMB, preface, reprinted in Xu Zongze, *Ming-Qing jian Yesuhuishi yizhu,* p. 123.

90. TJMB, preface, reprinted in ibid., p. 122.

91. See the discussion of the Nestorian Monument in Mungello, *Curious Land,* pp. 154-172.

92. TJMB, preface, reprinted in Xu Zongze, *Ming-Qing jian Yesuhuishi yizhu,* p. 122. Zhang has slightly condensed Lu Xiangshan's original quotation, which is found in Lu Jiuyuan, *Lu Xiangshan quanji* 35, p. 3.

93. TJMB, preface, reprinted in Xu Zongze, *Ming-Qing jian Yesuhuishi yizhu,* p. 123.

94. The description of Zhang's meditative stroll along West Lake is hypothetical and superimposed upon a description of a walk taken by the fictional literatus Ma Zhunshang (Ma Chun-shang) in the famous satirical novel *The Scholars (Rulin waishi).* This novel was written by Wu Jingzi (Wu Ching-tzu) (1701-1754) shortly after Zhang's death. See Wu Ching-tzu, *The Scholars,* translated by Yang Hsien-yi and Gladys Yang (Beijing, 1973), pp. 161-165.

CHAPTER 7

1. This prelude is not an imaginative reconstruction but rather a poem by Zhang on death, from his *Shengjiao zanming,* pp. 10b-11a.

2. Dehergne, *Répertoire,* p. 23; Dehergne, "La Chine centrale vers 1700," 2, p. 313.

3. Letter of Fr. J. Bouvet, dated 30 November 1699 at Beijing, published in *Der Neue Welt-Bott,* edited by Joseph Stöcklein, S.J. (Augsburg, 1726), vol. 1, part 1, letter 41, p. 25.

4. Dehergne, *Répertoire,* p. 107.

5. Ibid., p. 145; Dehergne, "La Chine centrale vers 1700," 2, p. 313.

6. Dehergne, "La Chine centrale vers 1700," 2, p. 313.

7. *Sinica Franciscana* (Rome), 7, 1 (1965): xlii.

8. Dehergne, *Répertoire,* p. 24; Pfister, *Notices biographiques,* p. 492.

9. Dehergne, "La Chine centrale vers 1700," 2, p. 314.

10. Fang, *Hangzhou Dafangjing Tianzhujiao gu mu zhi yan'ge,* p. 1945.

11. *Sinica Franciscana* (Rome), 8 (1975): 330-331.

12. Dehergne, "La Chine centrale vers 1700," 2, p. 314.

13. Sommervogel, *Bibliothèque* 4, p. 394; Robert Streit, O.M.I., *Bibliotheca Missionum* 7 (Freiburg, 1931), pp. 199-200, 290; Pfister, *Notices biographiques,* pp. 611-617. Fr. Joseph de Moyriac de Mailla (Feng Bingzheng, 1669-1748) and Fr. Jean-Baptiste Régis (Lei Xiaosi, 1663-1738) were both French Jesuits.

14. *Der Neue Welt-Bott,* edited by Joseph Stöcklein, S.J., and successors, 38+ vols. divided into 520 nos. (Augspurg and Grätz, later Vienna, 1728-1761). *Der Neue Welt-Bott* was a Jesuit attempt to publish in German selected letters and reports from missionaries throughout the world. It was probably inspired by the successful Jesuit production in French of *Lettres édifiantes et*

curieuses (Paris, 1707–1772), edited by Charles le Gobien and J. B. du Halde, from which many letters were translated.

15. Brunner, *L'euchologe*, pp. 124–129; Pfister, *Notices biographiques*, p. 617. The manuscript *Yu misa gongcheng* by De Ma'nuo (R. Hinderer) and Meng Youyi (Manuel Mendes, 1656–1741), dated 1721, is preserved in the Bibliothèque nationale, Paris, as ms. chinois 7438.

16. Dehergne, "La Chine centrale vers 1700," 2, pp. 314–315; ARSI, Jap. Sin. 117, f. 170r.

17. Letter of Fr. Roman Hinderer, dated 27 September 1719 at Hangzhou, in *Der Neue Welt-Bott* (Augsburg, 1726), vol. 1, part 7, letter 161, p. 44.

18. *Litterae Annuae 1678–1679*, ARSI, Jap. Sin. 117, f. 170r.

19. Hinderer's letter of 27 September 1719, *Der Neue Welt-Bott*, p. 44.

20. Pei Huang, *Autocracy at Work: A Study of the Yung-cheng Period, 1723–1735* (Bloomington, 1974), pp. 48–50.

21. Dehergne, *Répertoire*, p. 127.

22. Pfister, *Notices biographiques*, p. 613.

23. Li Wei's memorial to the Yongzheng emperor, 1730, translated in Lo-shu Fu, *Documentary Chronicle*, p. 164.

24. Hummel, *Eminent Chinese*, p. 793.

25. Dehergne, "La Chine centrale vers 1700," 2, p. 313.

26. This tablet was still in place in 1906. See Cloud, *Hangchow*, p. 32. Also, for Li Wei's relationship with the Yongzheng emperor, see Hummel, *Eminent Chinese*, pp. 720–721.

27. Dehergne, "La Chine centrale vers 1700," 2, p. 314. Cf. Cloud, *Hangchow*, p. 32.

28. See D. E. Mungello, "Unearthing the Manuscripts of Bouvet's *Gujin* after Nearly Three Centuries," *China Mission Studies (1550–1800) Bulletin* 10 (1988): 34–61. Also see the complementary article "*Tianxue benyi*—Joachim Bouvet's Forschungen zum Monotheismus in China," by Claudia von Collani in the same issue, pp. 9–33.

29. See C. von Collani, *P. Joachim Bouvet S.J., sein Leben und sein Werk* (Nettetal, 1985).

30. Fang, "Zhejiang Tianzhujiao lüeshi," pp. 62–66.

31. Fang notes that between 1885 and 1935 the number of Chinese priests increased from 7 to 116 while foreign priests increased only from 11 to 34. He also notes that there were increases in the number of Chinese nuns from zero to 167, foreign nuns from 30 to 48, Catholic schools from 32 to 278, Catholic school students from 588 to 12,773, and Catholic hospitals from 6 to 8 (ibid., p. 68).

32. Richard Madsen, "The Catholic Church in China: Cultural Contradictions, Institutional Survival, and Religious Renewal," in E. Perry Link, ed., *Unofficial China: Popular Culture and Thought in the People's Republic* (Boulder, 1989), p. 105.

33. Fr. Jean Charbonnier, publisher, *Guide to the Catholic Church in China* (Singapore, 1989), p. 291. A recent Protestant source estimates there to be in Zhejiang province 140,000 Catholics (including both those within and those outside of the Catholic Patriotic Association) and 900,000 Protestants (including both those who cooperate with the Three-Self Movement and those who do not). See Philip L. Wickeri, "Christianity in Zhejiang: A Report from a Recent Visit to Protestant Churches in China," *China Notes* (Spring and Summer 1990), p. 576. The Catholic Patriotic Association and the Three-Self Movement were organized soon after the Communist victory in China in 1949 in order to bring the Catholic and Protestant churches, respectively, under state control while breaking all ties with foreign churches. The term "Three-Self" referred to the autonomy of Chinese Protestant churches in terms of being self-supporting, self-governing, and self-propagating.

34. Madsen, "Catholic Church," pp. 104–105.

35. Ibid., p. 109.

36. Ibid., p. 116.

37. This refers to a famous cemetery on Beimang Mountain in the northern district of Luoyang in modern Henan province. In former times many kings and noble figures were buried there.

38. This final postlude is not an imaginative reconstruction but rather a poem by Zhang on heaven from his *Shengjiao zanming*, pp. 11a–11b.

GLOSSARY

Abida diyu　　阿鼻大地獄
Ai Rulüe　　艾儒略
Ai Siding　　艾斯玎
An Duo　　安多
Anhai　　安海
Anhui　　安徽
An Shigao　　安世高
Ao　　奡
ba　　跋
bai qian yi bei　　百千億倍
Baitou　　白頭
bao　　報
bei　　背,悖
Beiguan men　　北關門
Beimang　　北邙
Beiping Beitang tushuguan
　　zanbian Zhongwen shanben
　　shu mu (si)　　北平北堂圖書
館暫編中文善本書目(四)
Beitang　　北堂
benlai mianmu　　本來面目
biannian　　編年
Bianxue shugao　　辯學疏稿
Bigan　　比干
Bi Jia　　畢嘉
Bo Jin　　白晉
Bo Yi　　伯夷
Budeyi　　不得已
bu ke sheng shu　　不可勝數
buren　　不仁
bu Ru yi Fo　　補儒易佛
Cao Yuechuan　　曹月川
Changchunyuan　　暢春院
Changzhao he zhi gao　　常昭
合志稿
Chaoxing tang　　超性堂

Cheng Yi　　程頤
Chen Shidao　　陳師道
Chen Yuan　　陳垣
Chu　　楚
Chuan Gaisuwen　　船蓋蘇文
Chu Li　　曲禮
Cixi　　慈谿
Dafangjing　　大方井
Da Fumu　　大父母
Daguo　　大過
Da Hui　　大慧
Da jie　　大街
Da ke wen　　答客問
Damuqianlian mingjian jiu mu
　　bianwen　　大目乾連冥間救
　　母變文
dang　　黨
da xueshi　　大學士
Da zangjing　　大藏經
Dao de jing　　道德經
dao xi　　蹈襲
Dao Zhi　　盜跖
Daxi Tianxue xiushi yu ci
　　大西天學修士寓此
Daxue zhangju　　大學章句
De Ma'nuo　　德瑪諾
Di'er Zhongyao chang　　第二
　　中藥廠
Diguan　　地官
dihuang　　帝皇
Ding Richang　　丁日昌
Ding Yuntai (zi: Lü'an)
　　丁允泰(字履安)
Di Renjie (Liang Gong)
　　狄仁傑(梁公)
Ditang　　地堂

Dong Zhongshu　董仲舒
Dunhuang bianwen　敦煌變文
du zhi ren　塗之人
En Lige　恩理格
Er Duan　二端
Er Shi　二氏
ershi Shi Lao　二氏釋老
Fa Anduo　法安多
Fang Hao liushi zidinggao
　方豪六十自定稿
Fangjige xiansheng　方濟各
　先生
Fangjingnan　方井南
Fangjing taoyuan ling　方井
　桃源嶺
Fan Guoliang　潘國良
Fan seng　梵僧
Fei Lede　費樂德
Fei Qigui　費奇規
Fei Youlong　費毓龍
Feng Bingzheng　馮秉正
fengjiaozhe　奉教者
Fengshan men　風山門
fengshui　風水
Feng Zanzhang　馮瓚璋
Fo hui si　佛惠寺
Foshuo zuiye yingbao jiaohua
　diyu jing　佛說罪業應報教
　化地獄經
Fu Fanji　傅汎際
fuhuo　復活
fuhuo zhi ri　復活之日
Fu Ruowang　伏若望
Fushun　撫順
gaitong yizhe　改統易轍
Ganlusi　甘露寺
Ganzhou　贛州
Gao Yizhi　高一志
Gaozi　告子
Gengsang Chu　庚桑楚
Ge Qizhan　葛屺瞻
geyi　格義
gongan　空案

Gong Bai　恭伯
Gong Dangxin　龔[公]當信
gong fu　共父
Gong Jiazun　龔嘉儁
gongsheng　貢生
Guan hang　觀巷
Guan qiao　貫橋
Guan Yu　關羽
Gubadai　雇入代
gui　鬼
Gu jing　古經
Gujin jing Tian jian Tianxue
　benyi　古今敬天鑑天學本義
gu Ru　古儒
Guofeng yuekan　國風月刊
Guo Jujing　郭居靜
Guo Najue　郭納爵
Guo Ruowang　郭若望
Guo Zhongchuan　郭中傳
Guozi jian　國子監
Guwen　古文
Haining　海寧
Han Gaozi　漢高子
Hanghui gonglu　杭徽公路
Hangyu gonglu　杭餘公路
Hangzhou Dafangjing Tianzhu-
　jiao gu mu zhi yan'ge　杭州
　大方井天主教古墓之沿革
Hangzhou-fu zhi　杭州府志
Hangzhou pijiu chang　杭州
　啤酒廠
Han Lin　韓霖
Han Yu　韓愈
Hao Zhenhua　郝鎮华
Hasebe Yūkei　長谷部幽蹊
hengxing　恒性
Hong Duzhen　洪度貞
Hong Ji　洪濟
Hong Ruo[han]　洪若[翰]
Hong Zhong　洪鐘
Hou Ji　后稷
hou Ru　後儒
Hou shan ji　後山集

Hou Yi　后羿
Hu [Yuan] Anding　胡[瑗]
　安定
Huang Nie　黃蘖
Huayan jing　華嚴經
Huihuijiao　回回教
hun　魂
Hun Tian　渾天
Huo Shuchu　霍叔處
Ji　楫
Jiamiao　家廟
Jiangnan　江南
Jiangning　江寧
Jiangxi　江西
jian zhengmen　建正門
Jiaxing　嘉興
Jiaxue yuanliu　家學源流
Jieliu Xingce　截流行策
Ji Fa　祭法
Jie wang　桀王
Ji Jiongfan　計迥凡
Ji'nan　濟南
Jindai Ouzhou Hanxuejia de
　xianqu Maerdini　近代歐洲
　漢學家的先驅馬爾帝尼
Jingjiao bei　景教碑
Jingtu　淨土
Jin Hong　金宏
Jin Nige　金尼各
jinshi　進士
Jin Xian gong　晉獻公
Jin Yufa　金毓黻
jishi　記事
jishi benmo　紀事本末
jiu　仇
Jiujiang　九江
jiyan　記言
Jiyang　濟陽
Ji Yi　祭義
jiyue　極樂
Ji Zha　季札
jizhuan　紀傳
Jizi　箕子

juan　卷
juehun　覺魂
Ju gu　具故
juren　舉人
Kaijiao san dazhushi　開教三
　大柱石
kong　空
koubai　叩拜
laorenjia　老人家
lei　類
Lei feng ta　雷峰塔
Lei Xiaosi　雷孝思
Lengjia jing　楞伽經
li　理
Li　禮
Li Andang　利安當
Liang Wu di　梁武帝
libian　理編
Li bu　吏部
Li bu　禮部
Li Chengqian　李承乾
liexiu　列宿
Li Houzhu　李後主
Li Ji　驪姬
Li ji　禮記
Li Ke　里克
Li Leisi　利類思
Li Linfu　李林甫
Li Madou　利瑪竇
Lin'an　臨安
linghun　靈魂
Li Ningshi　黎寧石
Li [alias Xi] Shengxue
　利[習]聖學
Lishi yanjiu　歷史研究
Liu Bang　劉邦
Liu Wenbin (zi: Sudiao)
　柳文彬(字素調)
Liu Ying　劉應
Liu Zhongcao　劉中藻
Li Wei　李衛
Li Xitai xiansheng　利西泰
　先生

liyi　理義
Li Zhizao　李之藻
Li Zicheng　李自成
Li Zubo　利祖白
Long Huamin　龍華民
Longjing　龍井
Longwu　隆武
Lu Jiuyuan　陸九淵
Lu Xiangshan quanji　陸象
　山全集
Lunyu jizhu　論語集注
Luo Maodeng　羅懋登
Luo Ruwang　羅如望
luwei　祿位
lü　閭
Lü Miangang　呂勉剛
Ma Ruose　馬若瑟
Ma Tang　馬堂
Ma Yong　馬雍
Meng Youyi　孟由義
Mengzi jizhu　孟子集注
Mi Fu (Nangong)　米芾
　（南宮）
Minglun tang　明論堂
Ming-Qing jian Yesuhuishi yizhu
　tiyao　明清間耶穌會士譯著提要
Min Mingwo　閔明我
Min Pei (zi: Mingke)　閔珮
　（字鳴珂）
Min Shin Bukkyō shi kenkyū
　josetsu　明清佛教史研究
　序說
mixin ji shen　迷信極深
Mo Di　墨翟
Mo Youzhi　莫友芝
mubiao　暮標
Mu Jingyuan　穆敬遠
Nanchang　南昌
Nan Huairen　南懷仁
Nan Ming shilüe　南明史略
Nanxiong　南雄
nan xun　逎巡

Neige　內閣
Nongzheng quanshu　農政
　全書
paifang　牌坊
pailou　牌樓
Pang Diwo　龐迪我
Pan Guoliang　潘國艮
Pangzi yi quan　龐子遺詮
piao　票
Pi shishi zhu wang　闢釋氏
　諸妄
Pi lüeshuo tiaobo　闢略說條駁
Pingyang　平陽
po　魄
Poyang　波陽
Puren　晋仁
qi　氣
qi　祈
Qianqing gong　乾清宮
Qiantang　錢塘
Qiantang-xian zhi　錢塘縣志
qibian　器編
qing qing　輕清
Qing shi biannian　清史編年
Qintianjian　欽天監
Qiuyou pian　逑友篇
Qi Zheng　七政
ren　仁
Renhe　仁和
rouqu　肉軀
roushen　肉身
Ru　儒
Ruan Yuan　阮元
Rulin waishi　儒林外史
Ruoan Tongwen　箬菴通問
Sanbao taijian xia xiyang ji
　三寶太監下西洋紀
Sanshisan Tian　三十三天
Sanyin　三飲
Shalan　沙闌
Shan Duan　善端
Shangdi　上帝

Shang Huqing (Shiji) (zi: Weitang) 尚祜卿(識己)（字韋堂）

shangshu 尚書

Shang you Tiantang, xia you Su Hang 上有天堂下有蘇杭

Shao Jinhan 邵晉涵

shen 神

shenci 神祠

shendao bei 神道碑

shengci 生祠

Sheng Dian 聖殿

Shengfu 聖父

Shengjiao rike 聖教日課

Shengjiao zanming 聖教贊銘

Shengjing 聖經

Shengmu wuyuanzui tang 聖母無原罪堂

Shengren xingshi 聖人行實

shengti 聖體

shengxue 聖血

shenxian 神仙

shi 事

Shiba diyu miao 十入地獄廟

Shi Cheng 十誡

Shiji 史記

Shijing 詩經

shilu 實錄

Shiqi shiji Yidali Hanxuejia Wei Kuangguo mudi kao 十七世紀意大利漢學家衛匡國墓地考

Shisan jing zhu shu jiaokanji 十三經注疏校勘記

shishi yi nianlu 釋氏疑年錄

shiyuan 嗜欲

Shujing 書經

shulüe 疏略

Shu Qi 叔齊

shuren 庶人

Sidian shuo 祀典說

siduo 司鐸

Sima Guang 司馬光

Siming 司命

si shan 四善

Si shengsuo jizhe 四聖所紀者

Sishu jizhu 四書集註

Sishu zhangju jizhu 四書章句集註

song 頌

Songgotu 索額圖

Song Yuan jiu ben shujing yanlu 宋元舊本書經眼錄

suicha 歲差

Suzhou 蘇州

Taiji 太極

Taishō shinshū daizōkyō 大正新修大藏經

Taixi 泰西

Taixi shuifa 泰西水法

Taixi Yin Juesi xiansheng xinglüe 太西殷覺斯先生行略

Taixi zhu wei xiansheng 泰西諸位先生

Taixu 太虛

Taixue 太學

Tang [Wang] 唐[王]

Tang Ruowang 湯若望

Tianhou 天后

Tianjiao bu Ru 天教補儒

Tianjiao chao Ru 天教超儒

Tianjiao mingbian 天教明辨

Tian Ru yin 天儒印

Tianshen 天神

Tianshui qiao 天水橋

Tiantang zhi jing 天堂之靜

Tianxue chuan'gai 天學傳概

Tianxue chuhan 天學初函

Tianzhujiao dongchuan wenxian sanbian 天主教東傳文獻三編

Tianzhujiao dongchuan wenxian xubian 天主教東傳文獻續編

Tianzhujiao Rujiao tongyi kao
天主教儒教同異考
Tianzhujiao xiushi zhi mu
天主教修士之墓
Tianzhu Shengfu　　天主聖父
Tianzhu shengjiao nianjing
　zongdu　天主聖教念經總牘
Tianzhu shiyi　　天主實義
Tianzhu wuxian renci　　天主
無限仁慈
Tianzhuzi　　天主子
Tiechuang diyu　　鐵床地獄
Tong ban chao　　佟半朝
Tong Guoqi　　佟國器
Tong Guoyin　　佟國印
Tongjian jishi benmo buhoubian
通鑑紀事本末補後編
tongshi　　通史
Tubo　　土伯
Tudi miao　　土地廟
Wang Dun　　王敦
Wang Fangping　　王方平
Wang Huashi　　王華士
Wang Jun[lü]　　汪君[旅]
Wang Ruwang　　汪儒望
Wei Kuangguo　　衛匡國
Weishi　　唯識
Weixin　　唯心
Weizi　　微子
Wenzhou　　溫州
Wocun zazhi　　我存雜誌
wo Ru　　我儒
wo Zhongguo ren　　我中國人
Wu　　吳
Wu Chang　　五常
Wu deng quanshu　　五燈全書
Wu di　　武帝
Wu Jingzi　　吳敬梓
Wu Lun　　五倫
Wu Sangui　　吳三桂
Wu Yi (zi: Risheng)　　吳易
（字日生）

Wu Yuan　　伍員
Wu Zetian　　武則天
xian Ru　　先儒
xian zong dang hou lü li
先宗黨後閭里
Xiang Ji (zi: Yu)　　項籍(字羽)
Xiaokang　　孝康
Xiao Yu　　蕭瑀
Xichao dingan　　熙朝定案
xiegui　　邪鬼
Xie Guozhen　　謝國楨
Xiemo　　邪魔
Xifang wenda　　西方問答
Xiguo Ru　　西國儒
Xiguo shengxian　　西國聖賢
Xiguo xingfa　　西國刑法
Xihu　　西湖
Xin　　信
Xinhui　　新會
Xin jing　　新經
Xinwen　　新文
Xiong Sanba　　熊三拔
Xi Qi　　奚齊
Xi Rong　　西戎
Xi shi　　西士
Xi shi　　西史
Xi shi　　西師
Xitian　　西天
Xi you ji　　西游記
Xuanzang　　玄藏
Xu Guangqi (Wending)
徐光啟(文定)
Xu Guangqi ji　　徐光啟集
Xu Guangqi xinglüe　　徐光啟
行略
Xukong　　虛空
Xu Mingde　　徐明德
Xu Risheng　　徐日昇
Xu Wending gong shishi sanbai
nian jinian wen huibian
徐文定公逝世三百年紀念文
彙編

Xu Zongze　徐宗澤
Yajiada　亞加大
Yang Guangxian　楊光先
Yang Manuo　陽瑪諾
Yang Tingyun (hao: Qiyuan)　楊廷筠（號淇園）
Yang Yiyuan　楊漪園
Yang Zhu　楊朱
Yan Wuben　顏務本
yao[1]　曜
yao[2]　耀
yaoren　妖人
Yeshi　業識
Yesu　耶穌
Yesuhui lie　耶穌會例
Yi　義
Yidali Hanxuejia Wei Kuangguo mudi kao　意大利漢學家衛匡國墓地考
Yi di　義帝
yiduan　異端
Yi'na-zi　依納子
Yin Duoze (Juesi)　殷鐸澤（覺斯）
Yi Sang'a　伊桑阿
Youbei　有北
Youdida (Su Qinwang)　猶第大（肅親王）
Youhao　有昊
yu　雩
Yu　禹
Yuan Shu (zi: Jizhong)　遠樞（字機仲）
yuanzui　原罪
Yu Cang　玉蒼
yuhang　餘杭
Yulan [pen] hui　于蘭[盆]會
Yu misa gongcheng　與彌撒功程
Yu Wenhui　游文輝
Zangshi　藏識
zao gu　造故

Zhang Anmao　張安茂
Zhang Fuyan (zi: Yinfu; hao: Boyu)　張傅宕（字殷甫、號伯雨）
Zhang Pengge　張鵬翮
Zhang Xingfa　張星法
Zhang Xingyao[1] (zi: Zichen) [Yi'najue]　張星曜（字紫臣）[依納爵]
Zhang Xingyao[2] [Taigui] (zi: Zizhao [Dizhong])　張星耀[台桂]，（字紫昭[砥中]）
Zhang Xinwei　張辛煒
Zhang Youling (zi: Dujiu)　張又齡（字度九）
Zhao　趙
Zhao Chang　趙昌
Zhao Feipeng (zi: Fujiu)　趙飛鵬（字扶九）
Zhaoshi tang　超事堂
zhaoting　朝廷
Zhao Wang　昭王
Zhejiang Hangzhou-fu Tianzhutang kan shuban mulu　浙江杭州府天主堂刊書板目錄
Zhejiang Tianzhujiao lüeshi　浙江天主教略史
Zheng Dao　正道
Zhengjiao fengbao　正教奉褒
zhengshi　正史
Zhengshi lüeshuo　拯世略說
Zhengxue liushi　正學鑼石
Zhen Yan　眞言
Zhi　智
Zhongguo guojia tushuguan　中國國家圖書館
Zhongguo Ru　中國儒
Zhongguo shixue shi　中國史學史
Zhongguo Tianzhujiao shi renwu zhuan　中國天主教史人物傳

Zhong Mingren　鍾鳴仁
Zhongshan bei lu　中山北路
zhongsheng　衆生
Zhongyong zhangju　中庸
　章句
zhong zhuo　重濁
zhou　州
Zhou Wang　紂王
zhu　助
zhu　主
Zhuangzi　莊子
Zhu Chenhao　朱宸濠
Zhu Fangdan (hao: Shuqing)
　朱方旦 (號曙青)
zhufang ying cheng　駐防營城

Zhu Gaoxu　朱高煦
Zhu Ji'nan　諸際南
Zhu Xi　朱熹
Zhu Yujian　朱聿鍵
Zhu Zhifan　朱寘鐇
Zhu Zongyuan (zi: Weicheng)
　朱宗元 (字維城)
Zhuan Xu　顓頊
zhurong　祝融
Zizhi tongjian　資治通鑑
zongdong Tian　宗動天
zu　族
zuo dao　左道
Zuozhuan　左傳
zu tang　祖堂

BIBLIOGRAPHY

List of Works Consulted

PRIMARY LITERATURE

Bouvet, Joachim. *Eine wissenschaftliche Akademie für China: Briefe des Chinamissionars Joachim Bouvet S.J. an Gottfried Wilhelm Leibniz und Jean-Paul Bignon über die Erforschung der chinesischen Kultur, Sprache und Geschichte.* Edited with commentary by Claudia von Collani. Studia Leibnitiana Sonderheft 18. Stuttgart, 1989.

Capizzi, Carmelo. "La decorazione pittorica di una chiesa in Cina nella seconda metà del seicento: Una littera inedita del P. Prospero Intorcetta S.I." *Studi e ricerche sull'Oriente cristiano* 12 (1989): 3–21.

Confucius. *The Analects of Confucius.* Translated and edited by Arthur Waley. London, 1938.

d'Elia, Pasquale, S.J. *Fonti Ricciane: Storia dell'introduzione del Cristianesmo in Cina.* 3 volumes. Rome, 1942–1949.

Fu, Lo-shu, trans. *A Documentary Chronicle of Sino-Western Relations (1644–1820).* Tucson, 1966.

"The Great Maudgalyayana Rescues His Mother from Hell" (Damuqianlian mingjian jiu mu bianwen). Translated by Eugene Eoyang. In *Traditional Chinese Short Stories,* edited by Y. W. Ma and Joseph S. M. Lau. Boston, 1986.

Guo Zhujing (L. Cattaneo) et al., eds. [*Tianzhu*] *Shengjiao rike* (Jesuit prayerbook). 1665.

Hangzhou-fu zhi (Local history of Hangzhou prefecture). Compiled by Shao Jinhan et al. in 1784; edited by Gong Jiajun in 1888–1898. 178 *juan.*

Hinderer, Romain, S.J. [De Manuo], and Meng Youyi [Manuel Mendes, S.J.]. *Yu misa gongcheng* (A method for aiding the saying of mass). 1721. Double title page plus 19 double leaves. Manuscript in the Bibliothèque nationale, Paris, ms. chinois 7438.

Intorcetta, Prospero. *Compendiosa narratio de statu Missionis Chinensis. Ab anno 1581 usque ad annum 1669.* Rome, 1672.

———. "Compendiosa narrazione dello Stato della Missione Cinese cominciando dalt'anno 1581 fino al 1669" (Rome, 1671). Manuscript in the Biblioteca Nazionale di Napoli, ms. IX.

———. *Yesuhui lie* (Rules of the Society of Jesus). 2 *juan.* 36 and 54 double leaves. Manuscript in Bibliothèque nationale, Paris, ms. chinois 7445.

Karlgren, Bernard, trans. "The Book of Documents." In *Bulletin of the Museum of Far Eastern Antiquities (BMFEA)*, 22 (1950): 1–81, with glosses in *BMFEA* 20 (1948): 39–315, 21 (1949): 63–206. The glosses have been reprinted as a single volume entitled *Glosses on the Book of Documents*.

―――. *The Book of Odes: Chinese Text, Transcription and Translation*. Stockholm, 1950. Originally published in *Bulletin of the Museum of Far Eastern Antiquities* 16 (1945) and 17 (1946). The glosses appear in *BMFEA* 14 (1942): 71–247, 16 (1944): 55–169, and 18 (1946): 1–198; reprinted in one volume as *Glosses on the Book of Odes*. Stockholm, 1964.

Legge, James, trans. *The Chinese Classics*. 5 volumes. Oxford, 1893.

Le Gobien, Charles, S.J. *Histoire de l'édit de l'empereur de la Chine, en faveur de la Religion Chrestienne*. Paris, 1698.

Lettres édifiantes et curieuses. Edited by Charles le Gobien and J. B. du Halde. 26 volumes. Paris, 1707–1772.

Li Andang [A. Caballero a Santa Maria] and Shang Shiji. *Tian Ru yin* (A comparison of the Heavenly and Literati teachings) 1664. Reprinted in *Tianzhujiao dongchuan wenxian xubian* (A continuation of the collection of documents on the spread of Catholicism to the East) (3 vols.), edited by Wu Xiangxiang, 2, pp. 981–1042. Taipei, 1966.

―――. *Zhengxue liushi* (The touchstone of True Learning). 1698. Reprinted in *Tianzhujiao dongchuan wenxian sanbian* (The third collection of documents on the spread of Catholicism to the East) (3 vols.), 1, pp. 89–266. Taipei, 1972.

Li Zubo et al. *Tianxue chuan'gai* (A summary of the spread of the Heavenly Teaching). 1664. Reprinted in *Tianzhujiao dongchuan wenxian xubian*, edited by Wu Xiangxiang, 2, pp. 1043–1068. Taipei, 1966.

Litterae Annuae Vice Provinciae Sinicae. Ab 1677 ad 1680. Compiled by C. Herdtrich at Ganzhou in Jiangxi province, 6.i.1680. Archivum Romanum Societatis Iesu (ARSI), Jap. Sin. 116, ff. 214r–267v.

[*Litterae*] *Annuae V. Provinciae Sinensis Anni 1678–1679*. Archivum Romanum Societatis Iesu (ARSI), Jap. Sin. 117, ff. 161r–182r.

Lu Jiuyuan (Xiangshan). *Lu Xiangshan quanji* (The collected works of Lu Xiangshan). Compiled 1521–1553.

Martini, Martino. *De bello Tartarico historia*. Antwerp, 1654.

―――. *Novus atlas Sinensis*. Amsterdam, 1655. Published as part of Joannis Bleau's *Theatrum orbis terrarum sive novus atlas*.

Mémoires concernant l'histoire, les sciences, les arts, les moeurs, les usages, etc. des Chinois, par les missionnaires de Pékin. 17 volumes. Paris, 1718–1793.

Mo Youzhi. *Song Yuan jiu ben shujing yanlu* (A survey of old books from the Song and Yuan periods). 3 *juan*. 1873.

[*Der*] *Neue Welt-Bott.* Edited by Joseph Stöcklein, S.J., and successors. 38+
volumes. Augspurg, Grätz, and Vienna, 1728–1761+.

Qiantang-xian zhi (Local history of Qiantang district). First edition 1609;
1718 edition. 36 *juan.*

Ricci, Matteo. *China in the Sixteenth Century: The Journals of Matthew Ricci.*
Edited by N. Trigault; translated by L. J. Gallagher. New York,
1953.

—— [Li Madou]. *Tianzhu shiyi* (The true meaning of the Lord of
Heaven). 2 *juan.* 1603. Printed in *Tianxue chuhan* (The first collection
of writings on the Heavenly Learning) (52 *juan;* 6 vols.), edited by Li
Zhizao, 1, pp. 351–635. 1628; reprinted Taipei, 1965. English ver-
sion entitled *The True Meaning of the Lord of Heaven*, translated by
Douglas Lancashire and Peter Hu Kuo Chen, S.J.; edited by E. J.
Malatesta, S.J. St. Louis, 1985.

Sima Guang. *Zizhi tongjian* (The comprehensive mirror for aid in government). 1084.

Shisan jing zhu shu (Notes and commentary on the Thirteen Classics). A photolithographic edition based on *Shisan jing zhu shu jiaokanji.* Compiled
by Ruan Yuan and originally printed in 1806. 2 volumes. Beijing,
1980.

Sinica Franciscana (Rome). Vol. 7 (1965) and vol. 8 (1975).

"Taixi Yin Juesi xiansheng xinglüe" (A biography of Fr. P. Intorcetta).
Ca. 1696. 7 double leaves. Manuscript in Bibliothèque nationale,
Paris, ms. chinois 1096.

Wu Ch'eng-en. *Journey to the West.* Translated by Anthony C. Yu. 4 volumes. Chicago, 1977–1983.

——. *Monkey.* Translated by Arthur Waley. New York, 1943.

Wu Ching-tzu. *The Scholars (Rulin waishi).* Translated by Yang Hsien-yi and
Gladys Yang. Beijing, 1973.

Xu Guangqi. *Bianxue shugao* (Draft memorial in defense of [Christianity]).
1616. Reprinted in *Tianzhujiao dongchuan wenxian xubian*, edited by Wu
Xiangxiang, 1, pp. 19–36. Taipei, 1966.

——. *Nongzheng quanshu* (An encyclopedia on agriculture). 60 *juan.* 1625–
1628.

——. *Pi shishi zhu wang* (A refutation of all the falsehoods of the Buddha).
1 *juan.* Ca. 1614.

——. *Xu Guangqi ji* (Collected writings of Xu Guangqi). Edited by Wang
Zhongmin. 2 *juan.* Shanghai, 1963; reprinted 1984.

Xu Guangqi and Xiong Sanba (S. de Ursis). *Taixi shuifa* (Western hydraulics). In *Tianxue chuhan* (The first collection of writings on the Heavenly Learning), edited by Li Zhizao. 52 *juan.* 1628; reprinted Taipei,
1965.

Yang Guangxian. *Budeyi* (I cannot do otherwise). 1665. Reprinted in

Tianzhujiao dongchuan wenxian xubian, edited by Wu Xiangxiang, 3, pp. 1069–1332. Taipei, 1966.

Yuan Shu. *Tongjian jishi benmo* (Narratives from beginning to end from the *Comprehensive Mirror for Aid in Government*). 42 *juan*. 1176.

Zhang Xingyao. *Shengjiao zanming* (Inscriptions in praise of the Sage Teaching [i.e., Christianity]). 13 double leaves. Manuscript in the Bibliothèque nationale, Paris, ms. chinois 7067.

———. *Sidian shuo* (A discussion of sacrificial rites). 7 double leaves. Manuscript in the Archivum Romanum Societatis Iesu (ARSI), Jap. Sin. I, 40/7a.

———. *Tianjiao mingbian* (Clearly distinguishing the Heavenly Teaching [from heterodoxy]). 1711.

———. *Tianzhujiao Rujiao tongyi kao* (An examination of the similarities and differences between the Heavenly Teaching and the Literati Teaching). 3 *juan*. 1672–1715. Slightly variant manuscripts in the Xujiahui Library, Shanghai (84 double leaves), and the Bibliothèque nationale, Paris, ms. chinois 7171 (121 single sheets). The Xujiahui Library manuscript contains two prefaces to part 1, dated 1672 and 1715. The BNP manuscript contains the 1715 preface plus a preface dated 1702. Parts 2 and 3 also contain prefaces, but only a preface to part 2 contains a date (1705).

———. *Tongjian jishi benmo buhoubian* (Supplements to the history of the *Comprehensive Mirror* topically arranged). 50 *juan*. 1690.

Zhang Xingyao [arranger] and Bo Yingli (P. Couplet) [compiler]. *Xu Guangqi xinglüe* (A biography of Xu Guangqi). Manuscript in the Bibliothèque nationale, Paris, ms. chinois 1023. Published in *Xu Wending gong shishi sanbai nian jinian wen huibian* (A literary collection in commemoration of the 300th anniversary of the death of Xu Wending [Guangqi]), pp. 3–8. Shanghai, 1933.

Zhang Xingyao and Hong Ji. *Pi lüeshuo tiaobo* (An abridged refutation of several disputable points [held by the Buddhists]). Hangzhou, 1689. 47 double leaves. Printed together with Xu Guangqi's *Pi shishi zhu wang* (A refutation of all the falsehoods of the Buddha). 23 double leaves. Copies in the Xujiahui Library, Shanghai, and the Bibliothèque nationale, Paris, ms. chinois 7107, II.

Zhejiang Hangzhou-fu Tianzhutang kan shuban mulu (A list of books engraved at the Lord of Heaven Church in Hangzhou prefecture, Zhejiang). 2 sheets. Manuscript in the Bibliothèque nationale, Paris, ms. chinois 7044, X.

Zhu Xi. *Sishu zhangju jizhu* (Division into chapters and sentences and collected commentary on the Four Books). 1177–1189.

SECONDARY LITERATURE

Arlington, L. C. *In Search of Old Peking*. Beijing, 1935.

Beonio-Brocchieri, Paolo. "Prospero Intorcetta." In *Scienzati siciliani gesuiti in Cina nel secolo XVII: Atti del convegno a cura di alcide luini*. Palermo, 1983, pp. 171–182.

Boxer, C. R. "Some Sino-European Xylographic Works, 1662–1718," *Journal of the Royal Asiatic Society* [*of Great Britain and Ireland*], 1947, pp. 199–215.

Brunner, Paul, S.J. *L'euchologe de la Mission de Chine, editio princeps 1628 et développements jusqu'à nos jours*. Münster, Westfallen, Germany, 1964.

Chan, Wing-tsit. *A Source Book in Chinese Philosophy*. Princeton, 1963.

Chang, Garma C. C. *The Buddhist Teaching of Totality: The Philosophy of Hwa Yen Buddhism*. University Park, 1971.

Chang, K. C. *Early Chinese Civilization*. New Haven, 1976.

Changzhao he zhi gao. 1904 edition.

Charbonnier, Fr. Jean, publisher. *Guide to the Catholic Church in China*. Singapore, 1989.

Ch'en, Kenneth K. S. *Buddhism in China*. Princeton, 1964.

Chen Yuan. *Shishi yi nianlu*. Beijing, 1964.

Ch'u, T'ung-tsu. *Local Government in China under the Ch'ing*. Cambridge, Massachusetts, 1962.

Cloud, Frederick D. *Hangchow, the "City of Heaven."* Shanghai, 1906; reprinted Taipei, 1971.

Collani, Claudia von. *P. Joachim Bouvet S.J., sein Leben und sein Werk*. Nettetal, Germany 1985.

———. "*Tianxue benyi*—Joachim Bouvet's Forschungen zum Monotheismus in China." *China Mission Studies (1550–1800) Bulletin* 10 (1988): 9–33.

Crespigny, Rafe de. "Universal Histories." In *Essays on the Sources for Chinese History*, edited by D. D. Leslie, C. Mackerras, and G. W. Wang. Columbia, South Carolina, 1975.

Crossley, Pamela. "The Tong in Two Worlds: Cultural Identities in Liaodong and Nurgan during the 13th–17th Centuries." *Ch'ing-shih Wen-t'i* 4 (9) (1983): 21–46.

Cummins, J. S. *A Question of Rites: Friar Domingo Navarrete and the Jesuits in China*. Aldershot, England, 1993.

Dehergne, Joseph, S.J. "La Chine centrale vers 1700." 1, "L'Évêché de Nankin. Étude de géographie missionnaire." *Archivum Historicum Societatis Iesu* 28 (1959): 289–330; and 2, "Les vicariats apostoliques de la côte. Étude de géographie missionnaire." *Archivum Historicum Societatis Iesu* 30 (1961): 307–366.

————. "Les chrétientés de Chine de la période Ming (1581–1650)." *Monumenta Serica* 16 (1957): 1–136 plus map.

————. "Les lettres annuelles des missions jésuites de Chine au temps de Ming (1581–1644)." *Archivum Historicum Societatis Iesu* 49 (1980): 379–392; and "Lettres annuelles et sources complémentaires des missions jésuites de Chine (suite)." *Archivum Historicum Societatis Iesu* 51 (1982): 247–284.

————. *Répertoire des Jésuites de Chine de 1552 à1800*. Rome, 1973.

Di Giovanni, Vincenzo. "In To Çe Kio-ssé ouvero il Primo Traduttore europes di Confucio." *Archivo storico Siciliano* (Palermo) I (1873?): 35–48.

Dubs, H. H. "The Archaic Royal Jou Religion." *T'oung Pao* 46 (1958): 217–259.

Duyvendak, J. J. L. "A Chinese 'Divina Commedia.'" *T'oung Pao* 41 (1952): 255–316.

————. "Early Chinese Studies in Holland." *T'oung Pao* 32 (1936): 293–344.

Eberhard, Wolfram. *Guilt and Sin in Traditional China*. Berkeley, 1967.

Erkes, E. "The God of Death in Ancient China." *T'oung Pao* 35 (1940): 185–210.

Fang Hao. *Fang Hao liushi zidinggao* (The collected works of Marius Fang Hao, revised and edited by the author on his sixtieth birthday). Taipei, 1969.

————. "Hangzhou Dafangjing Tianzhujiao gu mu zhi yan'ge" (The development of the old Catholic cemetery Dafangjing at Hangzhou), originally published in *Wocun zazhi* (Hangzhou) 4 (8) (1936): 469–473; reprinted in *Fang Hao liushi zidinggao* (Taipei, 1969), pp. 1940–1946.

————. "Shiqi shiji shi de Hangzhou xiuyuan shiye" (The operation of educational academies in seventeenth-century Hangzhou). *Wocun zazhi* 4 (9) (1936): 537–541.

————. "Zhejiang Tianzhujiao lüeshi" (A brief history of the Catholic Church in Zhejiang province). *Guofeng yuekan* 8 (9–10) (1936): 62–75; reprinted in *Wocun zazhi* 5 (6) (1937): 335–350.

————. *Zhongguo Tianzhujiao shi renwu zhuan* (Biographies of historical personages in the Chinese Catholic Church). 3 volumes. Hong Kong, 1970–1973.

Feng Zanzhang. "Beiping Beitang tushuguan zanbian Zhongwen shanben shu mu (A brief catalogue of valuable Chinese books in the Beitang Library in Beijing)." *Shangzhi bianyiguan guankan* 2 (4–5) (1947): 363–368.

Fitzgerald, C. P. *Son of Heaven: A Biography of Li Shih-min, Founder of the T'ang Dynasty*. Cambridge, England, 1933.

Franke, O. "Das *Tse tschi t'ung kien* und das *T'ung kien kang-mu*, ihr Wesen, ihr Verhältnis zueinander und ihr Quellenwert." In *Sitzungsberichte der preussischen Akademie der Wissenschaften*. Phil.-Hist. Klasse Nr. 30. Berlin, 1930.

Gernet, Jacques. *Chine et Christianisme, action et réaction*. Paris, 1982. English version entitled *China and the Christian Impact: A Conflict of Cultures*, translated by Janet Lloyd. Cambridge, England, 1985.

————. *Daily Life in China on the Eve of the Mongol Invasion, 1250–1278*, translated by H. M. Wright. Stanford, 1962.

Giles, Herbert A. *A Chinese Biographical Dictionary*. Shanghai, 1892.

Goodrich, Anne Swann. *Chinese Hells: The Peking Temple of Eighteen Hells and Chinese Conceptions of Hell*. Nettetal, Germany, 1981.

Grootaers, Willem A., C.I.C.M., "Les deux steles de l'église du Nant'ang à Pekin." *Neue Zeitschrift für Missionswissenschaft* 6 (1950): 246–255.

Han, Yu-shan. *Elements of Chinese Historiography*. Hollywood, California, 1955.

Hasebe Yūkei. *Min Shin Bukkyō shi kenkyū jōsetsu*. Taipei, 1979.

Hervouet, Yves, ed. *A Sung Bibliography (Bibliographie des Sung)*. Initiated by E. Balazs. Hong Kong, 1978.

Hightower, James R. *Topics in Chinese Literature*. Cambridge, Massachusetts, 1950.

Ho, Ping-ti. *The Ladder of Success in Imperial China*. New York, 1962.

Höfer, Josef, and Karl Rahner, *Lexikon für Theologie und Kirche*. 2d edition. Freiburg, 1986.

Hou Wailu, ed. *Zhongguo sixiang tongshi* (A comprehensive intellectual history of China). Volume 4, part 2. Beijing, 1960.

Hsia, C. T. *The Classic Chinese Novel: A Critical Introduction*. Bloomington, 1980.

Huang, Pei. *Autocracy at Work: A Study of the Yung-cheng Period, 1723–1735*. Bloomington, 1974.

Hucker, Charles O. *A Dictionary of Official Titles in Imperial China*. Stanford, 1985.

Hummel, Arthur, ed. *Eminent Chinese of the Ch'ing Period (1644–1912)*. Washington, D.C., 1943.

Jin Yufa. *Zhongguo shixue shi* (A history of Chinese historiography). Shanghai, 1944.

Latourette, K. S. *A History of Christian Missions in China*. London, 1929.

Lee, Thomas H. C., ed. *China and Europe: Images and Influences in Sixteenth to Eighteenth Centuries*. Hong Kong, 1991.

Liang, Ssu-ch'ang. *A Pictorial History of Chinese Architecture*, edited by Wilma Fairbank. Cambridge, Massachusetts, 1984.

Liu, Wu-chi. *An Introduction to Chinese Literature*. Bloomington, 1966.

Lundbæk, Knud. "The First European Translations of Chinese Historical and Philosophical Works." In *China and Europe: Images and Influences in Sixteenth to Eighteenth Centuries,* edited by Thomas H. C. Lee. Hong Kong, 1991.

―――. *Joseph de Prémare (1666–1736) S.J.: Chinese Philology and Figurism.* Aarhus, 1991.

―――. "Notes sur l'image du néo-confucianisme dans la littérature euro-péene du XVIIe à la fin du XIXe siècle." In *Actes du IIIe colloque international de sinologie de Chantilly,* pp. 131–176. Paris, 1983.

―――. *The Traditional History of the Chinese Script from a Seventeenth Century Jesuit Manuscript.* Aarhus, 1988.

―――. *T. S. Bayer (1694–1738), Pioneer Sinologist.* Scandinavian Institute of Asian Studies Monograph Series no. 54. London, 1986.

Ma Yong. "Jindai Ouzhou Hanxuejia de xianqu Maerdini (Martini—pioneer of modern European sinology)." *Lishi yanjiu* 6 (1980): 153–168.

Madsen, Richard. "The Catholic Church in China: Cultural Contradictions, Institutional Survival, and Religious Renewal." In *Unofficial China: Popular Culture and Thought in the People's Republic,* edited by E. Perry Link. Boulder, 1989.

Matt, Leonard von, and Franco Barelli. *Rom, Kunst und Kultur der 'Ewigen Stadt' in mehr als 1000 Bildern.* Cologne, 1977.

Mayers, William Frederick. *The Chinese Reader's Manual.* Shanghai, 1874; reprinted Taipei, 1978.

Melis, Giorgio. "Martino Martini's Travels in China." In *Martino Martini, Geografo, Cartografo, Storico, Teologo: Atti del Convegno Internazionale,* edited by G. Melis. Trent, 1983.

―――, ed. *Martino Martini, Geografo, Cartografo, Storico, Teologo: Atti del Convegno Internazionale.* Trent, 1983.

Minamiki, George, S.J. *The Chinese Rites Controversy: From Its Beginnings to Modern Times.* Chicago, 1985.

Mirams, D. G. *A Brief History of Chinese Architecture.* Shanghai, 1940.

Mishima, Yukio. *The Sea of Fertility.* A tetralogy published in 4 volumes: Spring Snow, Runaway Horses, The Temple of Dawn, and The Decay of the Angel. New York, 1972–1974.

Moule, A. C. *Quinsai with Other Notes on Marco Polo.* Cambridge, England, 1957.

Moule, G. E. *Notes on Hangchow Past and Present.* 2d edition. Hangzhou, 1907.

―――. "A Roman Catholic Cemetery near Hangzhou," *Chinese Recorder* 21 (11) (November 1890): 509–512.

Mungello, D. E. *Curious Land: Jesuit Accommodation and the Origins of Sinology.* Stuttgart, 1985.

———. "The Reconciliation of Neo-Confucianism with Christianity in the Writings of Joseph de Prémare, S.J." *Philosophy East and West* 26 (1976): 389–410.

———. "Die Schrift T'ien-hsüeh ch'uan-kai als eine Zwischenformulierung der jesuitische Anpassungmethode im 17. Jahrhundert." *China Mission Studies (1550–1800) Bulletin* 4 (1982): 24–39.

———. "Unearthing the Manuscripts of Bouvet's *Gujin* after Nearly Three Centuries." *China Mission Studies (1550–1800) Bulletin* 10 (1988): 34–61.

Needham, Joseph. *Science and Civilisation in China.* 7 volumes in progress. Cambridge, England, 1954–.

Nienhauser, W. H., Jr., ed. *Indiana Companion to Traditional Chinese Literature.* Bloomington, 1986.

Nivison, David S. "Some Aspects of Traditional Chinese Biography." *Journal of Asian Studies* 21 (1962): 457–463.

Pelliot, Paul. "Une liasse d'anciens imprimés chinois des Jésuites retrouvée à Upsal." *T'oung Pao* 29 (1932): 114–118.

New Catholic Encyclopedia. Washington, D.C., 1967.

Peterson, Willard J. "Why Did They Become Christians? Yang Ting-yün, Li Chih-tsao and Hsü Kuang-ch'i." In *East Meets West: The Jesuits in China, 1582–1773,* edited by Charles E. Ronan, S.J., and Bonnie B. C. Ho. Chicago, 1988.

Pfister, Louis (Aloys), S.J. *Notices biographiques et bibliographiques sur les Jésuites de l'ancienne mission de Chine, 1552 à 1773.* 2 volumes. Shanghai, 1932–1934.

Pirazzoli-t'Serstevens, Michèle. *Living Architecture in Chinese.* Translated by Robert Allen. New York, 1971.

Polo, Marco. *The Travels of Marco Polo.* Translated by Robert Latham. Baltimore, 1958.

Presver, Nikolaus. *An Outline of European Architecture.* 7th edition. Middlesex, England, 1963.

Pulleyblank, E. G. "Chinese Historical Criticism: Liu Chih-chi and Ssuma Kuang." In *Historians of China and Japan,* edited by W. G. Beasley and E. G. Pulleyblank. London, 1961.

Qing shi biannian (The annals of Qing history). Edited by Lin Fujun and Shi Song. 3 volumes. Beijing, 1988.

Rawski, Evelyn Sakakida. *Education and Popular Literacy in Ch'ing China.* Ann Arbor, 1979.

Reinstra, M. H., ed. *Jesuit Letters from China, 1583–1584.* Minneapolis, 1986.

Rémusat, Abel. *Nouveaux mélanges asiatiques.* 2 volumes. Paris, 1829.

Ropp, Paul S. *Dissent in Early Modern China: Ju-lin wai-shih and Ch'ing Social Criticism.* Ann Arbor, 1981.

Rosso, Antonio Sisto, O.F.M. *Apostolic Legations to China of the Eighteenth Century.* South Pasadena, 1948.

Roth, Gertraude. "The Manchu-Chinese Relationship, 1618–1636. In *From Ming to Ch'ing: Conquest, Region, and Continuity in Seventeenth-Century China,* edited by Jonathan D. Spence and John E. Wills, Jr. New Haven, 1979.

Rowbotham, A. H. *Missionary and Mandarin: The Jesuits at the Court of China.* Berkeley, 1942.

Rule, P. A. "Jesuit Sources." In *Essays on the Sources for Chinese History,* edited by D. D. Leslie et al. Columbia, South Carolina, 1975.

Schlegel, G. "Les termes bouddhiques *Yulan Pen* et *Yulan Po.*" *T'oung Pao,* series 2, 2 (1901): 146–148, 394–397.

Sebes, J. S., S.J. *The Jesuits and the Sino-Russian Treaty of Nerchinsk.* Rome, 1961.

———. "Martino Martini's Role in the Controversy of the Chinese Rites." In *Martino Martini, Geografo, Cartografo, Storico, Teologo: Atti del Convegno Internazionale,* edited by G. Melis. Trent, 1983.

Sommervogel, Carlos, S.J. *Bibliothèque de la Compagnie de Jésus.* 12 volumes. Brussels and Paris, 1890–1932.

Soothill, W. E. *The Three Religions of China.* 2d edition. London, 1923.

Soothill, W. E., and L. Hodous. *A Dictionary of Chinese Buddhist Terms.* London, 1937.

Spence, Jonathan D. *The Memory Palace of Matteo Ricci.* New York, 1984.

———. *Ts'ao Yin and the K'ang-hsi Emperor.* New Haven, 1966.

Standaert, N. "Inculturation and Chinese-Christian Contacts in Late Ming and Early Qing." *Ching Feng* 34 (4) (December 1991): 1–16.

———. *Yang Tingyun, Confucian and Christian in Late Ming China.* Leiden, 1988.

Streit, Robert, O.M.I. *Bibliotheca Missionum.* Volume 5. Freiburg, 1929. Volume 7. Freiburg, 1931.

Struve, Lynn A. "Ambivalence and Action: Some Frustrated Scholars of the K'ang-hsi Period." In *From Ming to Ch'ing: Conquest, Region, and Continuity in Seventeenth-Century China,* edited by Jonathan Spence and John E. Wills, Jr. New Haven, 1979.

———. *The Southern Ming, 1644–1662.* New Haven, 1984.

Sung, Z. D. *The Text of the Yi King.* Shanghai, 1935.

Suzuki, D. T. *Studies in the Lankāvatāra Sūtra.* London, 1930.

Swann, Nancy Lee. "Seven Intimate Library Owners." *Harvard Journal of Asiatic Studies* 1 (1936): 363–390.

Teiser, Stephen F. " 'Having Once Died and Returned to Life': Representations of Hell in Medieval China." *Harvard Journal of Asiatic Studies* 48 (1988): 433–464.

Thompson, Laurence G. *Chinese Religion*. 4th edition. Belmont, California, 1989.

Vanderstappen, Harrie, S.V.D. "Chinese Art and the Jesuits in Peking." In *East Meets West: The Jesuits in China, 1582–1773*, edited by Charles E. Ronan, S.J., and Bonnie B. C. Oh, pp. 102–126. Chicago, 1988.

Wakeman, Frederic, Jr. *The Great Enterprise: The Manchu Reconstruction of Imperial Order in Seventeenth-Century China*. 2 volumes. Berkeley, 1985.

Watson, Burton. *Early Chinese Literature*. New York, 1962.

Watson, James, and Evelyn S. Rawski, eds. *Death Ritual in Late Imperial and Modern China*. Berkeley, 1988.

Wickeri, Philip L. "Christianity in Zhejiang: A Report from a Recent Visit to Protestant Churches in China." *China Notes,* Spring and Summer 1990, pp. 575–582.

Wilkinson, Endymion. *The History of Imperial China: A Research Guide*. Cambridge, Massachusetts, 1975.

Witek, John W., S.J. *Controversial Ideas in China and in Europe: A Biography of Jean-François Foucquet, S.J. (1665–1741)*. Rome, 1982.

———. "Understanding the Chinese: A Comparison of Matteo Ricci and the French Jesuit Mathematicians Sent by Louis XIV." In *East Meets West: The Jesuits in China, 1582–1773*, edited by Charles E. Ronan, S.J., and Bonnie B. C. Oh, pp. 62–102. Chicago, 1988.

Wright, Arthur F. *Buddhism in Chinese History*. Stanford, 1959.

Xie Guozhen. *Nan Ming shilüe* (A brief history of the Southern Ming). Shanghai, 1957.

Xu Mingde. "Yidali Hanxuejia Wei Kuangguo mudi kao (An investigation of the grave site of the Italian sinologist Wei Kuangguo [M. Martini])." *Lishi yanjiu* 1981 (4): 183–187; revised as "Shiqi shiji Yidali Hanxuejia Wei Kuangguo mudi kao (An investigation of the grave site of the seventeenth-century Italian sinologist Wei Kuangguo [M. Martini])." *Sino-Western Cultural Relations Journal* 11 (1989): 1–10.

Xu Zongze. *Ming-Qing jian Yesuhuishi yizhu tiyao* (A summary of Jesuit translations made in the late Ming and early Qing periods). Taipei, 1958.

Yang, C. K. *Religion in Chinese Society*. Berkeley, 1961.

Young, John D. *Confucianism and Christianity: The First Encounter*. Hong Kong, 1983.

Zürcher, E. *Bouddhisme, Christianisme et société chinoise*. Paris, 1990.

———. *The Buddhist Conquest of China*. Leiden, 1959.

INDEX

Agathe (Yajiada), 29, 30
agriculture, 154; five grains, 154
Aleni, Fr. G., 17, 18, 34, 165, 185 n. 35
Analects (Lunyu), 44, 98, 102, 104, 107, 110, 114, 151, 152, 154
ancestral hall, 160–163, 171; four benefits of, 161–162; rites, 130, 132, 138, 155, 159, 160, 163, 176; tablets, 162
Anhai (Quemoy), 25, 28
Anhui, 21, 23
An Shigao, 135
anti-Christian: feeling, 58, 62, 70, 102, 147; movements, 45, 47, 60, 61, 125, 172
anti-foreign feeling (by Chinese), 63
antiquity, Chinese, 101, 110, 129, 135, 158, 161, 166, 167; Ao (legendary figure), 106; Bo Yi, 106; Dao Zhi, 107; Gengsang Chu, 158–159; Gong Bai, 158; Guan Yu, 157; Hou Ji, 106; Hou Yi, 106; Huai (king of Chu), 111; Huo Shuchu, 140; Jie (Xia king), 131, 134; Jing (Han emperor), 140; Ji Zha, 158; Li Ji, 115; Liu Bang (Han Gaozi), 111; Liu Bei, 157; Mo Di, 82; Prince of Millet (Hou Ji), 154; Seven Kingdoms' rebels, 140; Shun (legendary emperor), 82, 124, 132, 148; Shu Qi, 106, 107; Tang (Shang founder), 82, 124; Three Dynasties, 152; three worthies of the Shang (Bigan, Weizi, and Jizi), 110; Wen (father of Zhou founder), 82, 124, 132; Wu Yuan, 158; Xian (duke of Jin), 115; Xiang Ji, 110, 111; Xi Qi, 115; Yang Zhu, 82; Yao (legendary emperor), 82, 99, 124, 132, 148; Yellow Emperor, 83; Yu (legendary emperor), 82, 106, 124, 132, 158; Yuan (Han emperor), 165; Zhang Fei, 157; Zhao (Zhou king), 81; Zhou, Duke of, 82, 124; Zhou (Shang king), 110, 131, 134
astronomy, 36, 37, 63; Bureau of (Qintianjian), 25, 62, 65, 88, 92; instrument of, 35

Astudillo (Dominican friar), 170
Augery, Fr. H. (Hong Duzhen), 30, 47, 54, 72

Baitou peasant uprising, 25
balance between love and morality, 154
baptism(s), 85, 150, 160, 171; of foundlings, 66–67, 196 n. 107; by Fr. Hinderer, 171; in Hangzhou, 172; of Zhang, 69, 112, 143, 156, 166, 167
Baptista, Fr. J. (Guo Ruowang), 170
Barelli, Fr. A. (Ai Siding), 55, 170
Beiguan (North Wall) Gate, 30, 61, 187 n. 74
Beijing, 16, 17, 18, 20, 24, 45, 55, 58, 59, 62, 65, 70, 73, 169, 173; Manchu court at, 60, 61, 123, 143, 147, 167, 174
Beimang Mountain, 177, 217 n. 37
Beitang (church), 31; (library), 145, 174
benevolence *(ren)*, 110, 117, 118, 123, 133, 153
Berkeley, Bishop G., 127
Bible, 90, 150, 151, 154; command to honor parents, 163; Corinthians (Epistle), 49, 84, 91; Exodus (Book of), 163; Mark (Gospel), 89, 116, 164; Matthew (Gospel), 89, 149; New Testament, 89, 90, 112; Old Testament, 89, 90; teaching of, 111
Blood Lake, 207 n. 15
Bom Jesus da Vidigueira, 44
Book of Changes (Yijing), 98, 99, 156; hexagram *Daguo*, 115
Book of Documents (Shujing), 98, 99, 104, 134, 156, 158, 202–203 n. 9
Book of Odes (Shijing), 98, 99, 118, 130, 154, 156, 202 n. 9
Book of Rites (Li ji), 98, 156, 157, 161, 162
Bouvet, Fr. J. (Bo Jin), 58, 173
Brossia, Fr. J.-C. de (Li [alias Xi] Shengxue), 170
Buddha, 111, 114, 121, 123, 130, 133,

239

ABOUT THE AUTHOR

D. E. Mungello received his Ph.D. from the University of California at Berkeley, where he was one of the last students of the China historian J. R. Levenson. In 1986 he was one of the first Western scholars to gain access to the famous former Jesuit library of Zikawei in Shanghai, where he discovered the manuscripts that form the core of this book. Dr. Mungello is also the author of *Leibniz and Confucianism: The Search for Accord,* and *Curious Land: Jesuit Accommodation and the Origins of Sinology.*

Production Notes

Composition and paging were done on the
Quadex Composing System and typesetting
on the Compugraphic 8400 by the design
and production staff of University of
Hawaii Press.

The text typeface is Baskerville and
the display typeface is Gill Sans.

Offset presswork and binding were done by
The Maple-Vail Book Manufacturing Group.
Text paper is Writers RR Offset,
basis 50.